Financial Planning

Profit Improvement through Modelling

Second Edition

DAVID ASCH and
G ROLAND KAYE

KOGAN
PAGE

First published in 1989
Reprinted in 1990
Second edition 1996

Apart from any fair dealing for the purposes of research or private study, or criticism or review, as permitted under the Copyright, Designs and Patents Act 1988, this publication may only be reproduced, stored or transmitted, in any form or by any means, with the prior permission in writing of the publishers, or in the case of reprographic reproduction in accordance with the terms and licences issued by the CLA. Enquiries concerning reproduction outside those terms should be sent to the publishers at the undermentioned address:

Kogan Page Limited
120 Pentonville Road
London N1 9JN

© David Asch and G Roland Kaye, 1989, 1996

British Library Cataloguing in Publication Data

A CIP record for this book is available from the British Library.

ISBN 0 7494 1634 3

Typeset by Palimpsest Book Production Limited,
Polmont, Stirlingshire
Printed in England by Clays Ltd, St Ives plc

LEEDS METROPOLITAN
UNIVERSITY LIBRARY

1701423988

B33BL

366145   17-5-96

7·6·96

658·15 ASC

Contents

Introduction; Financial planning and modelling; Profit improvements; Structure of the book; Summary; Further reading; References.

Introduction; Introducing financial statements; Published financial statements; Analysing financial statements; Summary; Further reading; References.

Introduction; Sources of funds; Leveraged and management buyouts; Cost of capital; Capital structure; Summary; Further reading; References.

9 Decision Making 219

10 Planning and Modelling Tools and Methods 235

Appendix: Discount Tables 255

Index 256

List of Figures

List of Tables

The Financial Skills Series

The rapidly-changing role of the finance function in modern organisations is creating greater and more varied demands upon the skills of everyone involved in the world of finance and accounting. To enable busy professionals to keep up with this pace of change, Kogan Page has joined forces with the Chartered Institute of Management Accountants (CIMA) to create a lively, up-to-the-minute series of books on financial skills.

Highly practical in nature, each book is packed with expert advice and information on a specific financial skill, while the lively style adopted reflects the current dynamism of the discipline.

Already published in the series are:

Cost Control: A Strategic Guide
David Doyle
ISBN 0 7494 1167 8

Quality in the Finance Function
David Lynch
ISBN 0 7494 1145 7

Implementing an Accounting System
A Practical Guide
Revised Edition
Ray Franks
ISBN 0 7494 1052 3

Investment Appraisal
A Guide for Managers
Revised Edition
Rob Dixon
ISBN 0 7494 1065 5

Strategic Financial Decisions
David Allen
ISBN 0 7494 1147 3

Financial Modelling for Business Decisions
Bryan Kefford
ISBN 0 7494 1635 1

If you would like to be kept fully informed of new books in the series please contact the Marketing Department at Kogan Page, 120 Pentonville Road, London N1 9JN, *Tel* 0171 278 0433, *Fax* 0171 837 6348. CIMA members can also contact the Publishing Department at the Institute for further details of the series.

1

Introduction

In this second edition we have refocused the text towards *Financial Planning: Profit improvement through modelling*. It has become increasingly obvious during the last ten years that an organisation's finances are crucial to its well-being. Of equal importance in our view is that managers should have some understanding of financial matters rather than leaving it to accountants. The objective is not to explain how accounts are constructed or how accountants do their work, but rather to use financial information to gain improvements in performance. Our intention in this book, therefore, is to introduce financial planning as a managerial tool to aid decision making within organisations. One consequence of this approach is that we will focus on issues which concern decision makers rather than on 'technical' accounting concerns.

The fundamental assumption which underlies this approach is that financial performance is a product of successful investment in new opportunities and exploitation of existing activities. At the same time the financial performance of the firm defines the cost of raising finance for new opportunities. (Poor financial performance leads to higher costs of borrowing or lower shares prices.) Consequently only a limited number of investment opportunities may emerge with sufficient earnings to cover the cost of capital (the interest on the loan or funding for a project). This in turn may restrict the firm's ability to generate an adequate financial performance to satisfy the expectation of the market-place for finance. Hence we may construct a virtuous circle in which successful investment leads to low costs of finance and improved investment opportunities which in turn improve performance. Alternatively we may enter a vicious spiral of financial underperformance and reducing opportunities to invest.

The linkage between the financial performance of the firm is reported to the investors through the annual reports. The investment communities' pricing attitude to the shares and loans to the firm are reflected in the cost of capital for the firm, ie interest rates on loans and dividend payments on shares. The cost of capital helps define the acceptability of an investment and hence may restrict new opportunities. The financial performance of the firm reflects its exploitation of its current investment base and the additional performance from the new investments.

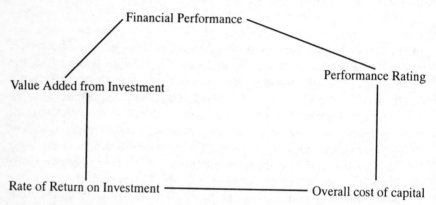

The importance of financial information should not be underrated. We have observed elsewhere that '. . . an insight into the financial situation can give a perspective on the state of the organisation . . . for most entities financial resources are the most flexible as they are generated by activities of the whole firm and are directly convertible into other types of resources.' (Bowman and Asch, 1987, pp 89–90). By its very nature, therefore, understanding accounting reports is fundamental to managing resources. In addition, research has shown that inadequate financial control is one of '. . . the most common characteristics of declining firms' (Slatter, 1984, p 30). Slatter observed in his study of forty firms that inadequate financial control may mean that the firm had absent or inadequate cash flow forecasts, costing systems and budgetary control.

However, a focus on the financial dimension of management should not be misconstrued. 'The function of financial management is as vital to the well being of the enterprise as the other major business functions such as marketing, production or personnel' (Otley, 1987, p 5). So we can distinguish between the use of financial information as an aid to decision making, and the contribution that properly managed financial resources can make to the organisation. We would argue that the latter involves all managers because their decisions determine the level of resource to be managed. But, we recognise that the situation is rarely as clear cut, since one of the major issues facing managers is choosing between alternative courses of action (or inaction), which are interactive, so it is often a chicken and egg situation. At any time the dimensions being explored are likely to be multiple, partially conflicting and ambiguous.

An argument often advanced is that those involved in making choices weigh objective economic evidence and make a logical choice. But as Donaldson and Lorsch (1983, p 9) argue '. . . strategic decisions are not the product of simple economic logic alone . . . they involve considerable uncertainty and ambiguity. To analyse these complexities top managers draw upon their experience and judgment . . . Thus to some extent their decisions always reflect non-rational considerations.' Because of this ambiguity, and because of the multiple dimensions to making management decisions we have also adopted a pragmatic approach to the use of accounting information. By this we mean that although we offer a number of prescriptions, we have done so only after careful thought as to their utility and in the hope that users of such tools and techniques will use them for enhancing their understanding of the problem or issue being examined rather than blindly believing the numbers produced. A degree of scepticism is necessary in interpreting the outcomes of any accounting information system.

Because we are adopting a managerial perspective in a pragmatic manner it seemed logical to us to adopt almost a non-accounting approach. As the title of the text implies we have adopted an approach based on modelling. We have done so to focus attention on the issue under discussion rather than on the accounting treatment thereof. In the light of what we have already said we would observe that although this may appear to be a logical/rational approach to decision making we have found it useful in capturing the richness and variety of problems encountered.

The next section will introduce financial planning through modelling and this will be followed by an overview of profit improvement and finally an introduction to the structure of the book as a whole.

FINANCIAL PLANNING AND MODELLING

In this section we will look at financial planning in the context of modelling. The strength of modelling on a computer lies in its ability to be flexible and permit adjustment and amendment.

Financial planning with computers permits alternative approaches to be pursued even though it is unlikely that an organisation will pursue more than one as it is likely to have a dominant philosophy or approach to planning and control. It is possible that identical planning tools may be in use by people and organisations facing similar planning problems but with different approaches. Equally an organisation may hold different planning philosophies towards different situations. For example, a firm may adopt a fairly rigid budget for control purposes while at the same time following an adaptive approach to production planning and to strategic decisions.

The way in which an organisation approaches decision making lies at the heart of the control or planning cycle. The planning cycle is the activity through which we attempt to control business activity. This is achieved by establishing plans which we seek to implement in the activity followed by an evaluation of the results through a measurement process. The results are compared to the plan − a process of either control through *feedback* which leads to reaction, or *feedforward* which leads to the amendment of plans in the light of experience.

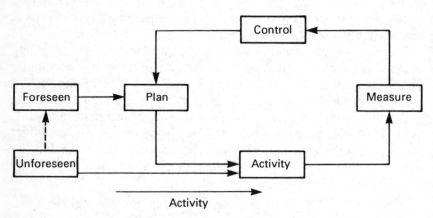

Figure 1.1 The control loop

Principles of modelling in financial planning

In everyday life we apply our knowledge, experience and skills to make decisions and solve problems. Most of the time this is undertaken intuitively as a matter of routine, on other occasions there is an explicit process. In all cases there are a series of activities which we know collectively as problem solving and decision making. Both have the same route but in problem solving there may be an absence of choice in the outcome.

Figure 1.2 shows the life cycle of a decision. The initial stage is problem identification. This may be signalled quite clearly (e.g. What should the selling price of the new product be?), or the problem may remain hidden for a while before some symptom reveals the existence of the problem (e.g. stocks have risen to the point of creating problems of storage and cash flow due to the poor performance of sales). The problem may exist in the real world or in the conceptual world.

Product pricing or stock problems are examples of real world problems. A conceptual problem may lie in our lack of understanding of the real world. In both cases the problems will be solved only after analysis of the real world. This analysis of the real world should lead to a synthesis of ideas which we call understanding. An alternative definition of this process is modelling.

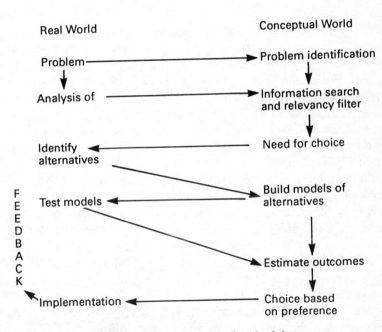

Figure 1.2 Life-cycle of a decision

Representing reality

A model is a representation of reality. It might be a physical model, such as a model of an aircraft undergoing wind tunnel testing, or an abstract model using mathematical formulae to represent size, shape, weight, relationships, etc.

Table 1.1 Types of model

Iconic	Looks like
Analog	Behaves like
Symbolic	Representative of
Mathematical	Mathematical representative of
Descriptive	Descriptive of behaviour, relationships, physical characteristics, etc.
Deterministic	Behaves in prescribed patterns
Probabilistic	Behaviour only predicts probabilities
Static	Static representation
Dynamic	Changing representation
Algorithmic	Optimised and structured
Heuristic	Trial and error

A further method of classifying models is based on their usage. Simulation models are used to simulate how a real item would behave. A key advantage of this approach is the reduction of risk and cost. For example, a model of an aircraft undergoes wind tunnel testing – the model simulates the aircraft flying – so reducing cost as well as risk. Recently Citroën announced the launch of a new car which had been designed by a computer using simulation techniques to test the characteristics of the car without the need to build a prototype. This resulted in a reduction of cost and time.

Optimising models are associated with the area of operational research in which models are built using mathematical representations, so that the processing of the model will permit the calculation of an optimal solution. This approach has been substantially developed since the last war in the areas of linear programming, queuing theory, economic order quantities, etc. The advantages of this approach are that it identifies the best decision, thus eliminating the judgement normally applied by the manager. However, the mathematical representation may lead to a simplification of reality. This could eliminate essential characteristics, thus resulting in an optimal solution which may not reflect the variety existing in the environment. Thus it is still up to the individual manager to add the essential ingredient of judgement.

Forecasting models have been available for some considerable time, either based on simple linear regression or multiple regression. The basic principle of forecasting is to project trends, cycles and seasonality into the future. This approach is often used in the areas of sales forecasting and budgeting decisions. However, it has received some bad press resulting from the use of historic data simply projected into the future, without consideration of possible changes on the horizon.

Today most models are built with the aid of computers which can be made to simulate, optimise or forecast in both a probabilistic or deterministic manner. Mathematical models are constructed in which procedures and processes are represented by algorithms reflecting causal relationships. These models are abstractions of reality and their ability to predict is used as the measure of representativeness. As humans we intuitively build models which we use to explain and predict events. These models are held in our minds and have been built up and maintained through both heuristics and exposure to logic in education. Modelling business activity requires the transfer of cognitive models (often steeped in implicit procedures) to explicit algorithms which may be encoded on to the computer.

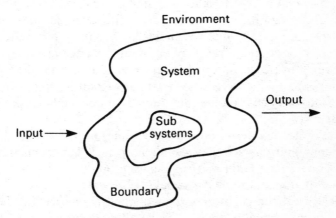

Figure 1.3 The business system

One of our prime concerns is the application of modelling to financial decision making. In order to understand the elements of the model and their inter-relationships, a systems approach can be utilised. The diagram in Figure 1.3 illustrates the basic assumptions of a business system. The systems view is reflected not only in the accounting system but also in the physical flows of activity through the business. A business model will seek to represent this system. A systems model is an abstract, simulating reality by feeding in data and predicting the likely outcome. Business models are probabilistic, – neither true nor false in their predictions. Their usefulness can only be established by comparing their predictions with reality; this probability is independent of how risk and uncertainty have been built into the model. Any abstraction must have a degree of probability associated with it, which reflects the degree of abstraction.

Modelling and decision support systems

A business model offers management one of the most powerful techniques for business planning; it is sometimes referred to as a decision support system. A business model allows management to test out the implications of their plans, strategies and tactics without committing the company either to expensive experiments or to irreparable steps into the unknown. This is achieved by producing alternative plans and testing out their effect on the business model. The model represents the firm and its behaviour and generates reports on the outcome of alternatives.

Business modelling is a tried and trusted management tool which has been available for decades. Computers have been programmed to offer these facilities for some years. However, as recently as a few years ago, to be able to undertake business modelling on a computer a large mainframe with highly sophisticated and very expensive software was needed. There was a significant price barrier for businesses seeking to enter the business modelling area, which was only recently broken with the introduction of personal computers and low cost software.

However, the model is only a model and is only as good as the assumptions and characteristics built into it. This fundamental rule must not be forgotten otherwise model users are in danger of believing the model is true and reality is false!

Typical of the type of report mentioned above is the development of a plan which allows the manager to see what happens to profit, assets, liabilities, etc, under various circumstances. Once these business variables have been entered into a model a number of different scenarios may be reviewed with changes being made to any input factors. Alternatively sensitivity analyses may be undertaken. Essentially, sensitivity analysis seeks to test the model to identify the model's outcomes and its degree of sensitivity to changes in the inputs (for example we could test the sensitivity of a cash flow model, to changes in the length of debtor's period in terms of the cash balance at the end of each month). Of course, the manager can always work backwards from a target profit and thus calculate requirements for sales, debtors, cash, production, inventory or any other business variable. The manager's ability to seek out answers to questions will depend on how the model was built and the model's capabilities. This particularly applies where models are built using standard software which may constrain the model's capabilities.

A model is built by a process of abstraction from reality, changing attributes and relationships into mathematical symbols. Symbolic models, though the mathematics might seem complex, are often much simpler to construct than physical models. It is the accounting information system which is embodied in this model and hence established accounting routines must be mathematically represented. The process of converting implicit accounting activities into explicit algorithms is perhaps the most difficult step for many accountants to take. But it is one which may be tackled in stages by developing simple models and subsequently amplifying them into more complex, detailed models. Modelling follows the same principles as many activities in data processing, in that data is captured, processed and stored, retrieved and reported. In so doing, data tends to be attenuated, i.e. compressed; this maintains the variety which is particularly pertinent to the model builder's task. However, in attenuation the process of variety reduction may lead to simplification which limits the potential of the model. The outcome of the model, where 'what if' questions are asked, is essentially data amplification. In other words a limited number of variables interact but produce a larger number of outcomes, thus providing us with the variety with which we need to make our choices. Some of the features, therefore, of decision making and problem solving may be described as data handling, variety handling and judgement. The data handling will be predominantly undertaken by the machine; the variety handling will be defined by our decisions in model building and model manipulation; and judgements will remain ours as managers. The computer frees the decision maker of the drudgery of 'number crunching' and exploits its speed and accuracy of processing. Modelling, like simulation, is a child of computer technology.

A model consists of a number of attributes, each of which relates to the others in some way which can usually be described mathematically. When data is fed to the model it is manipulated according to these rules and a result is produced. Both data and rules can be changed so that the model reflects the real world as closely as possible.

The best-known business model is the budget. Indeed, few people appreciate that a budget is a model but of course it is, for it seeks to represent the real activities of the business and to predict the likely outcome in the form of a profit. Its success, of course, depends largely on the model-builder's knowledge of the business and the way he or she abstracts it. It also depends on the data which is fed in and the accuracy of the rules portraying the relationship of attributes, e.g. what effect does a price increase have on the volume sold?

Models can be improved with experience but the past is not always the best guide to future events and so it is not possible to rely on experience alone. Some estimate or forecast of relationships has to be added to experience to make the model a valuable one.

Models are problem-solving tools which are used to try to predict what would happen in the real world if certain events took place. This is why models are often referred to as 'what if' models, the 'if' being the variable data and the 'what' being the outcome.

Advantages of computer models

- They provide a framework for examining problems. Though they may not always lead to solutions, they could highlight gaps in information.
- The process of building the model contributes significantly to a better understanding of the problem.
- They allow manipulation of both the rules and the data to test a wide variety of possible outcomes.
- They are easier and less expensive than carrying out a full-scale exercise, saving both time and money.

Other advantages include the ability to aid communication between managers within a business; the ability to consider a longer time horizon, and to act as a check on the consistency of plans. If the sales division is planning to sell X units and production division to produce Y units the discrepancy will soon show up in a model; that is not to say that the problem should not have been spotted without the aid of a model.

The above list is of course not exhaustive. If a computer will be doing the work, the modeller may be prepared to build in additional complexity (both in size and number of calculations), thus providing the business with the ability to explore more complex relationships and interrelationships between variables. By asking 'what if' type questions, managers can learn more about their business and hence re-define objectives, re-examine problems and search for new alternatives. Experiments such as sensitivity analysis (i.e. how sensitive is profit to a change in the pound/dollar exchange rate?) permit the manager to make a better assessment of the potential risks.

Anything the computer can do could be done manually, but it is the speed and accuracy of the computer which permits the model to be run under a wider set of assumptions and with more complexity as the arithmetic tedium is taken out of the job, so releasing valuable managerial time for more strategic and analytical thinking.

Disadvantages of computer models

- There is a danger of over-simplification. The model builder may leave out crucial factors for expediency.
- Symbolic language, though valuable, has its limitations, and not every relationship can be expressed mathematically.
- Model builders can become so enamoured of their models that they begin to believe they are better than reality; and the model may become rigid.
- Models produce only predictions of outcome. These might be a simple figure (as in a budget) or a range of results with an indication of the one most likely to occur.
- Models are never (or extremely rarely) absolutely right, leading some people to perceive them as inherently inaccurate.

One of the shortcomings of the modelling process is that it is prone to the 'garbage in, garbage out' syndrome. A salesman making absurdly optimistic assumptions will always produce an excellent profit forecast. Hence quality of the data and assumptions are extremely important. Sometimes models are used to 'prove a point' within an internal conflict whilst what is really at odds is not the model, but the underlying assumptions incorporated within the model. Project Z can be made to look profitable or unviable – depending on the sales forecasts input. Internal politics may lead to much waving of printouts while the real issue, say the level of sales that might be reasonably achieved in the future, is missed.

The decision-maker can get into a situation which is extremely difficult to model. For example, in modelling a timber merchant one might want to break down timber sales into three broad categories: softwood, hardwood and plywood. But cutting across each category there may be many different types of timber, different qualities, differing lengths/widths/depths, from different parts of the world.

Data availability is another problem. Ask for the price of Portuguese pine of certain width and length and you will probably get a straight answer. Ask for the average price of all Portuguese pine last year, and the business's data processing system may be incapable of supplying an answer. Data that is precisely relevant to the particular level at which a model is being built is rarely available. Either the data is too detailed or only readily available in too global a form. Frequently changes to the firm's data processing system have to be undertaken if the relevant data is to be correctly identified.

Sometimes, of course, the modeller has to adapt the model to reflect the availability of data.

The value of models lies not in their accuracy but in the use that is made of them in the problem-solving activities of managers. A model is a tool to be used with skill and understanding.

Many managers and accountants are now exploring the benefits of using models. They are aware of the advantages of using small computers to manipulate data within a prescribed framework. Modelling software is available which will operate on PCs, minis and mainframes. This software, sometimes referred to as modelling language, provides a means for constructing a model, without actually writing a program.

Capturing reality

One of the primary influences on attitudes towards financial modelling is the reality of the model. We have all experienced examples of models which fail to capture reality but yet have been applied and led to incorrect decisions. This failing often leads to the rejection of financial modelling. At the same time it has also led to excessive criticism of actual performance which has been out of line with some models' predictions. Both these reactions reflect a failure to understand the objectives and methods of modelling.

The objective of models is to permit the development and testing of ideas and beliefs without the costs and risks associated with building and testing examples in the real world. In the case of financial modelling the alternative is to implement decisions and risk the financial consequences.

In order for models to achieve the objective above, they must be sufficiently realistic to ensure that the results generated from the model are those which may be reasonably expected in reality. At the same time a model captures and affects our understanding and knowledge of the real world. If we had a total understanding and knowledge of the real world we would not need a model as we should be able to accurately predict the outcomes of our decisions. However we do not have this total knowledge and understanding and this results in risk and uncertainty.

It is through our model building, its repeated testing and improvement, that we seek to increase our knowledge and understanding. This process means that modelling is a learning process in which the current model represents our limited understanding and knowledge. Consequently the model will not fully capture reality and must result in a degree of uncertainty in its predictions as opposed to real world events.

A model can only predict and behave within its design constraints so the output from a financial model must be treated with a degree of caution. This rather negative view should not be interpreted as a rejection of modelling but rather as an encouragement to learn. This is because by learning about modelling we learn not only about the modelling process but also about our business and the world around us.

The Logic of Modelling

Growing uncertainty and the rapid rate of change combine to increase the need for prediction and the planning of tactics and strategies to survive and prosper. In solving a planning problem you have probably created another, i.e. insufficient time to evaluate the alternatives before you make a decision. The process of building financial models for planning and decision making requires an initial investment of time. Subsequently time will be saved without doubt, but the initial building of a computerised model may take as much as three times as long as for a manual model. While in the manual model subsequent changes which require re-calculation may take hours, microcomputer models will take fractions of a second.

The first step in building a model is to compile a complete list of variables which have been identified through the problem analysis process. Once the variables have been identified, their relationship must be analysed and made explicit in the form of mathematical relationships. These variables and their relationships represent rules by which calculations will be performed in order to arrive at the outcomes which are sought from the model. These interconnections must then be structured in a logical format so that they move in an ascending order from base input through their relationships to the output. This movement will be constrained by the processing capabilities of the software. In the case of financial modelling packages, where reporting and the logic are separate, greater freedom is available than is found in spreadsheets, where the logic and report format are merged.

1. Price 'A'
2. Quantity 'A'
3. Revenue 'A' = line 1 × line 2
4. Price 'B'
5. Quantity 'B'
6. Revenue 'B' = line 4 × line 5
7. Total Revenue = line 3 + line 6

The above example demonstrates a logical progression with statements including input, e.g. price and quantity, for product A + B, as well as calculations producing results such as line 3 Revenue 'A', line 6 Revenue 'B', line 7 Total Revenue. These are the basic logical relationships which we will use both in financial modelling packages and spreadsheets.

It must be emphasised at this stage that the process of defining logical relationships as algorithms is one which requires managers and accountants in particular to make explicit the implicit relationships which they assume daily. Once the process is begun it becomes a simple automatic exercise. With most modelling systems traditional expressions of $X = fy + e$ may be more easily understood by using

LABOUR COST = LABOUR RATE ×
LABOUR HOURS + GUARANTEED DAY RATE.

Most modelling systems are capable of testing either expression. However, in the case of the simpler spreadsheets we may have to re-express the formula as the representative row/column relationships.

PROFIT IMPROVEMENT

Profit improvement is one of the key objectives of managers today, whether a commercial organisation or a public service. In the latter case, profits represent surpluses which may be channelled into new activities and opportunities while in the former they may be similarly used, or used to reward shareholders and investors.

In everyday life we tend to measure success in terms of having greater wealth at the end of the day than at the beginning. This may be reflected in profits from trade, return on investments, as well as appreciation of assets from holding. This latter gain must be treated with caution as it may not reflect real gain where there has been a general increase in monetary values due to inflation.

When we look at investments we tend to judge them by the return, so an investment of 100 which yields 7.5 per cent per annum (i.e. after one year you will have £107.5) is viewed as better than one which only earns 6.5 per cent per annum (assuming they are both as secure). This fundamental principle may be applied to a business by comparing the level of profits made with the level of capital employed in the business, (e.g. a 7.5 per cent return on capital employed).

Return on capital employed = $\dfrac{\text{profit for period}}{\text{capital employed for period}}$ %

Clearly a business may improve its return by either reducing the capital employed or increasing the level of profit. In this book we will provide readers with an insight into how to achieve profit improvement through understanding the financial models of the firm.

STRUCTURE OF THE BOOK

We have already referred to the importance of financial information in organisations in our introduction to this chapter. The previous section introduced financial planning and modelling as a process. The published financial statements of an organisation are a model of the entity. The type of model will depend partly upon our view of the firm, and partly upon our purpose in considering the model in the first place. So we may see the published accounts as either a symbolic or static model for example. As a symbolic model they present one particular picture of the organisation to the world in general. As a static model the accounts represent the financial state of affairs at one particular point in time.

Figure 1.4 shows a plan of the book. The first part concentrates largely on organisation-wide financial matters, while the middle section seeks to explore a number of issues which, arguably, have a more internal focus. The last two chapters together seek to address some of the processes involved in financial planning.

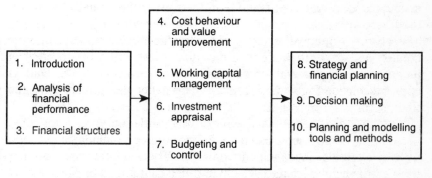

Figure 1.4 Plan of the book

Chapter 2 examines financial statements from an external 'macro' perspective. The chapter starts by looking at financial relationships and builds up to considering the complexity of published annual accounts and their analysis. This macro focus is continued in Chapter 3 where we examine the various sources of funds available to organisations, their relative costs and the relationship between the variety of sources represented by the firm's capital structure. These two chapters provide an organisation-wide backdrop to the rest of the text because decisions made by companies will be reflected ultimately in both their capital structure and their annual report. Decisions about which source of funds to use, for example, may well have a profound effect on the firm's cost structure and which opportunities (product and market) it develops.

Having discussed these broader issues the text then focuses on a range of issues largely within the organisation. In seeking to understand financial planning the remaining chapters seek to unpack much of the aggregate data which exist in the organisation and which are reflected in the published financial statements. Chapter 4 examines the need for information about costs and how this information is influenced by the costing system in the organisation. A range of topics related to costing and decision making are addressed and the chapter concludes by establishing some key linkages between capital structure discussed in Chapter 3 and fixed and variable costs. Chapter 5 examines the main elements in working capital management. The management of working capital is then discussed and a number of models relevant to that theme are introduced.

In Chapter 6 we discuss investment appraisal by first seeking to identify projects to which a variety of techniques could be applied. We then critically consider a number of methods (such as payback, discounting) and conclude by introducing the notion of financial models. Chapter 7 is about budgeting and control. The chapter commences by placing budgeting in a wider corporate context and by introducing some of the behavioural implications of the process. The actual process is then discussed and the chapter ends by considering some recent developments which managers may find useful.

The final chapters draw the somewhat disparate strands together. Chapter 8 commences by considering financial planning as part of the strategic management process. The chapter ends with a look at financial planning and modelling based on the privatisation of Jaguar. It concludes by looking at individual and group influences on decision making so that the reader is aware that such analytical and methodological approaches do not take place in a vacuum. Chapter 9 is focused on decision making and explores both the management role and decision processes. Chapter 10 introduces a methodological approach to modelling before contemplating some alternative approaches to modelling. As such it develops in much greater depth many of the issues raised in the earlier part of this chapter.

The text includes a number of 'real world' illustrations, for example the use of Anglian Water's annual report in Chapter 2, or the development of continuous business forecasting in Chapter 7 which we have included as examples of the use of the various methods and techniques in action. Each chapter also includes some ideas for further reading for those interested in exploring particular issues in more depth.

SUMMARY

In this, our introductory chapter, we have concentrated on setting out the nature and structure of the rest of the text. We commenced by establishing that we were adopting a managerial, pragmatic, modelling approach and followed this by introducing the concept of financial planning and modelling. A number of issues were raised, including some principles of modelling, problems of representing reality, plus an introduction to the logic of modelling. The plan of the text and some interrelationships between chapters were then outlined.

FURTHER READING

G R Kaye has written a more detailed text on *Financial Planning Models: Construction and Use* (1994), Academic Press in association with CIMA which develops computer models of the firm. G R Kaye and K N Bhaskar have written a series for Economist Publications Ltd, *Financial Planning with Personal Computers*, which explores the modelling aspects raised in more depth. There are numerous books on accounting for non-financial managers, for example: Sizer, J (1979) *An Insight into Management Accounting*, Penguin, Harmondsworth, or Wilson, R M S and McHugh, G (1987) *Financial Analysis: A Managerial Introduction*, Cassell, London, to mention two.

REFERENCES

Bowman, C and Asch, D (1987) *Strategic Management*, Macmillan, Houndmills, Basingstoke.
Donaldson, G and Lorsch, J W (1983) *Decision Making at the Top*, Basic Books, New York.
Otley, D (1987) *Accounting Control and Organisation Behaviour*, Heinemann, London.
Porter, M E (1980) *Competitive Strategy*, Free Press, New York.
Slatter, S (1984) *Corporate Recovery*, Penguin, Harmondsworth.

2

Analysis of Financial Performance

INTRODUCTION

In the introductory chapter we referred to the fact that financial statements were in effect a model of the organisation. In this chapter we will explore the main financial statements in order to understand the use that can be made of them for understanding business performance. The financial statement is one of the crucial documents used by both managers and owners, or potential owners, to evaluate the success or otherwise of the organisation. Research shows that the annual report is the key document for institutional investors in considering corporate performance (Lee and Tweedie, 1981, pp 77–91).

The chapter commences by considering what the main financial statements contain and the main accounting assumptions that are inherent in their construction. We then turn our attention to analysing a set of published accounts with a view to gaining some insight into the performance of the firm. Some of the issues involved in the use of financial ratios for assessing performance will also be addressed.

The main task of financial accounting is to communicate financial information to allow users to make decisions. Accounting is the activity of identifying, measuring, recording and reporting on the resources and performance of an enterprise. Consequently a central concern in the provision of useful reliable information relates to the best methods of measuring value and profit. As you would expect there are numerous ways in which those measurements could be made. In this book we will consider only the main issues arising out of the use of some of the approaches.

As our focus is on the use that can be made of financial information it is not our intention to go into a lengthy technical debate on accounting matters. In recognising that financial information is a vital part of information for management decision making it is equally important to recognise that true analysis will necessitate looking behind the figures to ascertain what is actually represented. 'Drawing quick conclusions is to be resisted as the information must be related to the situation in which the enterprise is, in terms of its competitive environment or stage of development' (Bowman and Asch, 1987, p 90).

INTRODUCING FINANCIAL STATEMENTS

Historically the production of periodic financial statements was designed to indicate to the owners the 'state of play' of the business. As the business world developed and as greater recognition was given to wider interests than the owners (e.g. to providers of loans), the amount of information provided, and the consistency of the information across and between firms became the subject of legislation – the Companies Acts. In addition the presentation of financial statements became influenced by the requirements of the Accounting Standard Board, defined in their Financial Reporting Standards (FRSs, which supersede the Statements of Standard Accounting Practice – SSAPs). Although not legally enforceable FRSs are intended to be complied with by those responsible for the preparation and presentation of financial statements. The three principal financial statements – the Balance Sheet, Profit and Loss Account and Cash Flow Statement (previously the Funds Flow Statement) – which are discussed below are all set out to comply with the essential requirements of the Companies Acts and FRSs, although some details have been omitted for the sake of clarity and brevity.

The balance sheet

A balance sheet is, quite simply, a list of everything a firm owns and everything that it owes at one particular point in time. Figure 2.1 displays a fairly typical balance sheet format and we will use it as an example to discuss the various measurement issues and assumptions inherent in its presentation. Normally the values shown are the historic cost, but where the current market value is less than cost then financial prudence would lead to the valuation being on the basis of net realisable value. This system of recording is useful because the amounts are recorded relatively easily when assets are initially acquired. Secondly, because the cost is certain, i.e. it can be checked against an invoice or other documentation, it is more reliable and easier to audit than, say, using replacement or selling prices. It is also simple and fits with the stewardship purpose of recording what the directors have done. The fact is that although historic costing enhances the reliability of the information it restricts its relevance.

Balance Sheet at 31st March 1995

	£000	£000
Fixed assets		
Land and Buildings		1800
Plant and Machinery		1600
Fixtures and Fittings		400
		3800
Current assets		
Stocks	1200	
Debtors	1200	
Cash	800	
	3200	
Current liabilities		
Bank Overdraft	400	
Trade Creditors	600	
	1000	
Net current assets		2200
Total assets less current liabilities		6000
Capital and reserves		
Issued share capital		2000
Reserves		2000
Shareholders interest		4000
Long term liabilities (over one year)		
Loan		2000
Total long-term capital		6000

Figure 2.1 Abbreviated balance sheet of any plc as at
31 March 1995

Perhaps the most crucial point about the numbers in the balance sheet
is that they do not represent, either individually or collectively, what
the business is worth as a whole or even what individual items may be
worth. In essence a business is only worth what someone is prepared
to pay for it. This would normally be determined by their judgement
concerning the amount of future profits, which may not necessarily
relate to the asset values disclosed in the balance sheet. This is an
issue that will be discussed when we examine the use of ratios.

Land and buildings are normally shown at their original cost less
a provision for depreciation. Depreciation is an annual adjustment

to take account of wear and tear. Depreciation also recognises that fixed assets are used over their expected life so the balance sheet valuation is steadily reduced over the years that the asset is owned. The profits will also be affected and will show depreciation as a cost of running the business. The value of land and buildings is volatile to economic cycles, thereby quoting the original purchase price of land and buildings is no use in determining their current worth. Some companies revalue their land and buildings and incorporate that in the balance sheet, in other words the asset is shown at valuation rather than original cost. In considering the accounts it is important to determine whether the asset has been revalued (and when) or whether it is shown at its historic cost.

Plant and machinery and *fixtures and fittings* are normally shown at their original cost less depreciation. Given the nature of these assets they are unlikely to appreciate so a revaluation is unnecessary.

Stocks may be of raw materials, work in progress or finished goods, and are generally valued at what they cost to acquire or produce, i.e. the cost of materials, production labour and so on. In the event that stocks have deteriorated, or been damaged, or gone out of fashion, then they are valued at their sale price less any disposal costs – net realisable value – where this is lower than their cost.

Debtors are customers who have yet to pay for the goods and services we have supplied. Debtors are shown at the amount anticipated to be received rather than what may be legally due.

Issued share capital is recorded at the amount paid in by the shareholders when they originally bought the shares in the company. In the case of public quoted companies that are traded in the Stock Exchange, the current market price of shares has no direct effect on the company, although as we will see in Chapter 3 it may well influence financial policy.

Reserves arise as a result of not distributing past profits to shareholders. These reserves primarily come from profits retained in the business (i.e. ploughed back) but other reserves may be built up from revaluation of land and buildings or other assets.

Many companies partially finance their business by borrowing money on a long-term basis. This long-term debt may take a variety of forms, but will be shown in the category of *long-term liabilities* and shown at the amount owed by the company that is due at some date in the future. The fact that for many firms such long-term loans have a market value and can be bought and sold in the same way that shares can does not affect the value shown in the balance sheet.

Cash flow statement

The balance sheet is effectively a snapshot of the state of affairs of the business at a particular time. Businesses are not static and between balance sheets there is continual movement in both assets and liabilities. Some of these movements will be associated with the operation of the firm and will be reflected in the operating profit, but others will reflect capital expenditure on new plant and equipment or the injection of further funds into the firm from loans or the disposal of redundant assets. This can be seen as different cash flows in and out of the firm. It is important to ensure that a firm has sufficient cash to meet day-to-day costs and to enable investment in appropriate fixed assets. An examination of the sources and uses of cash and working capital (net current assets) is an essential part of financial planning.

Cash Flow Statement for any plc for the year ended 31 March 1995

Net Cash Flow from Operating Activities			1300
Returns on Investments and servicing of finance:			
Interest received		100	
Interest paid		(250)	
Dividends paid		(600)	
Net Cash Outflow from returns on investments and servicing of finance			(750)
Taxation			
Corporation Tax paid (including ACT)			(750)
Investment Activities			
Payments to acquire assets		900	
Receipts from sales of tangible fixed assets		300	(600)
Net cash flow from operating activities			(800)
Financing			
Issue of Ordinary Share capital		425	
Issues of Debenture loan		460	
Expenses paid in connection with share issue		(25)	
Net cash inflow from financing			860
Increase in cash and cash equivalent			60

Figure 2.2 Cash Flow Statement

The cash flow statement is a vital means of monitoring all the changes in a firm's financial position during a year. It provides the essential information to reconcile the sources and applications of cash within the firm and explains why profits may be generated but cash may not be available for payment of dividends to shareholders due to its reuse in other types of assets or payments of liabilities. Figure 2.2 shows the general format of such statements. Note that there are sources of funds in addition to profit. Note also that the statement reveals quite clearly what funds have been raised and how they have been raised as well as clearly showing the uses to which the funds generated have been put. In this example we can see that the company has purchased some fixed assets as well as increasing the resources invested in working capital. The flow of cash through the firm is considered in more detail in Chapter 5.

Profit and loss account

Given that the balance sheet reveals the state of affairs at one point in time, and that the funds flow statement charts the movement of funds between balance sheet dates, the third statement – the profit and loss account – shows how much profit the business has made.

Profit for the period – profit and loss statements are normally prepared annually for publication – is worked out by matching the expenses of the year to the revenues of the year. Revenues are the receipts and expenses the payments (past, present and future) that relate to the accounting year. Profit (or loss) may result from two types of activity: operating profit resulting from normal trade, and/or profit on disposal of fixed assets including investments and associated reorganisation costs that are not likely to occur again. It is important to recognise that only operating profit is ongoing while profits from disposals or reorganisation distort the true performance of the business.

Figure 2.3 illustrates a profit and loss account, that is a record over a period of time of a firm's revenues and expenses. You can see that it begins with the turnover or sales figure. Cost of sales is then deducted. The costs of sales figure generally includes the cost of raw materials, production labour, power, and other factory costs including depreciation of machines. A non-manufacturer would only normally include the cost of goods purchased and resold during the period. In addition there are also administrative and selling costs that would normally include office salaries, rates, light and heat, insurance, motor vehicle expenses, depreciation of office equipment and so on. After taking into account interest on loans the net profit before tax is arrived at.

	000's	000's
Turnover		10000
less cost of sales		6500
Gross profit		3500
Less: Administration expenses	1000	
Selling and distribution costs	200	
Net interest on loans	150	
Expenses on share issue	25	
Loss on disposal of fixed assets	175	
		1550
Net profit before tax		1950
Corporation tax		750
Profit for the year		1200
Dividend		600
Transfer to reserves		600

Figure 2.3 Profit and loss account for any plc for the year
ended 31 March 1995

Accounting assumptions

There are a number of assumptions or conventions that underlie how
the above financial statements have been prepared. In order to better
understand financial information the main assumptions are briefly
outlined as they will influence the interpretation of the results.

Objectivity means that the financial statements are based upon 'facts'
which are measurable and verifiable. 'Objective' documents, such as
invoices, are used so that the figures are less easily manipulated
and less subject to judgement. Unfortunately this type of objective
information may not be very realistic in valuing the business. The
objectivity of the annual account is reflected in the auditor's report
which will accompany company accounts, where they certify the
accounts as a 'true and fair view' of the business. It must be
understood that this certification reflects the role of auditors as
'watchdog' in ensuring objectivity and compliance with the legislation
and recommended practices. Auditors are not there to search out fraud
or mismanagement.

Money measurement means that the firm's assets and liabilities are expressed in monetary terms. Money is the common unit of measurement for a variety of items like stock, office equipment, motor vehicles and so on. This appears quite logical and is consistent with being objective. Unfortunately it assumes that the money has a constant value over time, i.e. that the purchasing power of the currency, for us pounds sterling, remains constant. Clearly this is not and has not been the situation in the UK. As we have seen assets and liabilities are recorded and listed at their original cost, which is verifiable and not a matter of opinion, but which may therefore be misleading as their listed value probably bears little relationship to their worth. Furthermore, businesses that operate in a number of countries and currencies will have to reconcile their account to the parent company's currency. This can lead to significant distortions and needs careful monitoring if the reader is not to be misled.

Profits based on out-of-date costs and asset valuations based on historic costs reduce the usefulness of the financial statements. Various alternatives were explored in the 1970s and a system of *current cost accounting* was introduced for published accounts. As the rate of inflation declined in the mid-1980s and because of the amount of work involved in the preparation of current cost accounts the system was withdrawn. Interestingly Lee and Tweedie reported '. . . one of the least used sources of financial information was that concerned with inflation accounting . . .' (Lee and Tweedie, 1981, p 40). However, some companies continue to publish current cost statements.

Many important items of information – concerning the quality of management, or the firm's reputation for example – which have a considerable impact on the ability of the firm to make a profit and on its value, are not included in the financial reports because they cannot easily be measured and communicated in money terms. In addition some important assets may be excluded (e.g. employees' skill and commitment) while others have more recently started to be included, such as brand value (variety of valuation methods). However there is a trend to greater disclosure as a defence against under-valuation and the threat of takeover which is tempered by the needs of competition.

The going concern convention assumes that the business is going to continue to trade profitably for some considerable time to come. If a firm were to close down tomorrow then the most important information would be how much its assets could be sold for. If the firm intends to continue in business the saleable value is not so important because the company is not intending to sell its assets.

The realisation convention means that revenues are not recognised until a sale has been agreed so profit that has not been recognised is not recorded. If a sale is on credit, acquisition of the debt is considered sufficiently objective. Recognition occurs at the time when legal rights and obligations for the sale are set up. In practice the time of delivery is often used as the time of sale because it may fit more easily with the recording and invoice system.

In looking at the profit and loss account earlier in this chapter we noted that it *matched* the revenues and expenses for the year. Matching expenses and revenues (often known as the *accrual's convention*) involves recognising that receipts of a previous period may well relate to the current year. An example might be rent received in last year for this year as it may be payable in advance. The reverse could also occur, such as sales on credit. In the same way expenses may be paid in a period before or after the year in which they were incurred. Insurance payments paid in a previous year may well relate to part of the current year and many expenses (e.g. telephone, electricity, and so on) may be paid next year but relate to the current year as they are paid in arrears. *Depreciation,* the charging against profit of the cost of an asset over its useful life, is an example of matching cost to associated revenue. It would not be reasonable to charge the whole of the cost of a fixed asset as an expense of the period in which it was bought.

Prudence means providing for all possible losses and anticipating no profits. In choosing between two possible valuations the accountant will opt for the lower one, so making the profit less. It is believed safer to err on the side of caution than to overestimate.

There is a need for consistency in recording transactions, to avoid distortions in the accounting performance from year to year. As a result the accounting policies are published and care should be exercised to ensure a policy has not been changed which may distort the comparison. Financial statements should only include items significant enough to affect evaluation or decisions. So the purchase of minor items like a calculator for £10 should be recorded as an expense even though it may be a fixed asset. Such transactions would not make the balance sheet *materially* different.

PUBLISHED FINANCIAL STATEMENTS

Having considered the main features of the financial statements we are now in a position to look at the published accounts. Decisions about buying and selling shares and whether to lend money to a firm are often made on the basis of information disclosed in the published financial statements. We have already noted the assumptions under which such statements are prepared and it is worth recalling that such documents are deficient in terms of:

□ Assets are not normally recorded at a current value
□ Some important assets are not included, such as the skills of employees, their loyalty, the reputation of the firm and so on
□ There are no estimates of future profits.

Published annual accounts are drawn up in accordance with the Companies Acts (from 1948 to 1985) which have statutory force. They are also presented in accordance with the various FRSs in force at the time.

Many businesses operate as groups of companies, consequently they prepare *consolidated* financial statements. Often the holding or parent company does not own the means of production (factories, offices, equipment, stocks etc) itself. Subsidiaries own the assets and liabilities and trade themselves. The subsidiaries are controlled by the holding company; the shares in the subsidiaries are normally owned by the holding company. As they are part of the same business economically consolidated accounts are prepared. Such accounts are produced by adding together the balance sheets of all the companies in the group to form a group balance sheet. Cross-holdings of shares and loans to, from, and between group companies cancel themselves out. So the figures for fixed assets, current assets and current liabilities represent the sum of all such balances in the individual balance sheets.

As a result of consolidating the accounts an item called 'goodwill on consolidation' may arise. This is because in acquiring a subsidiary as a going concern the holding company may well have paid more for the business than the accounting value disclosed. In addition some subsidiaries may not be 100 per cent owned and there may be a few shareholders other than the parent company. As such they own a small part of the consolidated group and this is disclosed as 'minority interests' along with liabilities and capital.

Extracts from the annual report and accounts of Anglian Water Plc are set out on the following pages. We have included:

□ group balance sheet
□ group profit and loss account
□ group statement of source and application of funds
□ extracts from accounting policies
□ extracts from notes on the accounts, and
□ group current cost information.

Balance Sheets

At 31 March 1994	Notes	Group 1994 £m	1993 £m	Company 1994 £m	1993 £m
Fixed assets					
Tangible assets	13	**2,308.7**	2,049.6	**1.4**	2.8
Investments	14	**6.8**	3.9	**1,157.5**	1,125.5
		2,315.5	2,053.5	**1,158.9**	1,128.3
Current assets					
Stocks	16	**12.0**	10.9	–	–
Debtors	17	**124.2**	120.5	**62.1**	61.3
Cash and deposits		**101.5**	113.0	**139.0**	190.4
		237.7	244.4	**201.1**	251.7
Creditors: amounts falling due within one year					
Short term borrowings	18	**(17.1)**	(9.9)	**(100.8)**	(210.9)
Other creditors	18	**(298.1)**	(268.7)	**(93.3)**	(74.1)
Net current (liabilities)/assets		**(77.5)**	(34.2)	**7.0**	(33.3)
Total assets less current liabilities		**2,238.0**	2,019.3	**1,165.9**	1,095.0
Creditors: amounts falling due after more than one year					
Loans and other borrowings	19	**(587.4)**	(495.6)	**(301.8)**	(238.3)
Other creditors	20	**(66.4)**	(48.6)	–	–
		(653.8)	(544.2)	**(301.8)**	(238.3)
Provisions for liabilities and charges	21	**(171.4)**	(106.1)	–	(0.6)
		1,412.8	1,369.0	**864.1**	856.1
Capital and reserves					
Called up share capital	24	**296.2**	295.5	**296.2**	295.5
Share premium account	25	**4.0**	2.1	**4.0**	2.1
Profit and loss account	25	**1,103.8**	1,071.4	**555.1**	558.5
Other reserves	25	**8.8**	–	**8.8**	–
		1,412.8	1,369.0	**864.1**	856.1

The notes on pages 36 to 52 form part of these financial statements.

Approved by the Board on 6 June 1994

B V Henderson CBE

Chairman

C J Mellor

Group Finance Director

Group Profit and Loss Account

For the year ended 31 March 1994	Notes	Before exceptional restructuring charge 1994 £m	Exceptional restructuring charge (note 5) 1994 £m	Total 1994 £m	1993 £m
Turnover from continuing operations	2	687.9	–	687.9	583.2
Operating costs	3	(460.2)	(60.0)	(520.2)	(371.6)
Operating profit from continuing operations	2, 4	227.7	(60.0)	167.7	211.6
Profit on sales of assets in continuing operations		1.6	–	1.6	3.3
Profit on ordinary activities before interest		229.3	(60.0)	169.3	214.9
Interest payable (net)	6	(37.1)	–	(37.1)	(29.5)
Profit on ordinary activities before taxation		192.2	(60.0)	132.2	185.4
Taxation	7	(16.9)	–	(16.9)	(19.0)
Profit for the financial year	12	175.3	(60.0)	115.3	166.4
Dividends	8			(67.5)	(62.3)
Retained profit for the financial year				47.8	104.1
Earnings per share	9	59.2p		39.0p	56.4p

Total Recognised Gains and Losses

Statement of total recognised gains and losses for the year ended 31 March 1994	Notes	1994 £m	1993 £m
Profit for the financial year		115.3	166.4
Currency translation differences on foreign currency net investments		–	(0.2)
Total recognised gains relating to the year	12, 25	115.3	166.2

The notes on pages 41 to 48 form part of these financial statements.

Group Cash Flow Statement

For the year ended 31 March 1994	Notes	1994 £m	1993 £m
Net cash inflow from operating activities	28(a)	335.8	316.8
Returns on investments and servicing of finance			
Interest received		8.1	14.1
Interest paid		(34.0)	(35.0)
Interest element of finance lease rental payments		(7.4)	(1.2)
Dividends paid		(42.2)	(58.4)
Net cash outflow from returns on investments and servicing of finance		(75.5)	(80.5)
Taxation			
Advance Corporation Tax paid		(19.0)	(19.0)
Investing activities			
Purchase of tangible fixed assets		(348.3)	(288.8)
Investment in infrastructure renewals		(23.8)	(15.4)
Grants and contributions received		30.4	33.1
Purchase of subsidiary undertakings (net of cash and cash equivalents acquired)	28(b)	(19.0)	(27.3)
Sale of fixed assets		3.3	4.1
Investment in associated undertakings		(1.2)	–
Investment in other participating interests		(1.7)	(1.2)
Decrease/(increase) in short term deposits	28(c)	8.0	(15.0)
Net cash outflow from investing activities		(35.3)	(310.5)
Net cash outflow before financing		(111.0)	(93.2)
Financing			
Issue of 6 ½% Fixed Rate Bond 1998		62.0	–
Loans from the European Investment Bank		10.0	25.0
Other long term loans		–	20.0
Amounts received under finance lease arrangements		21.8	55.3
Repayments of amounts borrowed		(2.8)	(5.3)
Capital element of finance lease rental payments		(2.0)	(0.8)
Issue of warrants		8.8	–
New share capital subscribed		1.6	1.2
Net cash inflow from financing	28(d)	99.4	95.4
(Decrease)/increase in cash and cash equivalents	28(c)	(11.6)	2.2

The notes on pages 41 to 48 form part of these financial statements.

Notes to the Financial Statements

1. Accounting policies

The financial statements are prepared under the historical cost convention and in accordance with applicable accounting standards and, except as disclosed in note 1e below, in accordance with the Companies Act 1985. The following principal accounting policies have been applied:

a. Basis of consolidation
The Group accounts comprise a consolidation of the accounts of the Company and all of its subsidiaries to 31 March. The results of companies acquired or disposed of are consolidated from the effective date of the acquisition or to the effective date of disposal. The treatment of a company as an associated undertaking has regard to the Group's holding of at least 20% of the equity capital, representation on its board of directors and participation in policy making, including dividend policy. The Group's share of the profits or losses of these companies is included in the profit and loss account and the investments are included in the balance sheet at the Group's share of the net tangible assets of the companies.

b. Goodwill
On the acquisition of a subsidiary undertaking, fair values are attributed to the net assets acquired. Goodwill, which represents the difference between the purchase consideration and the fair values, is taken to reserves.

c. Turnover
Turnover represents the income receivable (excluding value added tax) in the ordinary course of business for goods and services provided and, in respect of contract work in progress, the value of work carried out.

d. Tangible fixed assets and depreciation
Tangible fixed assets comprise:

Infrastructure assets (being mains and sewers, impounding and pumped raw water storage reservoirs, dams, sludge pipelines and sea outfalls) comprise a network of systems. Investment expenditure on infrastructure assets relating to increases in capacity or enhancements of the network is treated as an addition and included at cost. Investment expenditure on maintaining the operating capability of the network in accordance with defined standards of service is charged as an operating cost. No depreciation is charged on infrastructure assets because the network of systems is required to be maintained in perpetuity and therefore has no finite economic life.

The charge for infrastructure renewals expenditure takes account of planned expenditure on maintaining the operating capability of infrastructure assets, in accordance with the operational policies and standards underlying Anglian Water Services Limited's asset management plan. The timing of the investment programme and other operational considerations result in unevern patterns of infrastructure renewals expenditure. Charges to the profit and loss account therefore comprise actual expenditure together with accruals which recognise planned expenditure identified in the asset management plan.

Other assets (including properties, overground plant and equipment) are included at cost less accumulated depreciation. Freehold land is not depreciated. Other assets are depreciated evenly over their estimated economic lives, which are principally as follows:

Operational structures	40 – 80 years
Buildings	30 – 60 years
Fixed plant	20 – 40 years
Vehicles, mobile plant and computers	3 – 10 years

Assets in the course of construction are not depreciated until they are commissioned.

e. Grants and contributions
Grants and contributions on capital expenditure, other than those relating to infrastructure assets, are credited to a deferral account and are released to revenue evenly over the expected useful life of the

42 / Financial Planning

relevant asset in accordance with the provisions of the Companies Act. Grants and contributions to capital expenditure on infrastructure assets are deducted from the cost of these assets. This policy is not in accordance with the provisions of the Companies Act but has been adopted in order to show a true and fair view since, as explained above, infrastructure assets have no finite economic life and hence no basis exists on which to recognise such contributions as deferred income. The financial effect of this departure is disclosed in note 13. Other grants and contributions are credited to the profit and loss account in the year to which they apply.

f. Leased assets
Where assets are financed by leasing arrangements which transfer substantially all the risks and rewards of ownership of an asset to the lessee (finance leases), the assets are treated as if they had been purchased and the corresponding capital cost is shown as an obligation to the lessor. Leasing payments are treated as consisting of a capital element and finance costs, the capital element reducing the obligation to the lessor, and the finance costs being written off to the profit and loss account over the period of the lease. The assets are depreciated over the shorter of their estimated useful lives and the lease period. All other leases are regarded as operating leases. Rental costs arising under operating leases are expensed over the term of the lease.

g. Investments
Investments held as fixed assets are stated at cost less provision for permanent diminution in value.

h. Stocks and work in progress
Stocks are stated at cost less any provision necessary to recognise damage and obsolescence. Work in progress, with the exception of long term contract work in progress, is valued at the lower of cost and net realisable value. Cost includes labour, materials, transport and an element of overheads.

i. Long term contracts
Amounts recoverable on long term contracts are stated at cost plus attributable profits less provision for any known or anticipated losses and payments on account and are included in debtors. Payments on account in excess of amounts recoverable on long term contracts are included in creditors.

j. Pension costs
Contributions to the Group's defined benefit pension schemes are charged to the profit and loss account so as to spread the regular cost of pensions over the average service lives of employees, in accordance with the advice of an independent qualified actuary. Actuarial surpluses and deficits are amortised, where appropriate, over the average remaining service lives of employees in proportion to their expected payroll costs. The cost of defined contribution schemes is charged to the profit and loss account in the year in respect of which the contributions become payable.

k. Research and development
Research and development expenditure is charged to the profit and loss account in the year in which it is incurred.

l. Foreign currencies
Transactions in foreign currencies are recorded at the rate of exchange at the date of the transaction or, if hedged forward, at the rate of exchange under the related forward currency contract. Assets and liabilities denominated in foreign currencies, including the Group's interest in the underlying net assets of overseas subsidiary and associated undertakings, are translated into sterling at the financial year end exchange rates. Profits and losses of overseas subsidiaries and associates are translated into sterling at average rates of exchange during the year. Gains or losses arising on the translation of the net assets of overseas subsidiaries and associates are taken to reserves, together with exchange differences arising on related foreign currency borrowings. Other exchange differences are taken to the profit and loss account.

m. Deferred taxation
Tax deferred as a result of timing differences is only provided for to the extent that there is a reasonable probability that such deferred taxation will be payable in the foreseeable future. Provision is made for potential taxation liabilities which could arise on the remittance of retained overseas earnings only to the extent that there is currently an intention to remit such earnings.

	Turnover		Operating profit		Net operating assets	
	1994	1993	1994	1993	1994	1993
2. Segmental analysis	£m	£m	£m	£m	£m	£m
By class of business						
Water supply and sewerage services	594.5	561.1	171.8	216.2	1,998.7	1,827.3
Process engineering	97.0	23.5	2.3	(3.2)	(2.1)	(12.4)
International	0.4	0.2	(1.5)	(0.6)	3.1	1.4
Other	5.0	5.4	(4.3)	(0.6)	0.5	6.4
Less intersegment trading	(9.0)	(7.0)	(0.6)	(0.2)	–	–
	687.9	583.2	167.7	211.6	2,000.2	1,822.7
By geographical origin						
United Kingdom	640.0	579.8	167.2	212.0	1,997.9	1,826.0
Other	47.9	3.4	0.5	(0.4)	2.3	(3.3)
	687.9	583.2	167.7	211.6	2,000.2	1,822.7

Other turnover arises principally in Europe. Turnover by destination is not significantly different from turnover by origin. Net operating assets are shown before deduction of net debt, dividends payable and advance corporation tax of £587.4m (1993–£453.7m). The acquisitions during the year described in note 15 relate to the process engineering segment. These businesses contributed £3.4m to net operating assets but their contributions to turnover and operating profit were immaterial. Process engineering and international operations have been analysed as separate business segments this year to reflect their increasing significance within the Group. Prior period figures have been restated accordingly.

	Before exceptional restructuring charge 1994	Exceptional restructuring charge (note 5) 1994	Total 1994	1993
3. Operating costs	£m	£m	£m	£m
Raw materials and consumables	88.8	–	88.8	44.4
Other external charges	185.5	14.3	199.8	163.3
Staff costs (see note 10)	127.3	45.7	173.0	108.4
Change in stocks of finished goods and work in progress	3.5	–	3.5	(0.7)
Own work capitalised	(47.2)	–	(47.2)	(38.8)
	357.9	60.0	417.9	276.6
Depreciation of tangible fixed assets	68.6	–	68.6	58.3
Amortisation of deferred grants and contributions	(1.8)	–	(1.8)	(1.2)
Infrastructure renewals	35.5	–	35.5	37.9
	460.2	60.0	520.2	371.6

4. Operating profit	1994 £m	1993 £m
Operating profit is stated after charging/(crediting):		
Share of losses of associated undertakings	1.1	0.2
Hire of plant and machinery	1.9	1.2
Other operating lease costs	2.0	1.0
Research and development expenditure	4.1	2.6
Grants and contributions	(0.4)	(0.4)
Closure costs of terminated businesses (including goodwill of £0.6m)	1.5	–
Fees paid to auditors:		
for audit work	0.4	0.5
for other work (including £0.1m overseas (1993 – £0.2m))	0.3	0.7
Included above are fees of £nil m charged to cost of investments (1993 – £0.4m)		

5. Exceptional restructuring charge	1994 £m	1993 £m
Provision for restructuring of the water and sewerage business:		
Severance and other reorganisation costs	60.0	–

6. Interest payable (net)	1994 £m	1993 £m
Overdrafts and other loans repayable wholly within five years	5.7	2.1
Long term loans (any part repayable after five years)	34.2	37.4
Finance leases	5.6	5.3
	45.5	44.8
Interest receivable	(8.4)	(15.3)
	37.1	29.5

Interest payable on long term loans includes the indexation element of the Index Linked Loan Stock (see note 19).

7. Taxation	1994 £m	1993 £m
Advance corporation tax	16.9	19.0

Taxation allowances on capital expenditure are sufficient to ensure that no UK mainstream corporation tax liability arises and consequently advance corporation tax for the year is written off. No provision for deferred taxation is required for the year ended 31 March 1994 (see note 22).

8. Dividends	1994 £m	1993 £m
Interim dividend 7.3p (1993 – 6.8p) per ordinary share	21.6	20.1
Proposed final dividend 15.5p (1993 – 14.3p) per ordinary share	45.9	42.2
	67.5	62.3

9. Earnings per share

Earnings per ordinary share has been calculated by dividing profit on ordinary activities after taxation of £115.3m (1993 – £166.4m) by 295.9m (1993 – 295.2m) being the weighted average number of ordinary shares in issue during the year. Earning per ordinary share in 1994 would have been 20.2p higher if calculated before the exceptional restructuring charge. On a nil distribution basis earnings per ordinary share is 44.7p (1993 – 62.8). Earnings per ordinary share are not materially affected if calculated on a fully diluted basis.

10. Employee information	Before exceptional restructuring charge 1994 £m	Exceptional restructuring charge 1994 £m	Total 1994 £m	1993 £m
Staff costs:				
Wages and salaries	105.7	20.5	126.2	91.2
Social security costs	10.4	–	10.4	7.1
Other pension costs (see note 26)	10.2	25.2	35.4	9.1
Employee profit share (see note 24)	1.0	–	1.0	1.0
	127.3	45.7	173.0	108.4

Average number of full time equivalent persons employed:	1994	1993
Water and sewerage services	5,180	5,147
Process engineering	729	289
International	10	5
Other	112	110
	6,031	5,551

The numbers include 414 full time equivalent persons employed outside the UK (1993–25).

13. Tangible fixed assets The Group	Land and buildings £m	Infrastructure assets £m	Operational structures £m	Vehicles, plant and equipment £m	Total £m
Cost					
At 31 March 1993	47.5	869.4	1,344.3	151.8	2,413.0
New subsidiaries	–	–	–	4.3	4.3
Additions	2.9	98.6	204.2	40.0	345.7
Disposals	(0.3)	–	–	(12.3)	(12.6)
At 31 March 1994	50.1	968.0	1,548.5	183.8	2,750.4
Grants and contributions					
At 31 March 1993	–	47.1	–	–	47.1
Additions	–	17.9	–	–	17.9
At 31 March 1994	–	65.0	–	–	65.0
Depreciation					
At 31 March 1993	7.6	–	230.3	78.4	316.3
New subsidiaries	–	–	–	2.7	2.7
Charge for the year	1.1	–	42.6	24.9	68.6
Disposals	–	–	–	(10.9)	(10.9)
At 31 March 1994	8.7	–	272.9	95.1	376.7
Net book amount					
At 31 March 1994	41.4	903.0	1,275.6	88.7	2,308.7
At 31 March 1993	39.9	822.3	1,114.0	73.4	2,049.6

Tangible fixed assets of the Group at 31 March 1994 include £382.7m of assets in the course of construction (1993 – £278.2m) and also include land £8.6m (1993 – £8.2m) which is not subject to depreciation. The Group's interests in land and buildings are almost entirely freehold. In accordance with the Group's accounting policy there is no provision for depreciation on infrastructure assets and the related grants and contributions are not amortised.

The net book value of the Group's tangible fixed assets held under finance leases at 31 March 1994 was £113.4m (1993 – £94.9m).

Depreciation charged on assets held under finance leases during the year ended 31 March 1994 amounted to £3.3m (1993 – £2.4m).

	Freehold land and buildings £m	Vehicles, plant and equipment £m	Total £m
The Company			
Cost			
At 31 March 1993	0.9	2.8	3.7
Additions	0.3	4.1	4.4
Transfer from/(to) subsidiaries	0.2	(6.5)	(6.3)
Disposals	–	(0.3)	(0.3)
At 31 March 1994	1.4	0.1	1.5
Depreciation			
At 31 March 1993	–	0.9	0.9
Charge for the year	0.1	0.6	0.7
Transfer to subsidiaries	–	(1.3)	(1.3)
Disposals	–	(0.2)	(0.2)
At 31 March 1994	0.1	–	0.1
Net book amount			
At 31 March 1994	**1.3**	**0.1**	**1.4**
At 31 March 1993	0.9	1.9	2.8

Investment commitments

As described more fully in the managing director's report, the Group has a substantial long term investment programme, which includes expenditure to meet regulatory requirements, shortfalls in performance and condition and to provide for new demand and growth.

The commitments shown below reflect the value of orders placed and expenditure specifically authorised but not placed at 31 March 1994.

Figures quoted for commitments in previous years have represented the value of the 5 year capital programme agreed in principle. The directors believe that the disclosure adopted in the figures below is more reflective of the actual commitments of the Group and prior year figures have been restated accordingly.

	Group		Company	
	1994 £m	1993 £m	1994 £m	1993 £m
Contracted for but not provided in the financial statements	**244.8**	283.5	–	–
Authorised but not yet contracted for	**325.2**	346.3	–	3.3

16. Stocks	Group	
	1994 **£m**	1993 £m
Work in progress	**2.2**	5.4
Payments on account	**(0.4)**	(4.7)
	1.8	0.7
Raw materials and consumables	**10.2**	10.2
	12.0	10.9

The current replacement cost of stocks does not materially exceed the historical costs stated above. There were no stocks in the Company.

17. Debtors	Group		Company	
	1994 **£m**	1993 £m	**1994** **£m**	1993 £m
Amounts falling due within one year				
Trade debtors	**92.4**	93.7	**–**	–
Amounts recoverable on contracts	**2.1**	4.1	**–**	–
Amounts owed by subsidiary undertakings	**–**	–	**59.9**	56.9
Other debtors	**21.3**	14.2	**–**	0.7
Prepayments and accrued income	**7.6**	8.0	**2.2**	3.7
	123.4	120.0	**62.1**	61.3
Amounts falling due after more than one year				
Trade debtors	**0.8**	0.3	**–**	–
Other debtors	**–**	0.2	**–**	–
	124.2	120.5	**62.1**	61.3

18. Creditors: amounts falling due within one year	Group		Company	
	1994 **£m**	1993 £m	**1994** **£m**	1993 £m
Bank loans, overdrafts and temporary borrowings	**16.2**	8.1	**100.4**	210.5
Current portion of long term loans	**0.8**	1.0	**0.4**	0.4
Obligations under finance leases	**0.1**	0.8	**–**	–
Short term borrowings	**17.1**	9.9	**100.8**	210.9
Trade creditors	**134.9**	128.2	**0.5**	5.4
Payments on account in excess of contract value	**9.3**	13.1	**–**	–
Amounts owed to subsidiary undertakings	**–**	–	**–**	1.3
Receipts in advance	**43.9**	45.1	**–**	–
Advance corporation tax	**16.9**	19.0	**16.9**	19.0
Other taxation and social security	**6.4**	7.0	**0.8**	0.9
Accruals and deferred income	**19.2**	14.1	**7.6**	5.3
Proposed dividends	**67.5**	42.2	**67.5**	42.2
Other creditors	**298.1**	268.7	**93.3**	74.1

The temporary borrowings of the Company include £100.0m (1993 – £210.0m) owed to a subsidiary undertaking.

	Group		Company	
	1994	1993	**1994**	1993
19. Loans and other borrowings falling due after more than one year	**£m**	**£m**	**£m**	**£m**
Repayable wholly after five years				
5 1/8% Index Linked Loan Stock 2008 (a)	**118.7**	117.1	**118.7**	117.1
12% Fixed Rate Bond 2014	**100.0**	100.0	**100.0**	100.0
European Investment Bank 1999	**25.0**	25.0	–	–
European Investment Bank 2003	**10.0**	–	–	–
Other	–	0.3	–	–
Repayable by instalments, any of which is due for repayment after five years				
European Investment Bank 1995/2007 (interest in the range 6.75 – 11.5%)	**105.0**	105.0	–	–
Finance leases (b)	**120.9**	100.3	–	–
Other borrowings	**24.9**	26.5	–	–
Repayable wholly within five years				
6 1/2% Fixed Rate Bond 1998 (c)	**62.3**	–	**62.3**	–
Other loans	**21.4**	22.2	**21.2**	21.6
Finance leases (b)	**0.1**	1.0	–	–
Total loans and other borrowings	**588.3**	497.4	**302.2**	238.7
Less amounts included in creditors falling due within one year	**(0.9)**	(1.8)	**(0.4)**	(0.4)
	587.4	495.6	**301.8**	238.3
Due for repayment as follows:				
Between one and two years	**2.0**	1.1	**0.4**	0.4
Between two and five years	**114.2**	40.1	**82.7**	20.8
After five years	**471.2**	454.4	**218.7**	217.1
	587.4	495.6	**301.8**	238.3

(a) The value of the capital and interest elements of the Index Linked Loan Stock are linked to movements in the Retail Price Index.

The increase in the capital value during the year of £1.6m (1993 – £4.2m) has been taken to the profit and loss account as part of interest payable.

(b) Amount due under finance leases include £3.7m (1993 – £0.2m) payable between one and five years and £117.2m (1993 – £100.3m) payable after five years.

(c) The Fixed Rate Bond was issued in conjunction with the warrants described in the directors' report. The net proceeds of the issue were used to refinance in full the 1993 acquisition of the Nordic Water companies, and for general corporate purposes.

(d) Of the unspecified loans and other borrowings £21.4m (1993 – £21.4m) are at fixed rates and the remainder are at variable rates.

Loans and other borrowings include £1.4m (1993 – £1.4m) secured on the revenues of a subsidiary undertaking.

	Group	
	1994	1993
20. Other creditors falling due after more than one year	**£m**	**£m**
Trade creditors	**4.7**	2.9
Receipts in advance	**4.3**	4.8
Accruals and deferred income	**1.8**	0.8
Deferred grants and contributions	**55.6**	40.1
	66.4	48.6

There were no other creditors falling due after more than one year in the Company.

The extract above from Anglian Water annual report is a fairly typical example of the annual report and accounts of a large public company. An interesting feature of this company is that it moved from state ownership to public share ownership in the recent privatisation activities. Clearly there will be variations from company to company, and we have only shown extracts as opposed to the report as a whole. It may be helpful here to briefly summarise what is normally included in a company's published accounts.

- Annual reports normally begin by listing the board of directors, noting the company's address, and providing an overview of the results. There will then be a chairman's statement that may be supplemented by a chief executive's report. Such a statement usually summarises key developments in the firm's progress. In the case of Anglian Water the chairman's statement is supplemented by information on the activities of subsidiaries and associates, details of community involvement, an employee review, and a ten-year summary of results and key retail statistics.
- The directors' report itemises disclosures required by the Companies Acts. These would include statements concerning profits and dividend, principal activity of the company/group, share capital and so on. The financial statements reproduced in part above normally follow. Note that in common with most large companies Anglia Water figures are rounded to the nearest million. Balance sheets for both company and group are shown. Both the profit and loss account and the source and application of funds statements relate to the group.
- The accounts are then followed by accounting policies, and notes to the accounts, both shown in abridged form here. There is also, in this case, a brief current cost statement that reveals the effect of inflation on reported profits and other important indicators. The published accounts also contain a report from the company's auditors.
- A segmental report is included which describes the market distribution of the turnover and operating profits of the business.
- The published accounts normally conclude with statements setting out shareholders' interests, including some form of analysis by category, details of the timing of dividend payments, and a formal notice for the annual general meeting.

ANALYSING FINANCIAL STATEMENTS

You should by now be reasonably familiar with financial statements. There are a number of clients for the financial statements and their needs are slightly different. The diagram below illustrates the range but we will concern ourselves with only a subset in undertaking analysis of performance.

The primary internal users of accounts are the management, but employees welcome being informed as to how well the employer is performing. However, the regular reporting will be to management on their own performance. Dupont Corporation devised a reporting system for management of its multi-site and multi-product business in the 1930s and it remains an important framework for reviewing performance (see Figure 2.4).

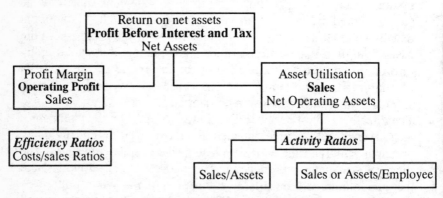

Figure 2.4 Dupont Pyramid

The ratios of themselves have little meaning and to extract the most meaning comparison with previous months/years, or with benchmarks of other companies is needed. The Dupont framework may be extended to the investor's perspective outside the firm by the addition of ratios reflecting the financing efficiency of the firm (see Figure 2.5).

The use of ratios to analyse a firm's performance over time, say five years, allows trends to be identified. Knowledge of these trends should assist management in planning future operations and may be of use in assessing the reasonableness of projected financial statements. A comparison of ratios with those of competitors may indicate differences which, if addressed, will increase efficiency. Comparing ratios to industry averages using publications like *Industrial Performance Analysis*, published by ICC Business Ratios, may also reveal variations that are worthy of further investigation. On-line data systems (Data stream) and databases available on CD-ROMs (Fame and Micro Exstat) have improved access and comparison as they perform consistent comparisons at the expense of some detail, thus jeopardising the usefulness of subsequent analysis.

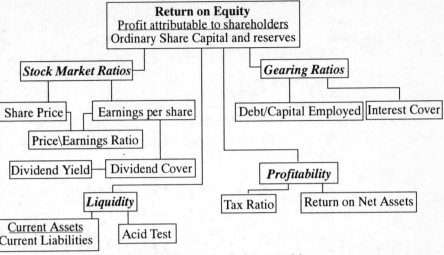

Figure 2.5 Extended Pyramid

Before looking at the ratios there are a number of cautionary points concerning their use that need to be identified:

☐ The dates and duration of the financial statements being compared should be the same. If not, the effects of seasonality may cause erroneous conclusions to be drawn.

☐ The accounts being compared should have been prepared on the same bases. Differing treatment of stocks or depreciation or asset valuations for example will distort the results.

☐ In order to judge the overall performance of the firm a group of ratios, as opposed to just one or two, should be used. In order to identify trends at least three years of ratios are normally needed.

Table 2.1 summarises some key ratios and sets out how they are calculated with a guide to their interpretation. The ratios have been divided into five groups: profitability, liquidity, gearing, activity, and investment ratios reflecting the interests of stakeholders. Clearly many stakeholders are interested in profitability but the relevance of the ratio will depend on their relationship to the business. In the case of shareholders their perspective is external to the business and hence return on equity, earnings per share and dividend are relevant to them, but for managers inside the business return on capital employed and liquidity are more appropriate. In the case of financiers such as bankers who extend loans to the firm, they are interested in the security of the loan, the coverage of the interest payment by the profits generated and the ability of the business to repay the loan through the cash flow. In contrast, trade creditors are interested in the reliability of the business

Table 2.1 Some Key Financial Ratios

Ratio	Calculation	Commentary
Return on equity	$\text{Return on Equity} = \dfrac{\text{Profits attributed to shareholders}}{\text{Ordinary Shares plus reserves}}$	Note: profit is after taxes, minority interest and preference dividend. The Key performance indicator that reflects not only operational efficiency but also the financial efficiency of the firm. Sometimes known as *return on net worth* this measures the rate of return on the shareholders (owners) investment in the firm.
Tax Ratio	$\text{Tax Ratio} = \dfrac{\text{Tax provision}}{\text{Profit before tax}}$	Measure the tax efficiency of the firm through time.
Return on Net Assets or Capital Employed	$\text{Return on net assets} = \dfrac{\text{Profits before tax and interest on debt}}{\text{Net assets}}$	Because there are many different ways of calculating return on capital employed it is important to ensure that you are consistent in using the same formula when comparing results over time or between companies. Measure the return on total investment in the enterprise. By adding interest to after-tax profits to form the numerator of the ratio recognises that total assets are funded by creditors as well as shareholders: the return provided in total is an appropriate measure of asset productivity.
Profit Margin	$\text{Net profit margin} = \dfrac{\text{Profit before interest and tax}}{\text{Sales}}$	Shows the profits from current operations without regard to interest charges arising due to the firm's capital structure. Below average margins indicate either relatively low sales prices or relatively high costs or a combination of both.
Efficiency Ratios	$\text{Gross profit margin} = \dfrac{\text{Sales-cost of sales}}{\text{Sales}}$	Indicates the margin available to cover operating expenses and yield a profit. *Operating costs to sales:* The costs of selling, administration, research and design would all be compared with sales and the trends analysed. *Production costs to sales:* Where information is available on the manufacturing costs then these should be compared with sales.

Table 2.1 continued

Ratio	Calculation	Commentary
Activity Ratios		
	Operating asset's turnover = $\dfrac{\text{Sales}}{\text{Operating assets}}$	Note that the returns on operating assets are a more accurate reflection of the manager's performance in operating the business (exclude investments and their income) is the product of: Return on Operating assets = Profit Margin × Asset Utilisation Operating assets are the fixed assets less any investments plus the working capital. Indicate the utilisation of all assets. If the ratio is below the industry average this indicates that the firm is not generating a sufficient volume of business given the size of its asset investment.
	Fixed asset's turnover = $\dfrac{\text{Sales}}{\text{Fixed assets}}$	Measures the productivity and utilisation of the fixed assets.
	Working Capital Turnover = $\dfrac{\text{Sales}}{\text{Working Capital (Current Assets} - \text{Current Liabilities)}}$	Working capital turnover reflects the intensity of utilisation of the current resources of the firm.
	Stock turnover = $\dfrac{\text{Cost of sales}}{\text{Stock}}$	Indicates the number of times in a year that the stock is turned over. Providing the firm is trading profitably, the higher the number the better. When compared to industry averages this ratio indicates whether the company is holding too much or too little stock.
	Average collection period = $\dfrac{\text{Trade Debtors} \cdot 365}{\text{Total sales}}$	Indicates the average length of time the firm must wait after making a sale before it receives payment.
	Average Payment period = $\dfrac{\text{Trade Creditors} \cdot 365}{\text{Cost of sales}}$	This indicates the extent of credit taken on suppliers.
	Inventory to working capital $\dfrac{\text{Inventory (stock)}}{\text{Current assets} - \text{current liabilities}}$	This ratio reflects the mix of assets and is a useful check on the trends. Measures the extent to which the firm's working capital is tied up in inventory. Similar mix ratios may be performed for other classes of assets and liabilities.

Table 2.1 continued

Ratio	Calculation	Commentary
Liquidity:	Current ratio = $\dfrac{\text{Current assets}}{\text{Current liabilities}}$	Indicates the extents to which the claims of short-term creditors are covered by assets that are expected to be converted to cash in a period roughly corresponding to the maturity of the liabilities.
	Quick, or Acid Test, ratio $\dfrac{(\text{Current assets} - \text{stocks})}{\text{Current liabilities}}$	Measures the ability of the firm to pay off short-term obligations without relying upon the sale of its inventories (stock).
Gearing ratios: Gearing is also referred to as financial leverage	Debt to asset's ratio $\dfrac{\text{Total debt}}{\text{Capital Employed}}$	Total debt may include overdraft and interest bearing current liabilities as this may represent an important element of the debt finance. Indicate the extent to which loans have been used to finance the firms' operations
	Long term debt to equity $\dfrac{\text{Long term debt}}{\text{Total shareholder's equity}}$	Measures the balance between loan and equity capital in the company's overall capital structure.
	Interest Cover $\dfrac{\text{Profit before tax and interest}}{\text{Total interest charges}}$	Measures the extent to which earnings can decline without the firm becoming unable to meet the annual interest costs.
Stock Market Ratios:	Earnings per share $\dfrac{\text{Profit after tax}}{\text{Number of ordinary shares in issue}}$	Shows the earnings available to the owners of ordinary shares.
	Dividend yield $\dfrac{\text{Annual dividend per share}}{\text{Current market price per share}}$	Measures the return to owners received in the form of dividends.
	Dividend Cover = $\dfrac{\text{Earnings per share}}{\text{Dividend per share}}$	Reflects the number of times the dividend is covered by earnings.
	Price-earnings (P/E) ratio $\dfrac{\text{Current market price per share}}{\text{Earnings per share}}$	The P/E ratio relates the Earnings per share (EPS) to the price the share sells for in the market and indicates the stock market's evaluation of the share. Faster growing or less risky firms tend to have higher P/E ratios than slower growing or more risky firms.

to pay for the goods and services and this is reflected in the liquidity and solvency of the business. However, creditors increasingly rely on credit reference agencies that use additional sources such as banks, county court records, debt agencies, etc.

As a first step in analysing the performance of business either a table or a graph should be drawn of the following:

- Turnover
- Net Assets
- Operating Profit.

It is worth comparing the relative growth of these factors with the overall movement in price levels to gain insight into the real performance of the business.

There are other useful ratios that are more related to the type of firm/industry that is the subject of analysis. For example, sales per square foot and sales per employee may be important performance indicators in the retail sector, whereas tonnes of output per employee may be important for a manufacturing enterprise.

The ratios outlined in Table 2.1 have been used to evaluate the performance of Anglia Water. Using the accounts set out earlier, and those of some previous years, the ratios in Table 2.2 have been prepared. The information in Table 2.2 represents the starting point for analysing Anglia's performance. The commentary on the ratios is based on this information. The next step would normally be to evaluate Anglia's performance in the light of averages for that industry and/or by comparing it with a major competitor – Severn Trent Water perhaps.

A Brief Commentary on Table 2.2

In undertaking our analysis we should reflect on the nature of the business under consideration. A water company has relatively low costs of material, as its basic material water is free in the environment. However, the cost of extracting from artesian wells or storing in reservoirs is relatively capital intense. At the other end of the process the distribution and subsequent drainage are both costly to maintain and increasingly environmentally sensitive. The customer, you and I, generally pay water rates in advance but some are metered including businesses and may pay in arrears. This payment pattern will have a consequence on the cash flow and working capital structure, while the nature of the assets (treatment works, pipelines, etc) will influence the balance sheet structure and financing.

Trend

The percentage increase year on year in turnover, net assets and

Table 2.2 Anglia Water Plc Some Key Financial Ratios

	1994	1993	1992	1991	1990
Trend % increase year on year					
Turnover	17.95	11.49	13.57	14.78	N/A
Net assets	10.83	11.09	15.33	28.66	N/A
Operating profit	−20.75	9.07	13.85	10.15	N/A
Profitability %					
Return on equity	8.16	12.15	11.64	11.16	10.25
Tax ratio	12.78	10.24	11.09	11.27	10.79
Return on net assets	7.56	10.64	10.68	10.83	12.66
Net profit margin	24.37	36.28	37.12	37.06	38.65
Efficiency Ratio %					
Gross profit margin	N/A				
Costs	N/A				
Activity Ratio					
Operating asset's turnover	.31	.29	.29	.33	.32
Fixed asset's turnover	.30	.28	.29	.29	.28
Working capital turnover	18.88	16.6	15.85	22.57	2.00
Stock turnover	57.33	53.5	78.07	60.61	59.01
Average collection period	49.01	58.83	61.53	66.39	61.21
Average payment period	71.57	80.22	67.67	87.96	59.67
Liquidity					
Current ratio	.75	.88	1.02	.90	.27
Quick, or acid, test	.72	.84	.98	.87	.25
Gearing ratios					
Debt to asset's ratio	.29	.27	.24	.20	.16
Long-term debt to equity	.46	.39	.32	.25	.05
Interest cover	4.56	7.28	8.48	6.87	2.23
Stock market ratios					
Earnings per share	39.0	56.4	51.7	45.9	42.1
Dividend yield	5.9				
Dividend cover	1.7				
Price-earnings (P/E)	11.2				

operating profit are important indicators of the general trend. If comparative data for price movements is available, a sense of real performance can be identified. In the period reported on, inflation and general price movements have been downward or relatively stable in single figures. The growth in turnover and net assets reflects real growth, however profits have been somewhat erratic, reflecting a number of factors. Firstly, 1990 was the first year of the privatised companies' activities and so the accounts have been influenced by a change process. In particular, 1994 results include provisions for restructuring of the business.

Profitability
Shareholders and investors will be interested in the return on equity and the related earnings per share. The general trend has been improving but the restructuring costs of £60m in 1994 resulted in a loss of earnings per share of 20.2p, nearly half the earnings on privatisation. However, this is not the only problem, as the profit margin has steadily been declining and examination of costs show that raw material and consumables doubled from 1993 to 1994.

Efficiency
It is difficult to compute the efficiency ratios for a water company as items such as raw material cost are relatively small (12.9 per cent of turnover – increase from 7.6 per cent in 1993). Staff and labour costs are exceptional – 25 per cent reflecting restructuring but would normally be approximately 18 per cent. Labour efficiency may usefully be measured in terms of sales or profit per employee, as well as fixed assets per employee, reflecting capital intensity.

Activity
The activity ratios reflect the capital intense nature of the industry with turnover only a third of operating assets. This contrasts with retail business where one may expect turnover to be three times the investment in operating assets. However, the water industry has an unusual balance of fixed assets to working capital.

Working capital has moved from a small positive proportion of net assets in 1990 to a –3.5 per cent in 1994. This reflects the small investment in stock and debtors and the extended credit from suppliers. Improved debt collection (now down to 49 days) further improves the financial position.

Liquidity
It has often been suggested that businesses need to ensure that current liabilities are fully covered by current assets but this fails to reflect the efficiency of the working capital cycle. Companies have shifted to just-in-time manufacturing and hence have minimised stocks while efficient cash movement systems have supported tighter credit control. The consequence is that the operating cycle for businesses is shorter and the level of cover required for liabilities has declined. The narrowness of gap between current ratio and acid test reflect the low

level of investment in stocks in Anglia. Retailers operate with even smaller ratios (current 0.5 and acid 0.2) while heavy manufacturing with slower operating cycles may be expected to have current ratios above 1.0.

Gearing
The gearing ratios show the increasing usage of debt to finance the business. This reflects the lower cost of debt finance (interest deducted pre-tax but dividends after tax) and recent economic trends. Interest cover is substantial but distorted in 1994 in line with restructuring adjustments.

Stock Market Ratios
These should be compared with other water companies to measure relative performance.

	Anglia	Yorkshire	Severn Trent	Chester
Earnings per share	39.0	68.0	59.0	10.0
Dividend yield	5.9	5.4	5.6	3.9
Dividend cover	1.7	2.3	2.2	1.9
Price-earnings (P/E)	11.2	7.9	8.8	17.0

The Stock Market has adjusted its expectations in line with the restructuring but has expectations of improvements in the future. As a result the P/E ratio suggests Anglia is rated more highly than Yorkshire or Severn Trent which is a small local water company.

Overall
The ratios reveal that Anglia has adapted to the new climate of privatisation and is producing the results expected of it by the market. Restructuring costs have distorted 1994 but are expected to improve efficiency in the future as reflected in the share price. However, the company needs to control its costs and improve its asset utilisation.

As we have already indicated the full set of financial statements provides a very comprehensive view of the firm's activities. Also remember that this would be the first stage in an assessment of the company; we would need to consider the ratios in Table 2.2 with those of a competitor or the industry in general.

Financial ratios can also be used to predict company failure. One of the better known attempts was the work of Altman who used five financial ratios and a statistical technique to calculate a Z-score that classified firms as solvent or insolvent (Altman EI, 1968). The Z-score was found not to be a good predictor for longer than two years before bankruptcy. Altman's work was applied to UK financial data by Argenti (1976) and Taffler (1977). Both recognised that the Z-scores used by Altman will be different in the UK, will differ by industry, and will change over time as economic conditions change. Ratios can only be used as a warning system rather than as a predictor.

Valuation of the business

A number of valuation methods are available that are likely to provide a range of results. This range is a basis on which to explore valuation but the only certain value is the price paid by a purchaser.

Market Capitalisation: Where a share is traded then an immediate valuation is available based on the market's view of the business. This price, which in theory should reflect future expectations of earnings, actually represents the traded price of shares. However, the theory is justified assuming that we all have equal knowledge as to future expectations.

Balance Sheet Value: It is generally agreed that the balance sheet is not a good guide for valuation and two approaches to adjusting the value may be taken. If a minimum price is sought then this is likely to be the value on break up which values all assets on the basis of individual realisation. Hence stock values and equipment will probably be written down. The alternative is to revalue the assets on the basis of going concern including any market value of intangible assets such as brands.

Price Earnings Ratio: An indicator of how the market values the share based on the current earning stream. Where a company's share is not traded then it is possible to estimate the likely valuation based on the company's actual earnings per share × an equivalent PE ratio (for a similar company whose share is traded).

Expected Future Cash Flow: Two approaches may be taken which reflect the degree of access the value has to internal company data. If we are external to the business then we may use Gordon's Dividend Growth model (Gordon and Shapiro, 1956) to calculate the likely share price based on the current dividend, the rate of growth of dividend and the required rate of return for this class of risk investment.

If we have access to internal information then we may estimate the future free cash flow after maintaining the business and meeting all payments on debt. The resulting income stream may be 'discounted' to provide a net present value for the business today (see Chapter 6 for an explanation of discounting).

The range of valuations should not be underestimated as in the case of the Ford Motor Company takeover of Jaguar. The range lay between £250m (market capitalisation) and £1.6bn (the price paid by Ford)! However, all value is in the 'eye of the beholder' and their expectations of what they can do with the prize.

The balanced scorecard first proposed by Kaplan and Norton in 1992 tries to redress the over-emphasis on financial performance associated with financial reporting and the short termism by incorporating a review reflecting the longer-term factors. The starting point of the review is the corporate objectives that may or may not be published externally. The firm's capacity to deliver these objectives will be reflected in four key areas of performance:

□ *Financial*: profitability, cash flow, reliability of performance
□ *Customer*: value for money, competitive position, innovation, satisfaction
□ *Internal*: quality, consistency, safety, efficiency
□ *Innovation and Learning*: Growth of new business, new products, staff attitudes, value of staff investment through training, improvements in productivity, innovation etc.

SUMMARY

We started this chapter by discussing the importance of the firm's financial statements. The major statements were then introduced, that is the profit and loss account, balance sheet, and cash flow statement. We also considered the key assumptions underpinning the construction of such statements and noted how this may mean that they are less than perfect tools for assessing the position of the company.

The use of financial ratios to evaluate performance was discussed. Some of the more important ratios were applied to Anglian Water plc as an example of how the technique may be used in practice. We can conclude by observing that such tools are widely used, even though there are important qualifications concerning the use of the annual accounts in assessing performance, which are due mainly to the lack of reality in some of the figures.

FURTHER READING

There are a number of books that deal with financial analysis. Readers may find the following useful:

Reid, W and Middleton, D R (1982) *The Meaning of Company Accounts*, Gower, Aldershot.

Sizer, J (1979) *An Insight into Management Accounting*, Penguin, Harmondsworth.

Wilson, R M S and McHugh, G (1987) *Financial Analysis: A Managerial Introduction*, Cassell, London.

REFERENCES

Altman, E I (1968) 'Financial ratios, discriminant analysis and the prediction of corporate bankruptcy', *Journal of Finance*, Vol 23, No 4: pp 589–609, September.

Argenti, J (1976) *Corporate Collapse: The Causes and Symptoms*, McGraw Hill, London.

Bowman, C and Asch, D (1987) *Strategic Management*, Macmillan, Houndmills, Basingstoke.

Lee, T A and Tweedie, D P (1981) *The Institutional Investor and Financial Information*, The Institute of Chartered Accountants in England and Wales, London.

Taffler, R J and Tisshaw, H J (1977) 'Going, going, gone: four factors which predict', *Accountancy*, March, pp 50–2, 54.

3

Financial Structures

INTRODUCTION

Chapter 2 stressed the importance of the annual financial statements in terms of presenting a picture of the performance of the firm to investors and potential investors. In this chapter we will explore some of the issues in how the firm is financed. The source of funds for future developments and the balance between sources are crucial to managers' future plans and to an investor's assessment of the firm. The chapter starts by considering the various sources of funds available and their relative costs before moving on to look at the financial structure of the business.

Before getting into the sources of funds available it is worth reflecting briefly on the role of the securities market.

> A market in securities performs two important functions. The first function (that of a primary market) is to provide both existing quoted companies and new companies with the facility for raising new capital. The second function is to permit holders of existing or outstanding securities to buy and sell, thus facilitating a change of ownership speedily and preferably at low cost. This latter function is usually described as the secondary market. (Franks and Broyles, 1979)

Most Stock Exchange activity represents purchases and sales of previously issued shares. Although we are primarily interested in new issues to provide finance it is important to recognise that if a company's share price falls because management pursues policies which are not perceived to be in the best interests of shareholders, new issues become more difficult. If the market value of a share falls below its par or nominal value, for example, a rights issue would not be permitted. It is possible during a slump when profits are reduced and loan finance may be difficult to obtain, that a company which has failed to maintain its stock market valuation may find few sources of loan capital which are not prohibitively expensive.

As well as acting as a potential source of funds the securities market does provide a convenient way of valuing a company by providing an 'objective' measure which can act as a guide to both management and owners. One consequence of this is the necessity for firms to keep stock exchange analysts, investment advisers and so on informed about future prospects. Indeed, other sources of financial information, such as financial press reports, occasional acquisition or merger reports, and stockbrokers' reports were found to be of considerable influence in investment decisions (Lee and Tweedie, 1981, p 95). In order to help shape advisers' perceptions of corporate performance most firms devote some time and energy ensuring that their view is clearly understood by institutional investors and their advisers. Many institutional investors make visits to the company to assess management and future prospects. Such visits were found to rank third in influence behind annual reports and other sources of financial information such as press reports (Lee and Tweedie, 1981, p 140).

SOURCES OF FUNDS

Most funds used by established firms are internally generated. Nevertheless, external sources of finance are a vital resource required from time to time by nearly all organisations. The clearing banks provide the bulk of short-term funds, such as bank overdrafts, and some bank loans are available for up to ten years. Table 3.1 summarises the sources and uses of funds by UK companies for the three years 1988 to 1990.

The figures are aggregates and as such may mask considerable variations. In general, however, they are confirmed by the findings of some research in America which noted that managers preferred internally generated funds supplemented by loan capital. The rationale for this was because such funds could be relied on with a high degree of certainty, and so were seen as assured or plannable sources of funds (Donaldson and Lorsch, 1983, p 52).

New issues

Before considering the types of finance available to the firm, and having briefly explained the function of the Stock Exchange, it is useful to review briefly the mechanisms available to an organisation which wishes to raise finance. Issuing houses, which are normally merchant banks, play a key role in new issues. They provide advice

Table 3.1 Companies – sources and uses of funds

	£m 1988	£m 1989	£m 1990
Sources			
Capital Issues	21,228	25,755	23,185
Short-term borrowing	34,031	51,636	8,474
Retained income	46,001	49,353	41,408
Other	769	2,597	(6,461)
	102,029	**129,341**	**66,606**
Uses			
Expenditure on fixed assets	71,605	92,022	65,239
Increase in current assets and investments	30,424	37,319	1,367
	102,029	**129,341**	**66,606**

Source: Annual Abstract of Statistics, HMSO, London 1994, Table 17.25

concerning the issue and act as middlemen in channelling funds to the purchase of new issues. They are involved in underwriting, marketing and pricing new issues. Whether the merchant bank is acting as the principal or merely the agent for a new issue, as an underwriter it guarantees that the money will be raised. To reduce its risk it will arrange with other financial institutions that they will underwrite the issue, for a fee of course. During periods of uncertainty or depression it is possible that a large proportion of a new issue may be left with the underwriters. Two recent examples would be the sale by the government of shares in Britoil in 1982, and in BP in 1987.

The issuing house has considerable discretion in the choice of security to be issued. The decision as to whether to issue equity or loan capital will take into account financial gearing (see Chapter 4) and the probable effect on the cost of capital. Once a decision has been made concerning the amount of finance required and the method of raising the capital, the price has to be set. Theoretically, the price of a new issue is largely set by the required rate of return that investors expect from that type of investment. However, although the issue price may be set with the best advice available and taking account of all probable stock market variations, it is still possible to pitch the price incorrectly.

From a company's standpoint when a new issue is oversubscribed and the price is, therefore, above the issue price, this would have the effect of lowering its cost of capital. This is because, in the future, it would have to issue fewer shares to obtain the same level of funding. Further issues would also tend to be more acceptable to the market. In situations where a large proportion of a new issue is left with the underwriters – who would probably wish to dispose of the shares as soon as it is feasible – the share price will tend to fall below the issue price, therefore increasing the cost of capital and making future issues more difficult.

The issue of shares does not necessarily raise funds for the company but for the holders of the shares. This is quite common for smaller enterprises and represents one method whereby the owners can realise some of their capital while concurrently raising further finance for the development and growth of the firm.

Set out below are the different methods of issuing shares in the United Kingdom.

- A *public issue by prospectus* uses an issuing house as an agent and attempts to persuade potential investors to buy shares in the shortest possible time. It has not been used much recently and has been superseded by the offer for sale method.
- An *offer for sale* is normally used when a large amount of capital is required. The issuing house, acting as principal, offers the shares at a fixed price. A detailed prospectus is issued and the offer is extensively advertised. In the event of an oversubscription, the issuing house allots the available shares to the applicants. To ensure that a ready market exists as many applications as possible get some shares, so applications for large holdings usually obtain only a small proportion of shares applied for and small applications are settled in full.
- A *private placing* can be used by unquoted companies who require a small amount of funds with the minimum of issue costs. Normally, an issuing house agrees to purchase a number of shares in the company with the intention of placing them with some institutional investors.
- A *Stock Exchange introduction* does not raise extra finance but does allow the company to obtain a Stock Exchange quotation. The shares become marketable – existing shareholders make some of their shares available – and their price tends to be higher than comparable unquoted shares.
- A *Stock Exchange placing* is a combination of a private placing and a Stock Exchange introduction. The company will need both a quotation and a small amount of capital which is usually raised from institutional investors.

□ *Issues by tender* are used when there is uncertainty over the issue price. A minimum price is set and the public invited to bid for the shares. Allotments are made at the price which will just clear all the shares, known as the striking price.

The *costs* of issuing new securities varies considerably depending on the method used and the type of security offered. In general, the cost of issuing ordinary shares is higher than for fixed interest stocks, and the cost of offers for sale as a percentage of gross proceeds is greater than the cost of placings.

Fixed interest stocks are usually bought in large blocks by relatively few institutional investors, whereas ordinary shares tend to be bought by large numbers of individuals. The relative underwriting risk of ordinary shares tends to reflect their greater volatility. Because many expenses associated with any issue tend to be fixed, their proportion of the total cost of flotation is high on small issues which typically relate to less well known companies.

Flotation costs are also affected by whether or not it is a rights issue and, if so, by the extent of underpricing. If there is an element of underpricing, the risk to the issuing house is reduced and less selling effort will be required. Such factors allow a company to float new securities to its own shareholders at a relatively low cost.

The advent of the Unlisted Securities Market (USM) in November 1980 was designed to assist the growth and development of small firms by making the availability of capital wider for them. The USM allows new entrants to raise equity without the need to satisfy all the onerous requirements of a full Stock Exchange listing. For example, a firm can put up a minimum of 10 per cent of its equity on the USM as opposed to 25 per cent for a full Stock Exchange listing. Should that 10 per cent already be in public hands the company does not even need an accountant's report for its introduction. The advertising requirement is also reduced so reducing some of the heavy costs of a public sale. Table 3.2 sets out the percentage costs of selling new issues.

We will now turn our attention to the distinguishing features of loan capital and share capital.

Loan capital

Loan capital can refer to many different sources of funds. All forms of loan capital do have one thing in common and that is lack of control. Loan capital carries no voting rights. However, in the event of a company defaulting on the terms of the loan, the holders may take effective control, often by the appointment of a receiver.

Table 3.2 Typical costs (per cent) of issues to raise £2m

1. Ordinary shares	
Offers or prospectuses	7.6
Placings	2.6
Rights	4.0
2. Fixed interest stock	
Placings	2.5
Offer	5.7

Source: Committee to review the financing of financial institutions, *Evidence of the Financing of Industry and Trade*, Vol 3, HMSO, London 1978

As a first step we will distinguish between short- and long-term loans. Short-term credit consists of obligations that are expected to mature in one year or less and generally such loans are unsecured. The management of short-term funds is dealt with in more detail in Chapter 5 on Working Capital Management. Suffice it to say that it is possible to identify three basic types of short-term finance which are briefly outlined below:

☐ Spontaneous sources, such as suppliers of goods and services, and accruals like employees' wages and salaries and government taxation. The use of trade credit from suppliers is widespread and a significant source of short-term funds. It involves no explicit cost except when a cash discount for early payment is offered. Accruals as a source of funds result from the fact that wages and taxes are paid at discrete points in time after the service has been rendered. This source of funding is hard to manipulate but does not incur any cost.
☐ Bank sources, such as the main clearing banks for overdraft facilities. These are often set up with a prearranged limit under which the company can borrow funds to meet seasonal needs. The cost is usually the bank's base rate plus a risk premium of 0–5 per cent. This is the most widely used and flexible source of short-term finance. Bank loans may be secured on the assets of the firm.
☐ Non-bank sources, such as the sale of commercial paper to other businesses, insurance companies and other financial institutions. Commercial paper is an unsecured short-term promissory note which may be placed directly or through the market. It can only be used by large financially strong firms. The cost to the firm is usually lower than any alternative form of negotiated short-term loan. Customer advances, where customers make an advance payment

on all or a portion of planned purchases, represent another potential source, as do loans from interested or concerned parties.

Long-term loan capital has a maturity in excess of one year. Such capital can be bought and sold on the stock market. Loan capital has a nominal value – though this may be in the form of stock rather than discrete share units – and this may differ from the market price. Holders of loan capital receive their income in the form of interest on the loan. This loan interest is a charge against revenue, it is not a share of profit. This implies that a fixed rate of interest is payable in full whether profits are made or not. Loan interest is also deductible for taxation purposes which will tend to reduce the cost of servicing the loan. There is also some security for the interest and capital arising primarily from the contract between firm and lender.

Loan capital can take many forms:

- The loan may be secured on particular assets of the company, often known as a mortgage debenture.
- It may be secured on all the assets of the company, other than those pledged to mortgage debentures, i.e. it has a floating charge.
- It may be unsecured, in which case it would rank after mortgage debentures and those with a floating charge in the event of a liquidation.

In addition a company may issue convertible loan stock. Convertible loans carry the right that they may be converted into ordinary shares at the option of the holder. The terms of the conversion and the dates on which it can be exercised are set out by the company. Normally the ratio in which the convertible security can be exchanged for equity is stated by indicating that the loan is convertible into *n* ordinary shares. A conversion feature enables the firm's capital structure to be changed without increasing the total financing.

Gitman (1982, pp 619–21) identified three reasons for using convertible loans. First, convertibles are a form of deferred equity finance, since both issuer and purchaser expect the security to be converted at some stage in the future. Without this expectation the purchaser would not accept the lower return normally associated with convertible loan stock. This leads into Gitman's second point, which is that the inclusion of a conversion feature reduces the effective interest cost as the purchaser sacrifices a portion of the fixed return to have the opportunity to become an equity shareholder at some future time. Finally, funds raised using convertible loans are temporarily cheap which may minimise the financial pressures on a firm during a project start-up period. During a period of tight money a conversion feature may enable loan capital to be successfully raised.

Share capital

Ordinary share capital, often referred to as equity, is the linchpin of a company's financial structure. Holders of ordinary shares have legal control of the company by virtue of their voting rights. The holder of one ordinary share has the right to cast one vote at the annual general meeting or at any special meetings which may be called. However, companies sometimes issue 'A' ordinary shares which do not possess voting rights but which are identical to ordinary shares in all other respects. The main characteristics of equity shares are as follows:

1. They must have a nominal or par value, i.e. they may be described as '50p shares' or as '£1 shares'. This nominal value is often the price at which the shares were first issued but it may not relate at all to their current market value.

2. Shares issued after a founding issue may be offered at a price equal to or at a price exceeding their nominal value. Issues may be offered generally as already discussed earlier in this chapter, or the issue may be restricted to the existing shareholders (a rights issue).

3. The shares of a quoted company may change hands frequently on the Stock Exchange. We referred in our introduction to the role played by the Stock Exchange and the importance of keeping analysts and advisers informed of corporate financial policy. Although there is no direct financial effect on the company of this trade in their shares the firm is required to maintain an up-to-date register of shareholders.

4. Normally a company is prohibited by law from repaying capital to its ordinary shareholders. So withdrawal of capital entails selling shares on the market. In the event of the firm being wound up the holders of the equity are entitled to the proceeds of the whole of the residual assets of the business. The law was amended in 1981 to allow companies to redeem its shares or to purchase and cancel them. The redemption or purchase must be either out of the proceeds of a fresh issue of shares made especially for the purpose or out of profits otherwise available for distribution. The total value of the capital fund must be conserved.

5. Bonus shares can only be issued to existing shareholders in proportion to their existing holdings. A bonus issue is not a source of finance, it is a bookkeeping operation designed to

recognise the fact that legally distributable reserves have become in effect permanent capital.

6. The holders of ordinary shares are entitled to any residual income, that is the amount remaining after all other expenses such as loan interest and corporate taxation have been paid. This may be actually paid in cash as a dividend, or it may be retained in the business for the ultimate benefit of the equity holders through providing funds for expansion. As Table 3.1 revealed retained earnings are the largest single source of funds.

There are a number of advantages to the firm of issuing equity. First there are no fixed charges – there is no legal obligation to pay a dividend. Second, equity has no fixed maturity date. Third, the issue of ordinary shares increases the credit-worthiness of the firm because they provide a cushion against losses for creditors. Finally, equity can often be sold more easily than debt because it would normally carry a higher expected return as well as a better hedge against inflation.

The disadvantages of issuing equity is first that it extends voting rights or control to additional members who are brought into the firm. Second, such extra shares extend the right to share with existing members in profits. Taken together, these points may lead to a significant dilution of existing shareholders' interest in the firm. Third, dividends payable on equity are not deductible as an expense for corporation tax whereas loan interest is. This will affect the relative cost of equity and loan capital. Finally, as Table 3.2 illustrated, it is cheaper to issue debt rather than equity.

A *rights issue* is where new equity is sold to existing shareholders. All existing members are given an option to buy a certain number of new shares, the number of which is determined by their existing holding. It is usual for new shares issued by means of a rights issue to be priced below the current market price. The rights issue should leave existing shareholders at least as well off as they were previously, even if they sell their rights rather than subscribe to the issue.

For example, assume a company has 40m ordinary shares in issue quoted at £1.50. It decides to raise £12m using a rights issue of one new share for every four held, i.e. 10m shares will be issued at £1.20. Theoretically, by raising an extra £12m the market value of the company should rise by exactly this amount giving an ex-rights price of £1.44 (60m + 12m/50m shares). The right itself then has a value of 24p, the difference between the ex-rights price (£1.44) and the issue price (£1.20). A shareholder can take up the rights or sell them. In either case the shareholder will neither benefit nor lose by the rights issue.

In the example above if a shareholder originally held 100 shares they had a market value of £1.50 and the holding was worth £150. If the owner exercises the right to buy then a further 25 shares at £1.20 each are acquired, an outlay of £30. The total investment is now £150 + £30 = £180. The investor now owns 125 shares with a theoretical ex-rights price of

$$(N_o \times P_o + N_n \times P_n)/N$$

where:

N_o = number of old shares
P_o = pre-issue price
N_n = number of new shares
P_n = new issue price
N = total number of shares

i.e. $(100 \times 1.5 + 25 \times 1.2)/125$ = £1.44

The value of the shares is £180 (125 × £1.44). If the rights to the 25 new shares had been sold the owner would have realised £6 (25 × (£1.44–1.2)) in cash. The original holding of 100 shares would now be worth £144 (100 × £1.44). This plus the cash from the sale of the rights, £6, is the same as the original investment. Remember this is the theoretical position. The market price of a share after a rights issue depends on the market's assessment of the future earnings prospects of the company.

There is a broader issue linked with the use of ordinary shares as a source of funds and that is their social impact. Weston and Brigham (1979, p 346) argue that companies funded by equity are less vulnerable to a downturn in performance because there are no fixed charges, the payment of which may precipitate liquidation. However, they point out that equity prices fall in a recession so causing the cost of capital to rise which in turn reduces investment. The reduction in investment will further aggravate the recession. An expanding economy is accompanied by rising share prices reducing the cost of capital so stimulating investment. This may add to the developing inflationary boom. Weston and Brigham conclude that ordinary share financing may tend to amplify cyclical fluctuations.

Preference shares are normally given preferential rights over profits, and, in the event of a winding up, over surplus assets. Because of the need to make their preferential rights attractive which is achieved by keeping the number issued low relative to equity they become virtually risk-free. They are not a popular source of funds now due to tax disadvantages relative to loan capital. For analysis purposes they are usually classified with loan capital.

Leasing

Leasing is a form of debt financing which provides for the effective acquisition of the asset. Unlike debt or equity financing, leasing is typically identified with particular assets. The risk to the lessor is reduced as if the lessee does not meet the contractual obligations, the lessor – as the legal owner of the item – has a stronger legal right to reclaim the asset.

It is possible to distinguish between an operating lease and a financial lease. An operating lease normally includes both financing and maintenance services. Normally the lessor agrees to maintain and service the item, the costs of which are built into the lease payments. In addition an operating lease is one where an asset is leased or hired for a period of time less than its useful life. The lessor expects to recover costs in subsequent renewal payments or on disposal.

A financial lease is one which lasts for the whole of an asset's estimated useful life and where the lessee in effect takes on all the risks and benefits associated with ownership. In substance a finance lease is the purchase of an asset financed by the lessor as lender. Such leases are now required to be shown on the balance sheet as assets at fair value and as liabilities for future lease payments.

A common misconception is that leasing allows the use of an asset without the firm having recourse to its own funds. However, lease payments are based on the price of the asset plus an interest factor, and it is also unlikely that the lessor would advance a loan for the total cost unless the proposed lessee had other assets or equity to support the loan.

LEVERAGED AND MANAGEMENT BUY-OUTS

The 1980s and 1990s have seen a significant increase in leveraged buy-outs and management buy-outs. The term leveraged buy-out is usually applied to US deals where the transaction has been initiated by a financial group rather than by management. A management buy-out is the purchase of a business by its management with the help of financial backers. The managers put up a relatively small amount of the finance but gain a disproportionately large share of the equity. A new development in this area has been management buy-ins in which a business is purchased by one or more outside managers with the help of financial backers. Pure buy-ins are often riskier than pure buy-outs because they involve outside management. Buy-ins, management buy-outs (commonly known as bimbos) are becoming increasingly popular as they combine internal and external management expertise.

Table 3.3 sets out estimates of total UK buyouts plus an analysis of their gearing.

Table 3.3 UK MBOs and their gearing

Year	Number	Total funding (£m)	Equity (£m)	Mezzanine (£m)	Debt (£m)	Gearing (M+D:E)
1989	500	5885	1055	864	3966	4.6
1990	550	2056	571	205	1280	2.6
1991	500	1922	775	140	1007	1.5
1992	520	2304	1003	96	1205	1.3
1993	510	2010	850	120	1040	1.4
1994	550	2772	1134	90	1548	1.4

Source: KPMG Corporate Finance, 1995

Mezzanine finance is usually used in larger deals where equity providers are not prepared to increase the amount of ordinary capital they will supply and the banks are not prepared to increase the amount of debt. Mezzanine finance fills the middle layer, taking a higher risk than banks for a higher return but a lower risk and return than equity holders. The attraction is that, in a mature business with sound cash flow characteristics, mezzanine provides a cheaper form of equity for expansion when banks still perceive risk is too high for debt finance.

The overall change in average gearing of MBOs over time is of interest – from 4.6 in 1989 down to 1.4 in 1994. However, if you recall that Anglian Water (Chapter 2) had gearing of less than 0.5, the benefits to the equity holders (and the risks) in an MBO of the increased proportion of loan capital should be clear. It should be noted that such high gearing tends to confound conventional financial theory. MBOs have proved popular as companies have sought to divest themselves of parts of their business and who better to run such firms than existing management. MBOs were also believed to free managers from the constraints of operating within a larger, perhaps more bureaucratic, corporate framework. Given the high levels of debt finance, and its associated cost, those managing MBOs would need to ensure that they competed effectively and efficiently if they were to stand a chance of reaping the rewards.

COST OF CAPITAL

Before any decisions can be made concerning the organisation's capital structure it is essential to understand some of the issues involved in determining the cost of capital. We will consider the cost of debt or loan capital, the cost of equity, and the weighted average cost of capital. The cost of preference shares will not be considered as they are so rarely used and do not form a major source of funds. Indeed we have already noted that preference capital is very similar in nature to loan capital with the exception of the taxation implications.

Cost of loan capital

The cost of loan capital is relatively straightforward because the amount receivable by the investor is known as it is set by the contract. It is reasonable to assume that the contractual return will be paid in estimating the interest cost of the capital even though the investor is not certain to receive this return as the company could go into liquidation. A simple equation will provide the cost of debt:

$$R_d = r/MV$$

where:

$$R_d = \text{cost of debt}$$
$$r = \text{the interest cost}$$
$$MV = \text{current market value}$$

In estimating the cost of debt an adjustment should be made for corporation tax as the amount of interest paid is deducted from earnings in computing the corporation tax liability. So if the basic cost of debt is r per cent and the rate of corporation tax is T, the after tax cost of debt becomes:

$$R_d = r(1-T)/MV$$

For example, if a company is paying £20,000 per annum on debt capital with a current market value of £180,000 and a corporation tax rate of 35 per cent, the after tax cost of debt is:

$$20,000(1-0.35)/180,000 = 7.2\%$$

Because the contractual obligations to holders of loan capital are invariably expressed as actual money sums and not at constant prices, the basic estimate of the cost of debt will in effect include an allowance for inflation. Where cash flow estimates have been made in terms of constant prices, the effective cost of debt should be expressed in real terms. So, if a company raises loan capital at 14 per cent with a corporation tax rate of 35 per cent, and inflation expected at a rate of 5 per cent, then the rate of return in real terms is 4.1 per cent (14 – (14 × 0.35 – 5)).

Cost of ordinary share capital

The cost of equity is clearly related to the rate of return equity shareholders consider satisfactory. The problem is to identify this rate. Just before we look at some approaches to this problem it is necessary to recall that much of a company's new funding derives from retained earnings (refer back to Table 3.1).

> The extent to which a company earns money that could be paid as dividend and refrains from doing so represents an increase in the equity investment in just the same way as if it were raising new capital. (Bowman and Asch, 1987, p 156)

If the money were paid out as dividend the shareholders could invest it and earn a rate of return on it. Therefore, the company must earn at least an equivalent rate of return to justify retaining the cash. As a consequence we can infer that the rate of return required on retained earnings is the same as that required on new issues. The fact that new issues incur costs (underwriting, advertising, etc) can be allowed for by adjusting the estimates of inflows arising from a new issue.

We will consider two methods of determining the cost of equity, the capital asset-pricing model, and the Gordon growth model. These two approaches are complementary rather than mutually exclusive, and should produce the same answer if all measurements involved could be made with perfect precision.

The *capital asset-pricing model* (CAPM) is based upon portfolio theory. This recognises an individual's dislike of risk, and that investors therefore require a higher rate of return on a higher risk security. Given risk aversion, CAPM recognises the effect of diversification whereby investors reduce the risk by spreading their investment in a range of securities. Risk reduction arises from the selection of investments – the *portfolio*. The assumption is that stocks can be combined so that the portfolio is less risky than its components. The power of diversification to reduce risk is dependent upon the relationship between the returns of individual securities –

diversification will not reduce risk if the alternatives do well or badly together.

It is impossible to diversify in such a way as to eliminate risk completely since some form of risk is inherent in any investment. This *systematic* risk is related to the overall movement of the stock market and as such cannot be diversified away. There is an element of risk involved in an investment which is particular to that specific company. This element of risk, *unsystematic* risk, is a function of the nature of the firm's industry, the degree of operating gearing, its diversification and so on, i.e. its business risk, and the degree of financial gearing, its financial risk. Unsystematic risk can be diversified away. Figure 3.1 illustrates the concept of the use of diversification to reduce unsystematic risk.

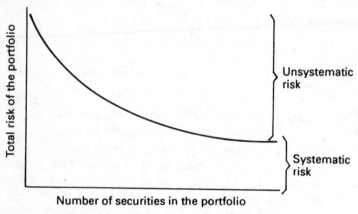

Figure 3.1 Diversification to reduce risk

CAPM recognises that risk can be diversified away and uses beta (β) as the measure of systematic risk. Beta derives from the correlation between the returns in the market portfolio and the returns in the security under consideration, and represents the power of diversification to eliminate the risk of the security concerned. The risk premium of a security is a function of the risk-free premium on the market. The risk-free premium, which varies directly with the level of beta, is the difference between the risk-free rate and the average rate of return expected in all securities in the market. CAPM expresses this as:

$$R = F + \beta(M-F)$$
where
R = expected rate of return
F = risk-free rate (e.g. on government securities)
M = average rate of return expected in all securities in the market

A high value for beta would be 1.6, which indicates that price changes for the share concerned average 1.6 times market changes. So if the market goes up or down 10 per cent the share price would go up or down 16 per cent. Such an investment would do little to reduce risk in the portfolio. A low value for beta would be 0.3. A security with such a beta would only move 3 per cent for each 10 per cent move in the market and would, therefore, be effective in reducing portfolio risk.

CAPM illustrates how returns on a security should be related to beta. For example if the risk-free rate is 7 per cent and the market as a whole offers a return of 16 per cent, then the return on a share with beta of 1.6 should be:

R = 7 + 1.6 (16–7)
  = 21.4%

The return on a share with a beta of 0.3 should be:

R = 7 + 0.3 (16–7)
  = 9.7%

To use CAPM to estimate the cost of capital requires estimates of the risk-free rate, the return on the overall market, and beta. The equation then provides the required return. There are a number of issues involved in the use of CAPM. First, the model relates to expected returns in the future which cannot be directly observed. As a consequence expected returns have to be inferred from historical data with adjustment for factors such as changes in the general level of interest rates. Second, beta should be estimated for expected future returns, but is usually estimated from historic data. Finally, the risk-free rate is usually estimated from the yield available on a short-term government security.

Despite these problems the use of CAPM to estimate the cost of equity has the advantage of being based on a careful and well-developed theory.

> We should not rely on CAPM as a precise algorithm for estimating the cost of equity capital . . . Financial decision makers can use the model in conjunction with the traditional techniques and sound judgement to develop realistic, useful estimates of the cost of equity capital. (Mullins, 1982)

The *Gordon growth model* commences with an expression for the valuation of an equity expressed in discounted cash flow terms:

$$V = D_1/(1 + i)^1 + D_2/(1 + i)^2 + D_3/(1 + i)^3 \ldots$$

where
   V = value of the equity
   D_1, D_2, etc = cash returns to the owner (usually dividends), assumed
   to be paid at annual intervals
   i = cost of equity

The underlying rationale for the model is that if the discount rate
represents the minimum acceptable rate of return, then the present
value of dividends will represent the maximum price that an investor
would be willing to pay for the share. If the price falls below the
maximum, buyers are likely to move in to restore the price. So, the
price can be assumed to equal the present value of future dividends.

Since the price of the share is known it should be possible to solve
the equation for i, providing some method can be found for predicting
investors' dividend expectations. Gordon suggested that a reasonable
approximation might be obtained by assuming a constant rate of growth
in dividends. This reduces the above valuation equation to:

$$V = D_o(1 + g)/i - g$$
where
   V = value of the equity
   D_o = last dividend actually paid
   g = growth rate
   i = cost of equity

The cost of equity can then be found by rearranging the equation:

$$i = D_o(1 - g)/V$$

Two assumptions may limit the usefulness of the growth model. The
assumption of a constant perpetual growth rate in dividends may
not always apply, and could not be applied to a firm not paying a
dividend. Second, the level or rate of dividend may not be the only
factor influencing share prices. The advantage of the growth model is
its directness and simplicity.

The weighted average cost of capital

Having considered the cost of specific sources of financing we are
now in a position to look at the overall cost of capital. Loan and
equity financing should not be looked at independently. It would be
inappropriate to relate different sources of funds to different investment
projects because in most cases the projects are in effect independent of
the funding source. The various sources of finance should be seen as

contributing to a pool from which all investments are financed because in the long run a balance will need to be maintained between equity and loan capital.

The cost of capital should be the weighted average cost of the various individual sources, weights used being in proportion to the market values of the respective classes of capital.

After calculating the cost of each specific source the calculation of the weighted average cost is quite straightforward:

$$K = (P_e \times C_e) + (P_d \times D_d)$$

where

K = weighted average cost of capital
P_e = proportion of equity capital
P_d = proportion of loan capital (note that $P_e + P_d$ must equal 1)
C_e = cost of equity
C_d = cost of loan capital

For example, if a firm has equity with a market value of £14m and a cost of 18 per cent, plus loan capital with a market value of £6m and a cost of 8 per cent, the weighted average cost would be:

$$K = (0.7 \times 18) + (0.3 \times 8)$$
$$= 15\%$$

In using weights based on market values we are assuming that the existing balance between loan and equity represents the desired capital structure. The cost of capital used in the above would also normally be the estimated marginal cost of each potential source.

CAPITAL STRUCTURE

In Chapter 2 we looked at measures of the firm's capital structure based on the published accounts, that is the relationship between loan capital and equity. In the next chapter we will look in more detail at the effect of financial gearing on profits and the risk to shareholders' earnings. We will also consider the trade-off, if any, between financial and operating gearing. In this section we will consider the effect of capital structure on the cost of capital.

It can be argued that the cost of equity and the cost of loan capital are determined independently. Because it represents a more risky investment we would expect the cost of equity to be greater than the cost of loan capital. Accordingly the more highly geared the company becomes, ie the more loan capital *vis-à-vis* equity it obtains, the lower its cost of capital. There must be some limit to this process otherwise all firms would be debt financed. So, at some stage the proportion of loan capital increases the level of risk to the potential lender. It also increases the risk to equity holders. The increased level of risk will cause the overall cost of capital to increase. On this basis, therefore, we can assume that a rational organisation will employ as much debt as is feasible. Figure 3.2 illustrates this traditional view which suggests that the cost of capital declines rapidly with increasing debt over a certain range and then begins to rise rapidly.

This traditional view has been challenged with the hypothesis that, except at extreme levels of gearing, the capital structure has no effect on the overall cost of capital. This theory states that the total value of the firm depends on its expected performance and its risk and is completely independent of the way in which it happens to be financed. Modigliani and Miller (MM) developed the very complex and rigorous theory in 1958 and while its logic may be impeccable it has been criticised for some of the assumptions on which it was based. Nevertheless the MM view has helped to develop thinking in the area.

Although difficult to prove empirically, there is some point between traditional and MM theories which reflects on the way that firms actually behave. The compromise argues that as financial gearing increases so does the cost of debt and equity resulting in a rather shallow average cost of capital curve. A graphical picture of this view is depicted in Figure 3.3. The implication of this is that there is an optimum capital structure so it is worthwhile giving consideration to the firm's capital structure. But as the curve is shallow the penalty for departing from the optimal point is not great. This allows some flexibility in the choice of new finance.

In conclusion the optimal capital structure for an actual firm has never been specified, nor has the precise cost of capital for any given capital structure. This should not be a surprise as decisions concerning the firm's capital structure are a matter of judgement. Such judgement should be informed by the sort of picture presented in this chapter. However, readers should be aware that the cost of capital and the effect of gearing on the capital structure is a very complex area which we have merely sought to introduce. The reader requiring further, more thorough analysis is advised to refer to the references at the end of the chapter.

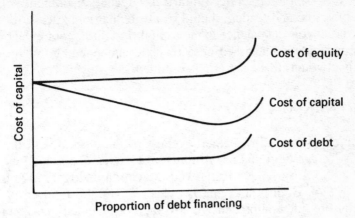

Figure 3.2 Feasibility of debt financing (traditional view)

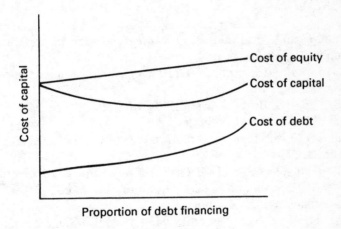

Figure 3.3 Feasibility of debt financing (compromise view)

SUMMARY

In order to set the financial requirements of the firm in a broader context this chapter has covered a very broad area. The variety of sources of funds available were identified, together with the issues involved in each particular case. We noted that, while most funds were internally generated, the firm could not ignore the influence of the market.

The cost of capital was considered by looking at two models for the cost of equity – CAPM and the Gordon Growth Model. We concluded by briefly considering the relationship between the cost of capital and the firm's capital structure. Empirical evidence of optimal structures is very scarce and readers should be aware that most decisions of this type, i.e. involving balance in the capital structure, require the exercise of sound judgement based on a realistic understanding of the issues involved which this chapter has outlined.

FURTHER READING

Comprehensive and readable coverage of the workings of the Stock Exchange can be found in *Introduction to Stock Exchange Investment* (2nd edition) by Janette Rutterford, Macmillan, Houndmills, Basingstoke, 1994. Both Franks and Broyles and Gitman referred to in this chapter provide comprehensive coverage of financial management.

REFERENCES

Bowman, C and Asch, D (1987) *Strategic Management*, Macmillan, Houndmills, Basingstoke.

Donaldson, G and Lorsch, J W (1983) *Decision Making at the Top*, Basic Books, New York.

Franks, J R and Broyles, J E (1979) *Modern Managerial Finance*, John Wiley & Son, Chichester.

Gitman, L J (1982) *Principles of Managerial Finance*, 3rd ed., Harper and Row, New York.

Lee, T A and Tweedie, D P (1981) *The Institutional Investor and Financial Information*, The Institute of Chartered Accountants in England and Wales, London.

Mullins, D W (1982) 'Does the capital asset-pricing model work? *Harvard Business Review*, January–February, pp 105–14.

Weston, J F and Brigham, E F (1982) *Managerial Finance*, 6th edition (British ed.), Holt, Rinehart & Winston, London.

4

Cost Behaviour and Value Improvement

INTRODUCTION

This chapter introduces the concepts of cost accountancy and links them to the operational characteristics of the firm. In this way we aim to establish a bridge between operational characteristics of the firm as portrayed in cost behaviour and the financial requirements of this activity.

The chapter commences by considering the need for costing information and considers cost accounting as one element in an organisation's information system. Costing systems are then considered and the differences between process and specific order costing identified. We then move on to look at methods for classifying costs and attempt to distinguish between direct and indirect, and fixed and variable costs.

Since writing the first edition a major debate has taken place in management accounting as to its relevance (Johnson and Kaplan, 1987). Essentially the debate questioned the validity of the information generated by accounting systems to support management decisions. The debate, while initiated in the USA, spread worldwide and corresponded with interest in the West with Japanese management practices. The results of the debate are additional costing methods and greater consciousness of the relevance of cost information in decisions on value improvement. The debate also confirmed that financial accounting information is inappropriate for internal management whether planning, controlling or decision making.

The use of cost information for short-term decision making is then addressed by considering the relationship between cost volume and contribution. A number of situations are looked at including accept/reject decisions, make or buy and so on. The chapter concludes by discussing the relationship between operating and financial gearing.

THE NEED FOR COST INFORMATION

If you were to start in business tomorrow either making or buying and selling goods, or services, your first considerations would be:

- ◻ How much do the goods/services cost?
- ◻ What price can I charge?
- ◻ How much profit will I make?

These basic questions apply no matter what your motives are.

Cost accounting emerged to answer these questions and, while much younger in formal literature than financial accounting, was in effect an underlying principle in trade and commerce. The need to formalise and increase the know-how came with the pressures of the industrial revolution when competition between producers led to a need for more information on costs and profits, and hence efficiency. This information is the backbone of any commercial organisation today. It is essential 'oxygen' that management need to control the organisation.

Traditionally pricing was undertaken on a 'cost plus' basis, i.e.:

$$\text{Cost} + \text{profit} = \text{price}$$

However in an increasingly competitive world, prices are set by the market in response to supply and demand. Only a few businesses in limited industries can be said to be 'price makers'; most businesses are 'price takers'. For the majority the formula may be revised to:

$$\text{Sales revenue} - \text{costs} = \text{profit}$$

Profit is the residue of trade, but this is unlikely to result in an adequate return on capital employed to satisfy our investors or the financiers. They demand that we earn a return sufficient to satisfy their expectations, i.e.:

$$\text{Income} - \text{required profit} = \text{costs}$$

The sales revenue will be the income we receive representing all the sales made at the market prices taken. This latter formula is closer to the Japanese philosophy of costing where:

$$\text{Price} - \text{profit} = \text{target costs}$$

The price and sales review are defined by the market, the resulting income must service our profit needs and the resulting costs may be viewed as the maximum costs of operations. This focus on target costs reflects an awareness that when we initially produce an item we will be learning how to. Later the costs will be lower as we have made improvements. The concept of costs declining with repetition has been noted for some time and targets may be set which reflect these improvements. Furthermore as the production continues ideas will be developed for further improvement leading to ever lower costs. This is the philosophy of Kaizen or improvement costing.

In this book we shall introduce the reader to financial models of the business which, when understood, will allow the reader to identify ways of improving profits through adding value, reducing costs and minimising the capital employed in the business. Through usage of these models the reader can move to a new understanding of profit improvement which is a virtuous circle in which increased profits allow investment in increasingly profitable opportunities.

The concept of the value chain has been around for some time. The value chain focuses on examining the operations of the business from purchasing of raw materials to the distribution and after-sales care of customers. Each activity within the firm should add value and competitive advantage will be gained by the business that can add the greatest amount of value between the input and outputs.

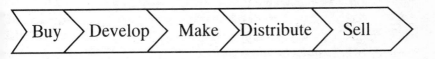

The focus of the value chain becomes each activity within the operation from initial purchase of materials through the operational cycles. Our concern is not only to minimise cost but to add value. Activities that add no value should be eliminated or the costs minimised if they cannot be eradicated. Activities that contribute to income generation such as selling and manufacturing clearly should add value but service departments that support the main activities will be highlighted and their costs minimised. We shall return later to this activity analysis approach when we examine activity-based costing.

In Chapter 2 we examined the profit and loss account produced retrospectively normally on an annual basis. This information, while useful to the steward and custodian of the assets, will not ensure that products or services provided today or tomorrow are made either at a profit or effectively (efficiently). Cost focuses on the present and future rather than the past. In addition, the emphasis is on individual goods and services rather than the business as a whole.

All organisations whether privately or publicly owned, need to make the best use of their resources. Measuring the effectiveness of the utilisation of scarce resources could be made in quantitative terms such as the number of tonnes or kilograms of minerals extracted from a mine. However, this would not necessarily provide a usable comparison due to the problems of measuring the resources in the process like land, machinery, labour and so on. The evaluation of the use of different economic factors is facilitated by the use of a common measure – money. In this way the cost of inputs is compared with the value of the output, and by recording monetary values the accountant is able to measure the results of activity, and present that information to those directing activities. In fact the success or failure of an enterprise may well depend on the measurement and recording of its activities because this will enable management to concentrate on those areas which require their attention. However, you should recall some of the problems inherent in using money as a measure from Chapter 2.

Internal management

Cost accounting is an element in the overall business information system which is primarily concerned with serving internal users of information, i.e. management.

Since an information system must serve the users of it, the requirements of management will form the primary definer of the contents of a cost accounting system.

It is the function of managers to manage those organisations, or parts of organisations, that are under their control. In order to carry out this function effectively information relating to all the relevant factors must be available. One of these factors is cost and it is the purpose of costing to provide management with information relating to costs. Therefore, costs are prepared for management to assist them in their function and not merely for the sake of preparing information.

Obviously cost is not the only factor that managers should consider in running a department or firm, but a manager can be more effective when using the best information it is possible to obtain.

The information should indicate the economic implications and consequences of their decisions even though, in some instances, the final decision may be made on other than economic grounds. Before considering costing in detail it is probably of use at this point to summarise the purposes of costing as these should be kept in mind throughout. The list is not exhaustive as each firm will have advantages arising from its own system:

- to disclose profitable and unprofitable activities to enable management to take corrective action as required;
- to provide information for comparison of costs;
- to analyse expenses incurred so that wastage can be traced and economies effected;
- to indicate the precise nature of an increase or decrease in the results disclosed by the financial accounts;
- to provide information upon which tenders, estimates and pricing may be based.

Cost accounting initially developed from *cost estimating*, reflecting the relatively uncertain nature of future costs. Financial accounting relies upon historic costs to give it a sense of certainty. The historic cost of operations may be analysed thereby implying accuracy to the financial accounting information. However, our previous chapters have suggested a degree of caution should be exercised in examining financial accounts as the historic costs may all be on different accounting bases and reflect different monetary units due to inflation.

Frequently cost accountants are required to estimate the future costs in order to quote for new business. This quotation may become the basis of the contract and hence an awareness of the confidence or accuracy of the costing is important. The traditional approach of estimate (or Americanism – guestimate) should not be lost in the computer printout of cost data. Where a business only produces a single product by a single process then the confidence in the cost estimates must be higher than if the business has multiple products and processes. Naturally if we have to estimate the cost of a single product out of many then we will encounter allocation of costs and these will always be liable to alternative interpretation and hence cost. A consciousness of this uncertainty is essential in gaining understanding and confidence in working with cost information.

COSTING SYSTEMS

The principles, conventions and objectives of all costing systems are the same, but their application will of necessity vary in accordance with circumstances. This does not mean, however, that the procedures in a firm must remain unaffected by the introduction of a system of cost accounting as it is quite possible that the installation of a costing system will reveal deficiencies which could adversely affect the accuracy of the costing records. With this reservation it is important to appreciate that the system must be designed to suit the business. Additionally the expense of operating the costing system must be considered in relation to the size of the enterprise and the expected benefits. The system should not be needlessly complex.

At this point it is worthwhile briefly considering the variety of production systems in existence. (In this context we will refer to production to cover the whole spectrum of operational systems from mass production and jobbing manufacture, to transport and service industries, e.g. insurance.)

Most industrial and commercial firms can be grouped together in that all the firms in a group will be involved in similar work processes having similar production and control problems. As a result methods have been developed which are of use in formulating a costing system for a particular business.

All 'business' systems have a unit of 'production':

a car;
a ton of coal;
a house built;
a life insurance policy;
a house conveyance;
an audit of a company;
a meal in a restaurant;
a surgical operation.

This unit of production has a cost (which we want to ascertain). This unit of production cost is called a *unit-cost*. A common feature of all the units given in the example is that they form the basis of a sale. In this way it will be ascertained for each commodity/transaction:

a unit cost;
a unit selling price;
a unit profit.

The problems arise when we study the methods of production and service. Here we find that the unit may be one of many produced in a continuous process, for example, a loaf of bread, a ton of coal, or it may have been produced discretely, for example, the Humber Bridge, the audit of Rover.

This characteristic division between mass and discrete has led to two distinct methods of cost accounting:

☐ *Specific order costing*, the basic costing method applicable where the work consists of separate contracts, jobs or batches, each of which is authorised by a special order or contract.

☐ *Continuous operation/process costing*, the basic costing method applicable where goods or services result from a sequence of continuous or repetitive operations or processes to which costs are charged before being averaged over the units produced during the period.

Both methods of cost accounting are in the initial stages similar in that costs are captured and recorded into the cost accounting system. They are then sorted and at this stage the techniques diverge.

In the case of specific order costing, costs are initially sorted and identified against specific units of production, e.g., window frame 6' × 4', House Contract No. 37 (37 Hill Road, Uptown).

Thus costs specific to a unit are collected in an account for the specific order. Costs which cannot be allocated to a specific unit will be collected separately and then shared between all the jobs.

Specific order costing is applicable where the work consists of separate contracts, jobs or batches, each of which is authorised by an order or contract. For example, in a jobbing business work proceeding through the factory can be clearly identified. Usually raw material is used at the start and is physically moved from one department to another while a variety of operations are performed in transforming the material input into the finished product. The identifiable direct costs are charged direct to the order, together with a share of the indirect costs. In some instances the nature of the business requires the operations to be performed outside the factory and each order is of a relatively long duration, e.g. house building and ship construction. The basic principles of job costing still apply, but with certain distinguishing features. Costing for construction contracts is normally known as contract costing.

To reduce set-up costs and make better use of available capacity it is beneficial to have as long a production run as possible. This emphasises standardisation of products, or if this is not feasible, the standardisation of component parts. In such cases batch costing is used, where a batch of identical components or products are treated as a job and costed as such. The total cost of the batch is then averaged over the number of components or products.

Process costing is the method applicable where standardised goods or services result from a sequence of repetitive or continuous operations or processes to which costs are charged before being averaged over the units produced during the period. It is possible, therefore, to add all the costs of the factory and divide the total by the units produced to arrive at a unit cost. Normally there is no problem of direct and indirect costs that may arise with specific order costing. Where the business, or a department within a firm, provides a service it is known as service costing. Service/function costing is the costing of specific services or functions, for example, canteens, maintenance, personnel, these may be referred to as service centres, departments or functions.

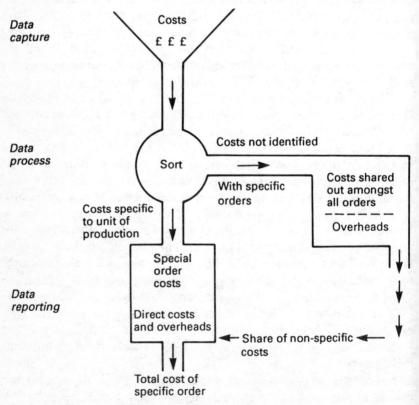

Figure 4.1 Specific order costing

Specific order costing and process costing are mainly concerned with the collection and assembly of cost data. In order to obtain the cost of a unit of product or cost of a process or department we must analyse the total costs of the business in such a way that we can identify cost with products, processes or departments. This is done by means of classifying costs, identifying users of costs (cost centres), coding cost units to the cost centres and then reassembling costs by products, processes or departments.

The design and installation of a costing system will need to consider the following factors:

- The views and suggestions of technical staff must be given consideration in designing the system as they are dealing with the day-to-day operations which will be recorded and reported on in economic terms. Their advice on the nature of materials used, the incidence of scrapped work and the point at which it is normally recognised, coupled with the deployment of the workforce, are invaluable in the design of the system. Furthermore, their knowledge of the production sequence is vital in establishing the points at which work has begun and finished and where the finished product of one section becomes the input to the next. Finally the managers and foremen will often be responsible for the supervision of data recorded for costing purposes by their clerical and non-clerical staff. They will ultimately use reports prepared from this information, and the system must be seen as an aid to their effective performance since their lack of co-operation may invalidate the results.

- No useful purpose will be served in analysing items of insignificant value. For instance the total cost of stationery is usually an adequate heading on an expense report with nothing to be gained from ascertaining the separate costs of paper, envelopes, paper clips, pens, etc.

- Where a business is related to others, i.e. as part of a group, there are advantages in adopting common cost accounting practices. The same would apply where a firm belonged to a trade association in that the adoption of common costing practices will facilitate the comparison of the firm's cost data with averages produced for the industry.

- Cost accounting is part of the overall management information service and care must be exercised to ensure that no duplication in reporting the same information in a different way takes place. Only information which is relevant in the context of assisting management to manage should be reported.

Furthermore, the costing system should be flexible and capable of adaptation to changing circumstances. It should be logical and simple and subject to periodical and skilled scrutiny to avoid the danger of obsolescence due to changes and developments in the business.

The cost accountant must be fully conversant with the areas within the business where large costs are incurred because their attention will often be focused on these areas in assisting management to control and reduce costs. It is important to remember that 80 to 90 per cent of the subsequent costs of operations are defined in the design phase. A reduction of the number of parts in an assembly will not only reduce the assembly cost but also reduce the number of potential parts to fail. Provision of easy servicing and repair will reduce subsequent running costs but must be built into the design phase. The involvement of cost accountants in the research, development and design phases may not only reduce costs but enhance value. It is their responsibility to advise managers of those areas where their concentrated efforts will be most effective. Cost accountants should not merely record data, but as a part of the management team, they must ensure that their function has an influence within the organisation.

COST CLASSIFICATION AND ELEMENTS OF MODEL

The financial accounts of a firm are designed to disclose the results of the firm as a whole and in respect of a definite period. The main items of income and expenditure are shown in the accounts under headings which describe their nature, for example, sales, purchases, wages, rent, etc. However detailed these statements are they only reveal the result of the activities of the firm as a whole. No detailed information is available as to the manner in which the net profit or loss has been made.

Total turnover may well be made up of many varied products, services, jobs or contracts, only some of which may be profitable. Considerable information will be derived from statements which reveal the separate result of each activity, while at the same time detailing how such a result has eventuated. The amount of analysis performed will be dependent upon the nature of the business and the degree of accuracy required. Ultimately expenditure will be charged to *cost units*.

A cost unit should not be confused with a *cost centre* which is usually an intermediate point to which expenditure can be charged for later distribution, if necessary, to cost units. Cost units and cost centres should be those natural to the business which are readily understood and accepted by all concerned. Cost centres can be defined as a location, function or items of equipment in respect of which costs may be ascertained and related to cost units for control purposes. This will also permit the cost of identifiable activities and departments to be disclosed so assisting in relating costs to the manager concerned.

The classification of costs is the basis of all costing systems and is an essential step in summarising detailed costs. Costs can be classified by function:

Production;
Sales/marketing;
Administration;
Research and Development.

Within functions costs are collected by cost centres and within cost centres by cost units. Costs collected in cost centres or cost units can be further classified into cost elements:

☐ material cost – which is the cost of goods used by a firm;
☐ labour cost – which is the cost of remuneration of the firm's employees (including wages, salaries, bonuses, commissions, National Insurance, etc);
☐ expenses – which are the cost of services used by the firm such as rates, insurance, telephone, etc.

These elements can be further classified depending on whether they are direct or indirect costs, i.e., direct or indirect material. A *direct cost* is one which can be allocated directly to a cost centre or cost unit. The cost can be directly associated with the production of a cost unit or with the activity of a cost centre. An *indirect cost* cannot be directly associated with the production of a cost unit or the activity of a cost centre, but has to be apportioned to the cost centre or absorbed by the cost unit on a suitable basis. Direct expenditure which can be directly identified with a cost centre or cost unit is allocated, whereas indirect expenditure is apportioned or absorbed.

Direct materials, direct labour, and direct expenses are *prime costs* which are directly related to the production of a cost unit or the activity of a cost centre. The sum of these direct costs for a period is known as the prime cost of production. The indirect costs of production, and all selling, distribution, research and development, and administration costs are often known as overheads. Ultimately all overheads that have been apportioned to cost centres have to be absorbed by cost units. Overhead absorption is usually achieved by the use of one or a combination of overhead rates, for example, labour hour rate, or machine hour rate.

Costs may be either fixed costs or variable costs, though some costs may have fixed and variable elements and are called semi-variable. A *fixed cost* is one which remains unchanged despite changes in activity; it is a cost of time in that it accumulates with the passage of time, e.g. rent, office salaries, insurance, etc. A fixed cost is not always fixed in amount as other factors, such as price-level changes, can cause fixed costs to change from period to period. If a sufficiently long time period is considered, virtually all costs become variable due to changes in the scale of the firm's operations. A *variable cost* will tend to follow (in the short term) the level of activity. Theoretically all prime costs are variable costs because their distinguishing characteristic is the fact that they can be directly related to cost units. In practice this may not necessarily be the case.

Total cost is the sum of prime costs and overheads attributable to the cost unit being considered. The unit may be the whole undertaking, a job, batch, contract, or group product. It may be a process or a service. Total cost can be made up as shown in Table 4.1.

Absorption costing. As has already been described, costs may be classified into direct costs and indirect costs. Direct costs are directly attributable and allocated to the specific cost unit. Indirect costs, the aggregate of which is overheads, must be shared equitably between all the cost units produced.

The technique used is called absorption costing. The indirect costs are amassed in an overhead account. A pre-estimate is made of the total indirect costs for the year and an absorption rate is calculated based on the estimate annual throughput of product. The overheads are then absorbed to the product on the basis of the absorption rate, e.g.:

Total factory overheads £100,000
Total direct labour hours 50,000 hours
Absorption rate £2 per direct labour hour
Product widget uses 5 direct labour hours
Therefore, each unit absorbs £10 factory overheads.

Note that if the pre-estimate of absorption rate is incorrect due to the total cost or the throughput being different, then the overheads would either be over- or under-absorbed. As a result the profit disclosed would be under- or overstated and, therefore, adjustments must be made periodically.

Table 4.1 Total cost

Direct costs	£	£
Material	4	
Labour	6	
Expense	1	
	—	
Prime cost		11
Overhead costs		
Production overheads:		
Indirect material	1	
Indirect labour	3	
Indirect expense	2	
	—	
		6
		—
Cost of production		17
Sales/marketing expenses	2	
Research and development costs	1	
Administration expenses	3	
	—	
		6
		—
Total cost		23
		—

Marginal costing. An alternative approach to absorption costing is to treat costs in the same manner as they behave. Costs tend to either vary with the level of output or remain constant in relation to output. The former are variable costs which may be directly attributable to products, but fixed costs are attributable to the time periods no matter what the output is.

Since fixed costs will remain constant no matter what level the output is then they may be ignored in decision making, as the level of final profit will depend on the relationship between variable costs, sales revenue and output. This relationship is called contribution.

The final level of profit will depend on the total contribution made in a period less the fixed costs attributable to the period. For useful management information to emerge some established techniques are available which have been devised to suit the purpose for which the information is required. At this stage a general understanding of the meaning of the terms is adequate. The main terms can be defined as follows:

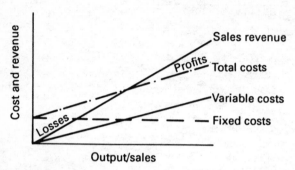

Figure 4.2 Fixed and variable costs

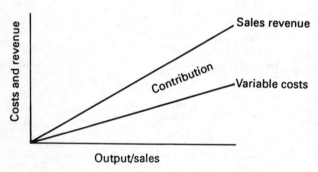

Figure 4.3 Contribution and variable costs

Historical costing, the actual cost of acquiring assets, or goods and services. The only advantage of this practice is its simplicity. The principal disadvantages are that the results are presented too late for effective action to be taken; there is no automatic analysis of the causes of excess costs; the only yardsticks existing for comparison are previous historical costs, or estimates based thereon; inaccurate estimates of operation times and overhead rates are not revealed; and in complex industries the clerical work involved usually means that only sample costing is undertaken.

Standard costing, a technique which uses standards for costs and revenues for the purpose of control through variance analysis.

Standard costing is the antithesis of historical costing, and its advantages are related to the disadvantages described in the preceding paragraph: promptness of presentation giving reasons for all digressions from targets which were predetermined in detail, with the minimum amount of clerical effort for complete and continuous coverage. The principle may be summed up as *management by exception*.

Budgetary control, the establishment of budgets relating the responsibilities of executives to the requirements of a policy, and the continuous comparison of actual with budgeted results, either to secure by individual action the objective of that policy, or to provide a basis for its revision.

Variance accounting, a technique whereby the planned activities of an undertaking are quantified in budgets, standard costs, standard selling prices, and standard profit margins, and the difference between these and actual results are compared. Management is periodically presented with an analysis of differences by causes and responsibility centres, such analysis usually commencing with the operating profit variance.

Variance analysis is that part of variance accounting which relates to the analysis into constituent parts of variances between planned and actual performance.

Differential costing, a technique used in the preparation of *ad hoc* information in which only cost and income differences between alternative courses of action are taken into consideration.

Incremental costing, a technique used in the preparation of *ad hoc* information where consideration is given to a range of graduated or stepped changes in the level or nature of activity and the additional costs and revenues likely to result from each degree of change are presented.

Uniform costing, the use by several undertakings of the same costing system, i.e. the same basic costing methods, principles and techniques.

Owing to its similarity of title, this is often confused with standard costing; it is not necessarily the same, for the costing principles adopted may take any form.

Large companies, having decentralised operating divisions, frequently maintain uniformity of costing procedure for administrative convenience, and to allow comparison of results thus detecting comparative inefficiency and stimulating competition within the group.

Uniform costing is also sponsored by many trade federations for two principal reasons. In times of depression many firms resort to selling at marginal prices often with inadequate cost information. If important items are left out of their calculations, their quotations will artificially depress the market price still further. Thus all members are urged to compute their costs in accordance with a formula considered to be sound for the particular industry, to avoid competition becoming 'cut-throat'. As a subsidiary object, cost information may be submitted by individual firms to the federation for analysis and issue of average figures to member for comparison with their own.

Activity based costing: we referred earlier to the value chain and the analysis of the business into the core activities that add value. This approach reflects a move away from the 'top down' approach adopted in much of cost accounting where costs are disaggregated and allocated and apportioned to cost units or centres. Even the marginal cost approach with its emphasis on cost behaviour and the incremental cost of the additional units relies on total cost information being analysed into categories of cost. These approaches run contrary to the traditional cost estimation approach that sought to build up cost from the elements as they were used. These latter approaches focused on activities necessary to achieve the outcome.

Activity based costing (ABC) emerged from the debate of management accounting in the late 1980s and has been described as 'back to basics', but this would not do justice to its contribution. ABC is based on a bottom-up build of costs from units of activity through batch activities to product, processes or facilities.

Unit level	Direct labour hour, machine hour.	An activity performed to enable a unit to be produced, e.g. drill a hole.
Batch level	Number of set-ups, distance moved, number of orders.	An activity performed to enable a batch to be produced – set up, move, order.
Product level	Number of parts, number of expedites.	An activity performed to enable a product to be produced – progress chase, design, manage, bills of material, process engineer.

Facilities level	An activity performed to enable operation, eg lighting, cleaning, engineering of factory

Each activity that takes place and incurs cost is identified and the cost driver identified. For example, the cost drivers for the second edition of this book included the number of days required for authoring, the number and degree of revisions and their impact on the original text, the editing, typesetting and proof reading. But these do not reflect either the printers' cost or the publishers' as many of their costs are driven by the number of books in process of publication and their associated states. Identifying, tracing and costing direct cost is relatively straightforward but the overheads have often been arbitrarily allocated apportioned costs, have increasingly formed a major element of cost and needed controlling and sharing more accurately if distortion in product profitability was not to result.

Early writers on costing were conscious of these problems and Church (1908) warned against using a simple method of on-cost to direct labour where there were multiple products going through different processes. Clark (1923) emphasises different costs for different purposes.

The focus of much of ABC is the 'burden' of overheads. The use of cost drivers to trace and bring to account the source of costs emphasises cost reduction while the more accurate allocation of overheads to activities that incur the costs leads to fairer distribution amongst the multiple products and processes. In particular, the linking of cost with value added emphasises the areas of the business that have competitive advantage.

Throughput accounting, the entire cost of the factory, excluding materials consumed, are fixed in the short to medium term provided that the labour is available. The factory, with its production lines and cells, is an integrated whole with a designed capacity. It is more useful and infinitely simpler to consider the entire costs excluding material as fixed and to call the cost the *total factory cost*. Throughput accounting seeks to maximise the throughput and hence profitability of the factory unit as a whole. It builds upon the contribution of marginal costing but incorporates the limiting factor of factory capacity and highlights operational response times and inventories. The recognition of the role of bottlenecks and their effect on profitability is attributed to Goldratt (1993), who sought to optimise production technology.

Backflush accounting, like throughput accounting backflush seeks to simplify the accounting approach but requires a *Just-in-Time* (JIT) manufacturing approach (see Chapter 5). JIT is based on immediate response from both manufacturing and supply chains resulting in zero inventories. In such environments there will be no work in progress to account for and the demand draws through the costs. Backflush focuses on the consumption and seeks to account for the items consumed by back working to explain costs. It greatly simplifies cost accounting, particularly where operations are clearly focused and cost easily traced. It has close affinity with some elements of specific order costing but may incorporate large batches.

The Chartered Institute of Management Accountants has for many years maintained an *Official Terminology* which is periodically reviewed and updated. The terms above are taken from this publication and readers are recommended to consult this publication for guidance on definitions.

COST BEHAVIOUR AND DECISION MAKING

Having described the systems of cost accounting we will now focus our attention on cost behaviour. The prediction of how costs behave is vital in the planning and decision-making activities of organisations. The prediction of cost behaviour is achieved by building models of costs which requires the identification of the variables, the estimation of the parameters and the validation of the model. Cost estimation may be undertaken in three distinct methods:

    analysis of historic data;
    engineering calculation;
    statistical methods.

Cost elements may be described as being fixed costs or variable costs. First, a fixed cost is one which, in a given period, is not expected to change and which remains fixed in relation to the volume of throughput. This picture is, however, only accurate if we recognise it in the context of a narrow band of feasibility, and a reasonably short time period, say, one year.

An example of a fixed cost could be rent in that it is fixed during an annual period and is unlikely to change in relation to the volume of throughput.

Variable costs are said to vary with the volume. Normally we are concerned with the product and sales volume. The cost, however, may vary more directly with some other intermediary variable. An example could be energy which varies with machine usage which is itself dependent on production volume although it may not be directly related.

As well as fixed and variable costs there are a multitude of semi-variable and semi-fixed costs, some of which are illustrated in Figure 4.4.

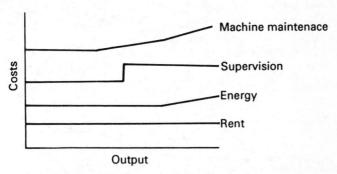

Figure 4.4 Semi-variable costs

A simplification often assumed by short-term decision makers is that costs are linear. Economists would suggest that this is not the case and that a curve-linear graph embodying some stepped functions is more appropriate. This would reflect the set-up costs, followed by the influence of learning curve effects and subsequent dis-economies of scale prior to rising to a new operational level (see Figure 4.5). The linear approximation may be justified by arguing that, within a narrow range, the economists' model would approximate to a straight line.

Cost volume behaviour

A major simplification of reality is, of course, the traditional break-even chart in which the revenue line reflects the prices and volumes and may be compared to the total cost or its elements. Where the total revenue exceeds the total cost the business is achieving profit and when reversed a loss. The point of equality is known as the break-even point. Figure 4.6 illustrates a break-even chart.

We may predict the effect of changes in the variables on the rate of profit (price-variable cost per unit) often referred to as the profit volume ratio (PV ratio) and on the relative break-even volume, and these are illustrated in Figure 4.7.

(a)

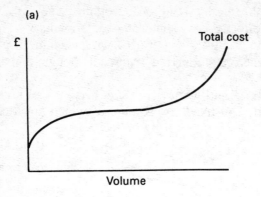

(b)

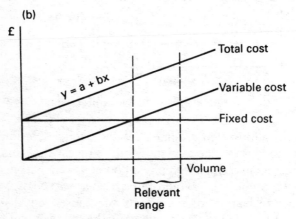

where y = total cost
       a = fixed cost
       b = variable cost
       x = volume (no. of units)

Figure 4.5 (a) The 'economist's' cost curve; (b) the 'accountant's' cost curve

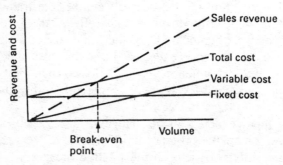

Figure 4.6 Break-even chart

Note that:
    Contribution = Sales revenue − Variable cost
    Contribution per unit = Sales price per unit − Variable cost per unit
    Profit or loss = Contribution − Fixed costs
At break-even:
    Contribution = Fixed costs
Therefore:
    Break-even = Fixed costs/contribution per unit

We may predict the effect of changes in the variables on the rate of profit (price-variable cost per unit) often referred to as the profit volume ratio (PV ratio) and on the relative break-even volume, and these are illustrated in Figure 4.7.

The sensitivity of the profit model

In planning and decision making it is important to be able to predict outcomes. It is also useful to know the consequences of actions if we are seeking control. It is therefore important that we should be aware of the sensitivity of the profit model.

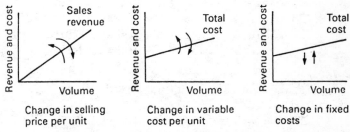

Figure 4.7 Effect of changes in variables

A measure which can be used for sensitivity is the *multiplier* (the multiplier is worked out by dividing the percentage change in the profit by the percentage change in the variable). Below is an example of a multiplier. Table 1 shows the control states: Table 2 reveals the effect of a 10 per cent change in quantity, which moves us from a loss situation through to a profit with the most dramatic changes in profit percentage around the break-even point.

Table 2 shows a 10 per cent change in price on the relative profitability, while Table 4 shows the effect on variable costs.

Table 1

Quantity steps % 0	Price 0	Variable	Contrib	Fixed	Profit	% Change
500	25	10	15	10000	-2500	0.00%
500	25	10	15	10000	-2500	0.00%
500	25	10	15	10000	-2500	0.00%
500	25	10	15	10000	-2500	0.00%
500	25	10	15	10000	-2500	0.00%

Table 2

Quantity steps % 10	Price 0	Variable	Contrib	Fixed	Profit	% Change
500	25	10	15	10000	-2500	
550	25	10	15	10000	-1750	-30.00%
605	25	10	15	10000	-925	-47.14%
666	25	10	15	10000	-18	-98.11%
732	25	10	15	10000	-981	*******
805	25	10	15	10000	2079	111.96%

Table 3

Quantity steps % 0	Price 10	Variable 0	Contrib	Fixed	Profit	% Change
500	25	10	15	10000	-2500	
500	28	10	18	10000	-1250	-50.00%
500	30	10	20	10000	125	-110.00%
500	33	10	23	10000	1637	1210.00%
500	37	10	27	10000	3301	101.60%
500	40	10	30	10000	5131	55.44%

Table 4

Quantity steps % 0	Price 0	Variable 10	Contrib	Fixed	Profit	% Change
750	25	10	15	10000	1250	
750	25	11	14	10000	500	-60.00%
750	25	12	13	10000	-325	-165.00%
750	25	13	12	10000	-1233	279.23%
750	25	15	10	10000	-2231	80.99%
750	25	16	9	10000	-3329	49.22%

Some uses of cost behaviour

While the ascertainment and control of costs may be either by absorption or marginal costing, only in the latter method are costs classified according to behaviour and so may be used for planning and decision making. However, a company may use both methods to enable both control and planning and while absorption costing may be preferred for control purposes the ability to classify costs according to behaviour is essential for planning and decision making and is facilitated with greater disaggregation of data possible in computerised systems.

Marginal costing has a wide variety of uses including: making accept or reject decisions; taking make or buy decisions; ranking products in their order of profitability; pricing goods for separate markets; and decisions concerning the use of limiting factors of production. Each of these uses will be examined, with the provision of an example to help explain any analysis concerned where necessary.

The accept or reject decision

Sometimes it will be beneficial for an organisation to sell the goods that it has in stock at a price which is below their production cost, or if the items still have to be produced below the absorption cost price as long as they provide a positive contribution to the fixed costs and profits of the firm. Where goods have already been produced, or are about to be produced in spare capacity situations, the organisation will sometimes benefit from the production and the sale (or simply the sale) of the goods, rather than doing nothing or leaving the stock on its shelves. However, care has to be taken in making such decision if there is already a regular market in the product. For such sales have to be isolated from the regular market; otherwise there could be an exchange between them, or the bottom will fall out of the established market if other users or consumers find out that the goods can be obtained elsewhere on more favourable terms.

From the following data the management of an organisation is deciding whether to accept a special order for 250,000 NELPS at a unit price of 43p. If the order is accepted the firm's fixed costs will not alter and there will be no effect on the existing market.

The standard costs of NELPS are set out below:

Selling price	0.55
Materials	0.30
Labour	0.10
Factory overheads:	
fixed	0.04
variable	0.01
Total standard cost	0.45
Standard profit	0.10

The budget facing the organisation is as follows:

Revenue	550,000
less: standard costs of production	450,000
Works Profit	100,000
less: administrative expenses	20,000
Budgeted Profit	80,000

Information for the decision can be presented in a number of ways. Two alternatives are set out in Figure 4.8. For illustrative purposes statements for both methods are provided, although in practice it would only be necessary to present figures for the approach preferred by management.

From both the approaches taken in Figure 4.8, it can be seen that if management accepts the order, the firm's profits will increase by £5,000.

The make or buy decision

Exactly the same analysis as that shown above for the accept or reject decision is also applicable to a make or buy decision. However, the question now becomes framed in terms of deciding whether to buy in a component or product, or to make it. Usually existing figures for internal production costs include overheads. Whereas the decisions should be based, if there is spare capacity, upon whether the buying-in price is actually greater than the marginal cost of producing the item concerned. If the buying-in price is greater than marginal costs of production the firm should produce the item themselves. Again the use of similar statements to those provided in Figure 4.8 for the accept or reject situation highlight which course of action will be the most beneficial.

(i) The 'have and 'have not' statement for the organisation

	Have	*Have not*
Revenue	657,500	550,000
less: costs of production	552,500	450,000
Works profit	105,000	100,000
less: administrative expenses	20,000	20,000
Budgeted Profit	85,000	80,000

(ii) The contribution statement for the product

Revenue per unit	0.43
less: variable production costs	0.41
Contribution per unit	0.02
Additional volume = 250,000	
Additional annual profit	£5,000

Figure 4.8 The accept or reject decision

Making for separate markets

It is possible that an organisation can sell the same product in quite different markets, for example, in home or overseas markets. Even when goods are sold in the same locality it might be possible to differentiate between various markets through branding or selling the same product in different ways. The former is where the same product is sold under a number of different names. The latter is where different channels of distribution, such as stores or mail order houses, are used to sell the product, or where different types of consumers are aimed at, for example as when selling jars of coffee to the householder, or selling the coffee in catering packs to the hotel trade.

It may be possible through the use of a judicious pricing policy for one market to absorb the majority, if not all, of the fixed production costs of the product. If this is possible then any income acquired from the additional market above that which covers the product's marginal cost of production, will be acceptable as this adds to the organisation's profit. However, the capacity situation, and whether there is any better use for the resources involved, must all come into the analysis. When this approach is used, or appears to be used, in overseas trading it may be referred to as dumping. This concerns the situation where a country's producers sell a product for a higher price in their home market than that which they charge to overseas buyers. There may be a number of reasons as to why they should do this. One of them, especially if under government influence, would be to bring in foreign exchange. Then as long as the producers are able to recover their fixed costs from the home market, anything that they can get above marginal cost on overseas markets will be beneficial to their country's currency or exchange.

Ranking products

Marginal costing can be used to rank products in order of those providing the greatest contributions. However, the question arises as to whether this contribution should be measured in absolute terms or in some other way. Nevertheless, as long as there are no limiting factors, an organisation should produce all the products that it can sell as long as these have a positive contribution. But rarely will there be no limits to an organisation's factors of production so the concept of the limiting factor is likely to have to be brought into the analysis.

The limiting factor situation

If an organisation has limits of any of its factors of production, such as capacity, the supply of specialist labour, supplies of raw materials, etc, the factor concerned is referred to as the *key* or *limiting factor* of production. It is important in such situations to ensure that the products which are produced are those which make the most efficient use of any such limiting factor. This analysis could take place using the principle behind 'have' and 'have not' statements, in this case by having 'have' statements for each of the possible products and comparing the results shown. At more advanced stages of such analysis quantitative techniques can be used and the notion of dual prices introduced. However, here the matter will be dealt with at a more simple level by looking at the contribution per limiting factor for each product. Nevertheless, it should be remembered that if there is more than one limiting factor this makes the analysis much more complex. It should be noted that the higher the contribution per limiting factor is for a product the more beneficial it will be to the organisation to produce that product.

An example best illustrates this approach of using contribution per limiting factor: management is deciding which product to produce in a situation where the supply of L is limited to 300 kilos per week. The following information is available:

	Product A	*Product B*
Selling price	50	50
Direct costs of production	20	10
Kilos of factor L required in the production of 1 unit of the product	10kg	15kg

The first step is to produce a marginal cost statement as follows:

Marginal Cost Statement

	Product A	Product B
Selling price	50	50
Direct costs of production	20	10
Contribution	30	40

This would seem to indicate that the best product to produce would be B because its contribution is 10 more than A's. However, if 'have' statements are drawn up for both products the total situation is shown as follows:

Availability of limiting factor	300kg	300kg
Limiting factor required per unit	10kg	15kg
Total units that could be produced	30	20
× contribution per unit	30	40
Total contribution of product	900	800

This shows that because one factor of production is in limited supply, and as each unit of A requires less of this factor, it will be more profitable to produce A on an overall basis.

A contribution per limiting factor can be worked out for each product which shows the contribution arising from each unit of the limiting factor consumed. This ratio is obtained from:

$$\frac{\text{Overall contribution of product}}{\text{Units of limiting factor required in product's manufacture}}$$

In the case of A this is: $30/10 = £3$
for B it is $40/15 = £2.67$

Once these ratios have been computed decisions are made based on ranking products in order of the contribution per unit of limiting factor. Those products at the top of the list are those which should be produced first.

Knowledge of marginal costing and the use of the marginal cost statement, and other appropriate devices, to isolate contributions and calculate contributions per limiting factors will help to ensure that an organisation's management make better overall decisions about the operation of departments, the manufacture of products, and the use of resources. Basically this is all about the use of relevant information. However, if the decision maker uses marginal costing this will at least ensure that a relevant approach is adopted.

FINANCIAL GEARING AND OPERATIONAL GEARING

Many organisations have some control over production methods – that is, they can use either a highly automated process with its associated high fixed costs, but low variable costs, or alternatively, a less-automated process with lower fixed costs, but higher variable costs. If the enterprise chooses to use the method involving a high level of automation its break-even point is at a relatively high sales level, and changes in the level of sales have a magnified effect on profits, in other words, the degree of operating gearing is high. This is the same effect as that produced with financial gearing in that the higher the gearing factor the higher the break-even sales volume and the greater the impact on profits.

The degree of operating gearing can be defined as the percentage change in operating profits associated with a given percentage change in sales volume. Operating gearing can be calculated using the following formula:

Degree of operating gearing = $(S - VC)/(S - VC - FC)$

Where S represents the level of sales (quantity × value), VC is total variable cost, and FC is total fixed cost.

For example: let us suppose that a firm has a level of sales of 100,000, total variable costs of 50,000 and total fixed costs of 20,000. Its degree of operating gearing would be:

$(100,000 - 50,000)/(100,000 - 50,000 - 20,000) = 1.67$ or 167%

Therefore, if sales increase by 100 per cent, profit increases by 167 per cent. Operating gearing affects earnings before interest and taxes

(EBIT), whereas financial gearing affects earnings after interest and taxes, that is, the amount available to equity. Financial gearing will intensify the effects on earnings available to equity after the effect of operating gearing has been taken into account.

The degree of financial gearing can be defined as: the percentage change in earnings available to equity that is associated with a given percentage change in earnings before interest and taxes (EBIT). An equation has been developed for calculating the degree of financial earning:

Degree of financial gearing = EBIT/(EBIT – I)

where EBIT is earnings before interest and taxation and I is interest paid.

Thus in our earlier example we can compute the degree of financial gearing if we now assume that further debt is required involving interest payments (I) of 5,000. The degree of financial gearing would be:

30,000/(30,000 – 5,000) = 1.2 or 120%

If EBIT were to increase by 100 per cent this would result in an increase of 120 per cent in the amount available to equity. We can combine operating and financial gearing to reveal the overall effect of a given change in sales on earnings available to the owners as follows (which in effect merely reflects the addition of the interest cost to fixed costs):

Combined gearing effect = (S – VC)/(S – VC – FC – I)

which for our example would be:

(100,000 – 50,000)/(100,000 – 50,000 – 20,000 – 5,000) = 2 or 200%

Therefore, if sales change by 100 per cent this would cause the earnings available to equity investors to change by 200 per cent.

In this example the combined gearing effect of 2 was obtained from a degree of operating gearing of 1.67 and financial gearing of 1.2, but clearly other combinations would have produced the same effect. It is possible to make trade-offs between financial and operating gearing.

The concept of the degree of gearing allows an organisation to predict the effect of change in sales on the earnings available to ordinary shareholders in addition to revealing the interrelationship between financial and operating gearing. The concept can be used to predict, for example, that a decision to finance new plant and equipment with debt may result in a situation where a small change in sales volume will produce a large variation in earnings, whereas a different operating and financial gearing combination may reduce the effect on earnings.

SUMMARY

The chapter has discussed a number of important issues which relate to financial planning and managerial decision making. The way in which costs behave, and indeed our ability to model such behaviour, has been a central concern as it affects decisions and their impact on the organisation. In addition the chapter makes important links between the preceding 'macro' focus, for example in Chapter 2, and the more disaggregated (from an organisational point) managerial concerns which follow, for example in Chapters 6 and 7. The chapter concluded by relating some of the issues in short-term decisions to their potential effects on the firm as a whole by considering the links between operating and financial gearing. The fact that an organisation may be able to make trade-offs between the two is clearly of significance and may mean that seemingly short-term decisions have an impact on the strategic development of the organisation.

FURTHER READING

There are a number of books which discuss cost behaviour. One of the most readable is Arnold J and Hope T, *Accounting for Management Decisions*, Prentice Hall, London 1983, Chapters 7, 9 and 10. More comprehensive coverage is arguably provided by Colin Drury, *Management and Cost Accounting*, Van Nostrand Reinhold, Wokingham, Berks 1985, Chapters 9, 10 and 11.

Management Accounting – Official Terminology, The Chartered Institute of Management Accountants, September 1984.

REFERENCES

Bromwich, M and Bhimani, A (1989) *Management Accounting: Evolution not Revolution*, Chartered Institute of Management Accountants, London, 112pp.

Goldratt, E M and Cox, J (1993) *The Goal* (2nd edition), Gower, London.

Johnson, H T and Kaplan, R S (1987) 'Relevance lost: the rise and fall of management accounting', *Harvard Business Press*, 269pp.

5

Working Capital Management

INTRODUCTION

Typically companies have 40 per cent of their capital invested in working capital. But unlike their investment in fixed assets that are often subject to rigorous investment appraisal decisions the investment in working capital is a series of apparently unconnected decisions in respect of sales, production, purchasing, inventories and cash. However, all these decisions may have a consequence on the level of investment in working capital and hence on the overall investment in the firm. While individual managers should indeed make their own decisions, a comprehensive and co-ordinated policy is needed alongside appropriate monitoring.

Gitman and Maxwell (1985) found that financial managers spent 32 per cent of their time on managing working capital which, along with financial planning and budgeting (35 per cent), took up the greatest proportion of their time. In the light of this emphasis and the sharing of responsibility with line managers it is surprising to find that the literature, although while comprehensive, is scattered in its source and lacks integration into an overall framework.

This chapter provides an overview to the management of working capital and provides an insight into the constituent parts. An introduction to some of the complex relationships and models thereof is also provided. It is hoped by providing some of the specific relationships the reader will be encouraged to develop models of the elements and relate them to the overall management of working capital. Many of the relationships which reflect the working capital elements have already been introduced in Chapter 2 with the discussion of financial statement analysis. For example, the simple ratio of current assets to current liabilities reflects the key relationship between the elements of working capital. However, it must be remembered that financial statement analysis is primarily practised on annual accounts and thus the dynamic relationships may become partially masked particularly in seasonal industries.

THE ELEMENTS OF WORKING CAPITAL

The management of working capital is of equal importance in both manufacturing and service industries. The main difference lies in the fact that whereas a manufacturer may have funds tied up in physical stocks (raw material and finished goods) a service organisation (e.g. a solicitor or accountant) may have funds tied up in work in progress (i.e. work done but not yet invoiced to the customer). As we saw in Chapter 2 funds for working capital derive primarily from permanent sources (share and loan capital), which, as Chapter 3 demonstrated, have a certain cost that will need to be met. The permanent funds may be used for the provision of adequate fixed assets (land, buildings and machinery, etc). However, over–investment in fixed assets must mean that the working capital which generates the profit may be underfunded. Figure 5.1 illustrates the various factors which affect the flow of cash in the firm and demonstrate the key linkages between these and working capital.

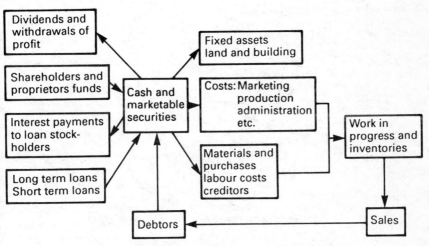

Figure 5.1 Flow of funds through a firm

Working capital is the fund required to support the expenses of production, sales, distribution and administration required prior to the receipt of the cash from the sale of finished goods. Thus a firm which has a longer lead time between production and sale will require a greater investment in working capital. The cash which we have spent on these items we hope to quickly turn back into cash through the sale of outputs to customers who subsequently pay us. The profit at the end of the cycle enables us to pay interest on the loans and even pay a dividend to the shareholders. The level of working capital is also closely related to the volume of production and sales. For example, J Sainsbury plc is able to effectively partially finance its store expansion programme out of working capital which is in fact negative, because of the way cash flows through the company, (i.e. cash received from sales (no debtors) before the goods sold are paid for).

Cash flows at different speeds in different parts of the same system and it is essential that control is exercised to ensure matching of flows and maintenance of solvency. Cash flows in the case of fixed assets are long term while cash outlays on production items will be relatively short term.

An analogy for the working capital cycle is the wheel in Figure 5.2, in which the fixed assets form the axle (subject to wear and tear) while the wheel spinning on the axle is our investment in working capital. In order to maximise return on capital employed not only do we need to have the minimum amount of capital employed in fixed assets and working capital, but we also need to maximise our return on each revolution of the working capital cycle. This we can achieve by:

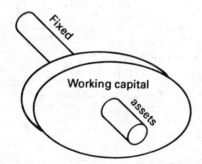

Figure 5.2 A working capital analogy

☐ ensuring the relative mark up from cost to revenue is at a maximum; but
☐ the working capital cycle takes the least possible time thus permitting within a given time period the maximum return.

At any one time, the capital employed in working capital may be identified from a balance sheet by deducting the current liabilities from the current assets. However, this single snapshot fails to portray the perpetually changing balance and mix of elements which form working capital. While some further insight into the change can be obtained by studying the cash flow statement this again fails to reflect the calculations within the business cycle stimulated by seasonality as well as the changing economic states and the management process. Figure 5.4 attempts to illustrate this using a graph of fluctuating net assets. The management of this vital element of the business combines operations management, finance and management accounting and its success can be enhanced through the use of appropriate modelling and planning.

Management requires cost data essentially to control costs in order to optimise resource usage and ROCE (return on capital employed). So, having considered the detail of cost control in Chapter 4, it is only necessary for us to reaffirm the need for appropriate information to assist management in controlling the investment in working capital.

Operational control

In order for an effective working capital management system to be introduced, a clear understanding of the operational process must exist. The operational process is a system consisting of:

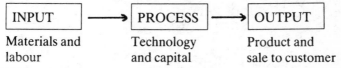

INPUT	PROCESS	OUTPUT
Materials and labour	Technology and capital	Product and sale to customer

It is also made up of departments and the structure can range from a simple organisation such as a packing operation, through the complexities of mass production, to the organisation of service provision. The operational process runs from acquisition of materials, the recruitment of labour, the organisation and control of production to the preparation of product for sale. Operational control is the direction of the material procurement and operational activities of the business in order to ensure that material and operational facilities, as specified by the technical functions, are available to carry out the planned programme of the business and that the maximum utilisation of operational facilities is achieved.

The stages, therefore, are as follows:

Material procurement and control ⎫
  labour recruitment and control ⎭   – Inputs

Control of

Production planning and control   – Process
Selling and distribution   – Outputs
Administration   – System

Two useful concepts that help managers focus on the activities that add value are:

core business
logistics.

If we examine the activities in a business then we may classify all activities which are performed into three categories:

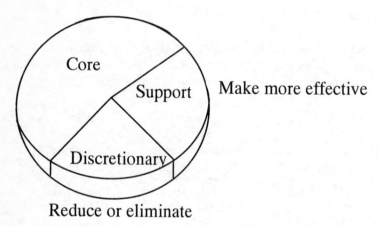

Core activities are those necessary to achieve the outcome of satisfied customers, products delivered to the right customer at the right time, etc. Failure to perform a core activity results in failure to achieve the objective.

Support activities are those which support core activities by ensuring the infrastructure is in place, that materials are available when required and that staff get paid for the work performed. While failure to perform support activities will not immediately lead to unfulfilment of the objective the long-term effect will be failure.

Discretionary activities are those which are not necessary and are merely performed because resources are available. Unfortunately too frequently discretionary means diversionary. While a customer complaint's department may be thought of as supporting, frequently it reflects failure of core activities and the discretionary resources to allow it to be performed. In fact it is a diversionary activity removing pressure from the core activity to 'get it right first time'.

Discretionary is a luxury which businesses can ill afford. Either the activity is core or it should be support. Discretionary spending on training is either necessary for staff to perform their core activities or is supportive of the corporate culture. Ill defined and unfocused activity is diversionary and unprofitable.

Logistics is the management of adding value in an activity or service from order to delivery. The emphasis, as in activity based costing, is on the activity flow through the business (in line with product service management and the value chain).

Firm Infrastructure					Margin
Human Resource Management					
Technology Development					
Procurement					
Inbound Logistics	Operations	Outbound Logistics	Marketing & Sales	Service	

Inbound logistics is concerned with planning, obtaining and specifying inputs including the use of just-in-time (JIT, see Chapter 4). The operations stage is concerned with the process and activities of adding value while outbound logistics focuses on customers, channels of distribution, etc.

Logistics is a stepping stone to the bottom-up approach of activity based costing (covered in Chapter 4) which focuses on the lowest common denominators and builds from these units through the batch activity to the production facilities and the customers and channels. They are in many respects complementary. Logistics emphasises the organising of the activity, whether manufacturing or service, to achieve the objective of satisfying the customer.

Cash conversion cycle

In this chapter we are focusing on the working capital cycle, not the overall cash flow. However, the interconnection between cash flow and working capital must not be lost as it forms a vital basis on which financial planning models build.

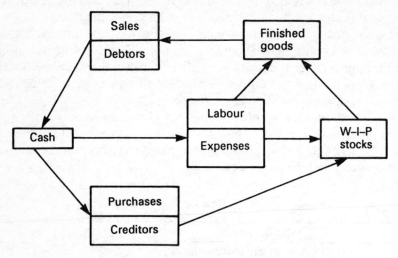

Figure 5.3 The working capital cycle

Richards and Laughlin (1980) suggested that the cash flow cycle could be modelled on the basis of its elements, which they identified as:

(a) Inventory conversion period – the time taken to convert raw materials to finished goods and despatch them to fulfil customers' orders.

(b) Receivables conversion period – the time taken to convert sales into cash received.

(c) Payables deferral period – average time from purchase/usage of raw materials, labour and expenses to payment.

(d) Cash conversion cycle – the net period of a + b – c to give the actual working capital cycle.

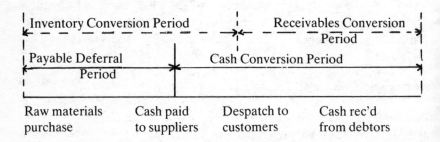

The policy for working capital management will therefore be towards minimising those cycles (i.e. a and b) which require investment and maximising that (i.e. c) which generates finance. However this must be balanced against the needs of other areas of the business. For example it is reasonable to assume that the terms of credit offered to customers form part of the overall marketing mix and unilateral action by credit controllers to restrict credit will almost certainly lead to the loss of sales that may have a more far-reaching effect on overall profitability. Likewise inventory management must balance the needs of production against those of finance.

Figure 5.4 illustrates the varying levels of capital employed which result primarily from the seasonal and trade cycle effects on working capital. A moderate finance policy which results in reasonably stable returns on investment would be to finance all of the permanent fixed and current assets from long-term finance thus only using the short-term finance for the temporary movements in current assets. A more aggressive policy would be to use short-term finance for both the temporary current assets and part of the permanent current assets. Such a policy would maximise the ROI but would require tight control over the working capital to avoid insolvency and high finance charges. A loose policy would provide finance for part of the trade cycle leaving only the temporary peaks to be financed by short-term finance. Clearly these policies have a direct bearing on the level of cash held, and consequently the ability to utilise buffer stocks etc. The degree of uncertainty prevailing will influence the policy adopted as with a high degree of uncertainty and cyclical trade patterns the provision of adequate finance to meet sudden and unexpected changes will encourage moderate to loose policies.

The short-term financing line for any specific company can be higher or lower than that shown – in fact, some companies may have some fixed assets financed by short-term debt while others will have only a portion of their fluctuating current assets financed from this source. The level of short-term debt financing depends on the business the company is in, the risk it is prepared to adopt and the relative costs of its short- and long-term debt.

The management of working capital is concerned with maximising the return to shareholders within the accepted risk constraints carried by the participants in the company. Just as excessive long-term debt puts a company at risk, so an inordinate quantity of short-term debt also increases the risk to a company by straining its solvency.

Two definitions are appropriate at this point:

(a) Moderate approach (maturity matching)

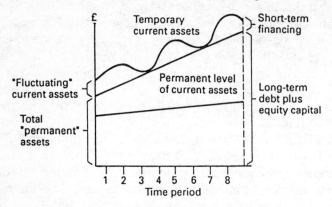

(b) Aggressive approach

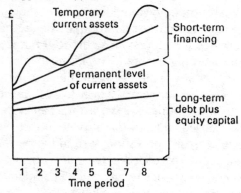

(c) Conservative approach

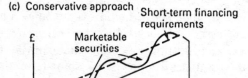

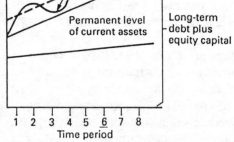

Figure 5.4 Alternative working capital policies

1. *Liquidity* – the nearness to cash of assets is a measure of their liquidity.
2. *Solvency* – the ability to meet debt payments on the due date by payments in cash.

Technical insolvency occurs when a firm has sufficient assets to meet all financial obligations, but not enough time to convert those assets to cash. This is an embarrassing position for any company to be in, but the risk can be minimised with adequate cash flow planning and control.

THE MANAGEMENT OF CURRENT ASSETS

Current assets are those which can be expected to be turned over into cash within a year. In the UK current assets represent more than half the total assets of business firms and the control of this large and volatile investment warrants considerable attention.

The total amount of current assets required by an organisation is related to the volume of sales and output. If a company increases its sales it will require a higher level of stock to service production and sales facilities and a higher level of debtors to maintain the increased sales volume.

However, management still has some discretion over the level of current assets at any particular level of output – and again a risk/return trade-off is involved. The lower the level of current assets the more profitable the company will be (as asset turnover will be increased), but there will also exist a higher risk of running short of stock or cash in the event of an unexpected increase in demand or claim from a supplier.

Similarly, a reduced level of debtors may increase the asset turnover of the company, but adversely affect profits through a drop in sales. A credit policy is part of a company's 'marketing mix' and they may lose sales to competitors who offer more attractive terms.

The general rule with current assets is to determine the minimum required quantity at the expected level of output and add a safety margin to cover any contingencies, the size of the safety margin being dependent on management's attitude to risk.

Managing stocks and work-in-progress

The amount of capital employed that is 'locked up' in stocks of one sort or another will, as illustrated above, affect profitability.

The amount of money invested in stocks in this country has historically been large (25 per cent of total assets to take an average figure of leading British companies) in the post-war period. However, increasingly this figure has been reduced due to economic pressure, reduction in the manufacturing base and changes in work practice in the 1980s. The adequacy of managerial control over this use of funds has, therefore, a considerable effect on rate of return and, historically, British companies compare unfavourably with American and Japanese companies as regards stock-turn.

Stocks fall into categories:

Finished goods
Work in progress
Raw materials
Miscellaneous.

Finished goods are goods ready for sale and it is normal to follow a stock-holding policy based on number of weeks' sale. This policy allows regular production of batches without excessive re-tooling associated with small batches, and yet permits flexibility in respect of sales and marketing. Work in progress will include product still in progress at period ends that will depend on the relative length of the production cycle. In addition, products which may be sold in various packages may be held as interim stocks prior to repacking to final order, thereby reducing finished stock holding and increasing production flexibility.

Raw material stocks may well reflect not only supply conditions and production requirements, but also opportunistic exploitation of market prices. However, these must be balanced against the costs of stock holding including the cost of financing such stocks. If just-in-time (JIT) stocking policies are possible (i.e., stocks are only taken in just when required) then significant reductions in stocks are possible.

Miscellaneous stocks include not only the small consumable materials, but the maintenance and engineering spares as well as packaging and stationery supplies for administration.

A certain level of stocks is necessary because, *inter alia*:

□ materials and parts can be purchased more cheaply in large lots and anticipated increases in material prices might be avoided
□ reserve stocks will be required to avoid stoppages in production through interruptions in deliveries
□ the length of production time cycles can vary
□ the production flows from different manufacturing stages will not match and the imbalance is adjusted through intermediate stock holdings
□ the order pattern is not even – orders arrive in irregular flows and to maintain customer goodwill quick deliveries are essential

□ there may be difficulties in forecasting future demand patterns
□ economies of scale may be lost.

If we could synchronise all the stages of production from the buying of raw materials to the final demand of the customers then there would be no need for stocks to be kept at any stage in the production–distribution system. This is the principle on which concepts such as just-in-time manufacturing builds upon. Essential to such approaches are advanced manufacturing technology, particularly flexible manufacturing systems and continuous flow where it is possible to reduce the set-up costs between batches and eliminate the need for stock-holding to match production rates. Using such technologies a batch of one unit may become economic. However, this is almost a Utopian situation to which organisations aspire, so we must consider not whether to keep stocks, but how to minimise the costs associated with such stocks. But first we must establish a model of stock movements and the cost relationships.

Variables in the stock control problem

Having introduced the reasons for stock keeping and said a little about the problem, it is useful to take an overall look to see how complex it can become and to indicate the variables which can be associated with such problems.

The main characteristics of controlling stocks usually involve some of the following variables:

□ demand or usage, and the rate of usage
□ delivery rate
□ cost of buying or making one unit
□ cost of storing one unit during unit time
□ cost of being out of stock, and
□ re-order lead time.

Demand or usage

Demand can be either known for certain or it can be an estimated figure. Note that estimates both regarding demand and rate of demand could be completely wrong and lead to losing money either by not having enough in stock or having too much in stock. For simplicity demand is often assumed to be at a constant rate as in Figure 5.5. However a more realistic pattern of consumption is probably that shown in Figure 5.6, but for simplicity of the model we will assume Figure 5.5 for the time being.

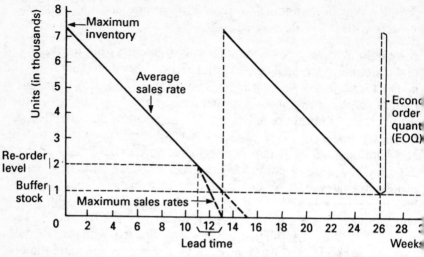

Figure 5.5 Stock position (including safety stocks)

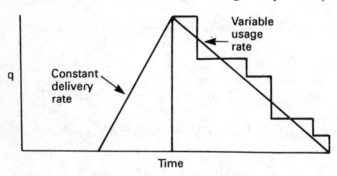

Figure 5.6 Stock demands

Delivery Rate

In some instances the delivery of materials into stock may be considered to take place instantaneously at some point in time. In other cases, delivery of a fixed amount may take place over a period of time – see Figures 5.5 and 5.6.

Cost of Buying (or Making)

If we order units from an outside supplier then we have two costs associated with this operation. In the first place we have the cost of raising the order, which can be considerable and the price which we pay for each unit, which might vary because of price discounts.

Cost of Storing One Unit for Unit Time

This cost is made up of a number of costs such as storage space, clerical costs, rent and rates, etc. It may be a difficult cost to ascertain, but in many cases not impossible.

The following list, while not exhaustive, is indicative of some of the costs to be considered:

Cost of finance for stocks held.
Cost of storage space whether rented or owned.
Cost of insurance.
Cost of depreciation associated with deterioration and obsolescence and wear and tear.
Cost of special storage conditions.
Cost of labour and freight associated with stock movements.
Costs of stock management.

Cost of Being Out of Stock

This is a much more difficult cost to find. For instance, if a motor car firm runs out of tyres on its production line the cost to the company could be astronomical. On the other hand, if a supermarket runs out of a certain brand of margarine then customers may buy another brand although in some cases such shortages could lead to loss of profit.

Re-order Lead Time

Since time will usually elapse between placing an order and receiving it, we require to know the duration of this time. In some cases this lead time will be known and certain, but in others it may be variable.

Other relevant measures include the following:

☐ *Re-order level.* A quantity fixed at which re-ordering procedures should be commenced. It is a level higher than minimum stock, such that given normal delivery no out of stock situation will occur.
☐ *Minimum stock.* A buffer stock level below which stores should not fall.
☐ *Maximum stock.* Stocks should not be allowed to rise above this level without special authority. Set by considering: rate of consumption; re-order time; finance; storage space; loss due to evaporation and deterioration; price fluctuations; obsolescence; market shortages; EOQ.
☐ *Average stock.* Max. stock + min. stock

2

□ *Rate of stock turnover.* $\dfrac{\text{consumption of materials}}{\text{average stock of materials}}$

A useful measure for controlling the quantity of stock carried from month to month is the average age of stocks:

$$\text{Average age of stock} = \dfrac{\text{Stock balance at beginning of period}}{\text{Purchases of stock during the period}} \times 30 \text{days}$$

This equation gives an approximate measure of the average age of stocks. Within the stock balance figure there may be items which have lain idle for 18 months and these should be identified and treated separately. However, it does give a guide for corrective action, since if it is increasing over time, it would indicate a less efficient use of stock which should warrant management attention. The age of stock that must be carried depends on the length of the production cycle and so considerable variations may occur.

It is possible to establish the number of weeks' work on the factory floor by relating the current quantity of work-in-progress to transfers into finished goods stock.

$$\text{No. of weeks work on factory floor} \quad \dfrac{\text{Current quantity of WIP}}{\text{Weekly rate of transfer into finished goods}}$$

Sharp increases in the ratio will indicate the presence and severity of bottlenecks.

Use of production planning techniques such as critical path analysis, pert and queuing theory may improve work flow. A useful guide to raw material stocking is *utility* and *availability*. It is reasonable to concede that stocks have no economic value if they have no utility (i.e. not what is wanted) or no availability (not available when required, where required).

Limitations of the quantity of finished goods held can be achieved by relating the rate of transfers into finished goods (by product groups) to cost of sales. Rises in the ratio will indicate either:

1. stockpiling of goods for which demand is falling away – danger of obsolescence; or
2. the general level of sales falling indicating contraction of production or drive on sales; or
3. stocks are again being built up for a particular purpose. From a working capital standpoint the importance here attaches to

whether advance payments can be obtained from customers on whose behalf stocking is taking place.

The higher rate of stock turnover, the greater the sales revenue obtainable. The objects of measuring stock rate of turnover are, therefore, twofold:

☐ the conservation of working capital; and
☐ the increase in revenue obtainable and the maximising of profit.

Use of number of weeks' or days' stock based on average and/or current or forecast sales will assist in control of stock build-ups.

Mathematical and graphical models

A knowledge of the relationships between demand, supply and costs enables us to build a model of the situation. This may be done in two ways: either mathematical or graphical. First let us select a solution to the following problem by inspection.

Suppose we have the following conditions:

1. We want to order 3600 units over a period of one year and these units are used at a constant rate during the year.
2. As soon as our supply has dropped to zero a quantity of a fixed ordered amount is received instantaneously.
3. Cost of sending out an order is £5. Cost of holding one unit in stock for one year is £0.8.

Using this information we can construct a simple working model:

Order	Number of orders	Cost of ordering	Average stock	Cost of holding	Total cost
1	2	3	4	5	(col 3 + 5)
		(col 2 × £5)		(col 4 × £0.8)	
		£		£	£
100	36	180	50	40	220
150	24	120	75	60	180
200	18	90	100	80	170
250	15	76	125	100	176
300	12	60	150	120	180
350	11	51	175	140	191
400	9	45	200	160	205
500	8	36	250	200	236
600	6	30	300	240	270
900	4	20	450	360	380
1200	3	15	600	480	495
3600	1	5	1800	1440	1445

Average stock is given by the quantity ordered divided by two (assuming constant rate of demand and instantaneous supply).

From the table we can see that the cost will be at a minimum if we place orders in lots of 200. If we were to plot this as a graph then we would produce Figure 5.7 below:

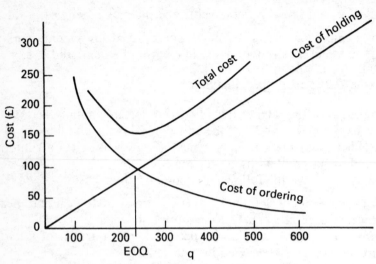

Figure 5.7 Stock holding costs

The least-cost position is where the total cost line turns, which is slightly above 200 units. With accurate drawing of the graph, or if the data in the table was more sensitive it would be possible to identify the minimum point. Alternatively we may use mathematics to solve the problem since the minimum cost point will be where the total cost turns from a downward slope to an upward slope. It will also be where the cost of holding and cost of ordering are equal.

Using the notation:

T = Total planning period
R = Total demand during T
q = Quantity ordered each time
t = Time between each order
C_o= Cost placing one order
C_s= Cost storing one unit for period T

Then the number of orders placed in period T would be R/q and the cost of orders in period t will be:

$R/q \times C_o$

If we order R/q times then the interval between each order will be:

$t = T/No\ of\ orders\ (R/q) = Tq/R$

If the interval starts with q units in stock and ends with zero units in stock then the average stock during period t is $q/2$.

The total cost of storing will be:

$q/2 \times C_s \times t \times R/q$

Which if we substitute for t simplifies to:

$q/2 \times C_s \times T$

So the total cost will be:

Total cost = holding cost + ordering cost

$$TC = \frac{q\,C_s\,T}{2} + \frac{C_o\,R}{q}$$

Which may be solved by differentiation to find the minimum cost. The value of q associated with this is called the *economic order quantity*:

$$q = \sqrt{\frac{2\,C_o\,R}{C_s\,T}}$$

If we apply it to the above data then we find the results:

T = one year
R = 3600 units
q = 212 units
t = 17.7 days
C_o = £5
C_s = £0.8
TC = £169.7

The economic order quantity is a guide in that it is based on various assumptions and the data applied is estimated. Thus while accuracy is implied by the output from the model it should be treated with the same degree of caution as is applied to the underlying elements.

The above example is deliberately simplified and the model may be refined to incorporate:

☐ stock-out costs reflecting shortages
☐ constant rates of replenishment and usage
☐ uncertainty.

Just-in-time Manufacturing

Just-in-time (JIT) manufacturing is the management of production and inventories such that the inventories of raw materials, work in progress and finished goods are reduced to zero. The principle is that demand should pull through production, rather than production maintaining stocks ready for call-off by customers. JIT demands that production and suppliers be responsive to the demands of customers and this requires production to be both flexible and continuous. Production and suppliers must be able to quickly set up machinery, clean down and change over from one production run to another, and receive prompt supply of small batches of raw materials. JIT demands short operating cycles, which may be achieved by advanced manufacturing and flexible working practices from staff.

Advanced manufacturing implies investing in technology with the associated fixed cost structures. Such capital intense industries require high volumes of throughput and consequent large market shares in order to justify the investment. Competitive advantage through either higher value or lower cost is essential. Alternatively, the use of flexible staff demands a return towards piecework methods and is the frequent basis of the suppliers supporting advanced manufacturers in the Far East.

Design allows the development of products with minimum set-up time and changeover costs and frequently permits reduction in number of parts in finished product. This reduction often assists the improvement in quality as there are fewer parts to fail.

Prompt supply demands good relationships between suppliers and buyers. An example of this can be seen in the retail sector in the UK where frequently the stockholding and distribution of goods are the responsibility of the supplier up until delivery to the supermarket for consumption the following day. In this way retailers have reduced their investment in working capital to the point where trading is financed by the suppliers and the cash receipts from sales finance new developments before being used to pay suppliers.

In reflecting on the economics of JIT it should be noted that ordering costs are assumed to be such that the minimum total cost (i.e. cost of ordering plus holding) will be at an economic order quantity of one unit.

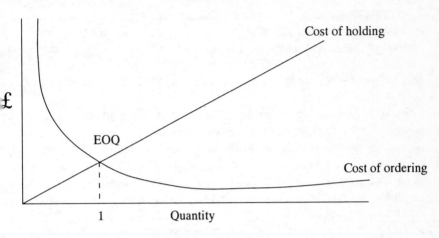

Kanban

An alternative to the JIT manufacturing and the EOQ approach to inventory system is the Kanaban. Essentially the Kanaban is a system of inventory management based on small physical stockpiles held in clearly marked areas. The stocks are constrained by the physical space but may be called off when required. The supply department is required to maintain the stock levels and may organise itself to refill as and when required in line with its own optimum operation. It relies on mutual responsibility to avoid over- and under-stocking.

Materials Resource Planning

Materials resource planning (MRP) was devised in the 1960s as a method of calculating the total quantities of material required to manufacture the finished products by 'exploding' the build quantities through the bills of materials, allowing for manufacturing processes, yields and waste. Enhancement in the 1970s and 1980s incorporated production planning and scheduling as well as shop floor control. MRPII calculates the materials, components and manufacturing capacity required to complete the production plan and schedules each activity on the shop-floor from sub-assemblies to finished product. It utilises sophisticated computer databases and planning models that can be interfaced with distribution, accounting, design and manufacturing systems. Combined with strategies for reducing complexity of design and JIT operating cycles are reduced and demand pull achieved.

Total Quality Management

The philosophy of total quality management has been an important contributor to the reduction of operating cycle time and the improved effectiveness of production. The embedding of quality in the production and operation cycles has reduced the necessity for separate quality control points that represented natural bottlenecks and potential stockpiles.

Before leaving inventories it is perhaps worth recalling that inventories may themselves be the subject of separate financing agreements, particularly with factors. Practice in the retail trade is the financing of inventories by the suppliers reflecting the relative negotiating power of the supplier and retailer. The shift in the focus of business activity to service industries has stressed the demand pull basis on which most inventory systems are now based. The economics of EOQ are still valid; however, the objective of management is to reduce the total costs of inventories and wherever possible finance them from suppliers or customers.

Debtors and credit control

The amount of a business's funds 'locked up' in debtors at any time is determined by:

- the volume of sales
- the credit policy
- the efficiency of the debt collection, and
- the occurrence of bad debts.

Again, historically, British companies have compared unfavourably with American companies regarding sales:debtors' ratios. In the case of manufacturing companies approximately 20 per cent of the companies' assets may be held as debtors.

The ratchet effect of credit policy should not be ignored in that an increase in sales will naturally lead to an increase in the level of debtors if credit terms are maintained. Consequently there will be a need for an increase in the level of finance for debtors, plus it is likely that increased sales will place demands on production and purchasing which in turn may require additional finance. Furthermore it is likely that there will be an increase in the doubtful debt provision and discounts.

To effect close control over the funds invested in debtors, management must make a number of decisions relating to the credit period, the progressing of paper work leading to the collection of cash, and the procedures for slow payers. Management must also determine what information feedback it needs if it is to exercise full control. As with the management of stock levels, a monthly statement of the average age of debts outstanding is a useful control document to determine whether the trend in the collection period is moving in an adverse way or not and how the achieved collection period compares with any standard set. Seasonal adjustments can be catered for in this simple moving averages-styled exercise.

$$\text{Average age of debts} = \frac{\text{Debtors' balance at beginning of period}}{\text{Credit sales during period}} \times 30 \text{ days}$$

The analysis of debtor by month, i.e. one month, two months, etc is often provided in total as well as by customer and sub-groups. While a normal distribution curve might be expected, it is likely that the efficiency of debt collection as perceived by the customers will lead to the skewing of the distribution towards the due credit date. If the credit collection is inefficient then a long tail to the distribution as well as the peak being after the due date is likely (see Figure 5.8).

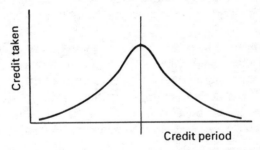

Figure 5.8 Inefficient credit collection graph

The granting of credit should be clearly specified as the responsibility of a specific post in the organisation so that the person in that post has a standard of performance to maintain that it is measurable.

Where the values of orders are such that they become individually significant for the company then some formal system of vetting customers is desirable. The firm need not rely solely upon its own staff to appraise the creditworthiness of its customers. There are a number of agencies which specialise in providing such information.

The practice of customer modelling in which the profitability of customers is evaluated by including not only the mix of products taken but also the discounts and special prices as well as the cost of finance associated with the credit terms taken. Trade practice tends to be the driving force for the granting of credit but clearly it is a part of the marketing mix and as such should be evaluated. Clearly companies should model their credit policy and consider the cost of giving credit as well as reviewing periodically the length of credit given.

A common cause of delay in collecting amounts due is slackness in rendering invoices to customers and delays in sending out statements. When the customer has not paid the account within the allowed credit period, there should be an automatic follow-up procedure, usually a sequence of letters, personal calls, etc, prior to the account being handed to solicitors or other collection agents. Perhaps the most important weapon in the credit controller's arsenal is the withholding of supply to debtors. While this is an extreme action the knowledge of its availability when used in conjunction with real-time sales order processing systems in which current information is available to sales negotiators can lead to effective control of poor payers.

One method frequently adopted to secure earlier payment of sums due is, of course, an offer of a cash discount for prompt payment. Naturally, the cost of this discount should be considered in fixing the price of the product initially. Unless the cost has been allowed for, it can more than wipe out its advantages in terms of speedier payments.

Doubtful debts are to be avoided as they may lead to bad debts but they have a value which can be measured in terms of their current value after discounting and adjustment for probability.

The overall marketing strategy of the business should include some decisions as to the credit period to be adopted. The granting of long-term credit can be used as a key selling point, but the cost should be weighed against that of other forms of sales promotion. The firm could, in fact, by offering only a very short credit period, say seven days, use the advantages of increased capital utilisation to provide a competitive advantage in quality or price and expand its market share by this means rather than by offering longer than average credit facilities.

The cost of a credit policy is often lost in the overall costs of the business and while specific reference above to the cost of credit in terms of finance has been made there are other costs of credit management. These costs include not only the manpower and establishment costs of operating a credit control department but also the costs of information systems and communications both internal and external to the company. A measure of the average cost of debtors may be arrived at as follows:

$$\text{Annual cost of debtors} = \text{average level debt} \times \text{variable cost ratio} \times \text{cost of finance}$$

An alternative to the operation of your own credit control department and to avoid the financing of debtors is to employ a factor to undertake this task. This method of financing debtors can be particularly useful to the smaller business but there is an opportunity cost in the income foregone which the factor claims as his margin.

The granting of credit is a lending decision when the net effect is merely to change the size of the debtors. If refusal of credit would not result in loss of business, and if the customer has alternative sources of funds, then the extension of credit is the same as granting a loan. In such a case we need to ask three questions:

☐ What is the principal and term of the loan?
☐ What effective rate of interest is required?
☐ How much credit can be extended?

In this chapter we have already contrasted the rigorous approach adopted to investment decisions involving, say, new equipment with a less rigorous approach involving working capital decisions. We can illustrate this using the organisation's credit terms. If the answer to any of the following four questions is *yes*, then the granting of trade credit is an investment decision and should be treated accordingly (see Chapter 6):

☐ Will the customer's buying decision be influenced by the credit terms?
☐ Is the customer short of funds?
☐ Is the supplier operating below capacity?
☐ Are the supplier's competitors operating below capacity?

Short-term investments

If a company has a surplus of cash and does not expect this surplus to be used in the near future it should invest the funds in the short-term money market. A small return on these funds is better than the nil return obtained in a current bank account.

The investments open to a company are:

☐ bank deposit accounts
☐ local authority deposits from two days to two years

- finance house deposits from one month to a year
- inter-company loans from two days to two years
- treasury bills.

The return obtained on these deposits depends on the period of deposit and the repayment notice required. The longer the term of the loan generally the higher the rate of interest.

Management of cash

It is pointless to absorb too much working capital by holding it in the form of cash and bank balances. Cash is a non-earning asset, therefore the natural policy is to minimise it. Any such surplus should be suitably invested having regard to whether this is of a temporary, semi-permanent or permanent nature, for instance dividend payments, capital investment. The choice of investment portfolio will, of course, depend upon the extent of the surplus and degree of permanence available. Use of a short- and mid-term cash flow forecast will highlight fluctuations in cash and bank balances and must be used in some form or another by a business as the first test of liquidity.

The cost of holding cash is not only the profit that could have been earned had the funds been put to other uses, but also the depreciation due to inflation and possible changes in exchange rates. However there are some good reasons for holding cash:

- A cash balance is required to meet transactions.
- The banks appreciate the holding of cash balances as collateral against borrowings and services.
- Cash balances provide precautionary balances to meet uncertainties and emergencies.
- Cash balances provide funds for speculative opportunities.
- Cash balances provide facilities to exploit discounts for prompt payment.
- Cash balances help improve a firm's credit rating.

Essentially the efficient management of cash is the synchronisation of the cash flows. This is achieved not only by the careful management of the cash conversion cycle but also the management of the float. The float is the time taken to clear and deposit cheques. It includes the mail float, the processing float through the company as well as the clearing float. Through the management of the floats significant finance may be generated, i.e. through prompt depositing of collections and deferment of payments. This may be assisted by the use of direct debiting as well as careful selection of a clearing bank.

In the case of divisionalised companies, special problems of compensating balances may be required. The growth of on-line cash management schemes now being offered by the banks reflects the increasing problems of cash flow management. The cost of cash management may be measured in the company in the opportunities foregone as well as in terms of the additional bank charges and interest lost or gained. The cost of a shortage of cash is measured in the cost of raising finance or ultimately in the cost of bankruptcy or restructuring. The cost of surplus is the cost of interest/opportunities foregone.

Baumol (1952) suggested that cash may be managed in the same way as any other inventory and that the inventory model could reasonably reflect the cost volume relationships as well as the cash flows. In this way, the economic order quantity could be applied to cash management. This, however, may be inadequate to reflect the complex mix of flows, and so dynamic programming methods have been used as well as LP and decision trees. The use of simulation and analytical forecasting techniques holds strong possibilities today.

Before leaving current assets we must emphasise that while the individual elements require special management as in the case of inventory, the collective also require management. In particular, there exists relationships between debtors, stocks and cash. This can be illustrated by considering the case of a wholesale company faced with decreasing cash, increasing stocks and static debtors. This could possibly be explained by a decline in sales to the retail customers who in turn are facing declining demand for the product line. Consequently, the retailers, while buying less, defer payment resulting in an apparent steady debtor's level, but increasing stock. The result for the wholesaler is a shortage of cash. These interrelationships emerge by considering the flows within the working capital cycle and the analysis of performance through ratios over time demonstrates the shift.

ABC/Pareto analysis or the 80:20 rule

Finally, before leaving the assets element of working capital management it is worth mentioning the 80:20 rule which can apply to both stocks and debtors. Figure 5.9 illustrates the 'rule' in the form of a graph. For example according to the rule 20 per cent of the stocks will represent 80 per cent of the turnover or value. Accordingly it is to this 20 per cent that the effect of stock control is applied to ensure economic stocking policies. Meanwhile, the 80 per cent that represents only 20 per cent of the turnover should be subject to scrutiny to verify its value to the organisation. On a similar principle, debtors may be reviewed while always remembering they are customers.

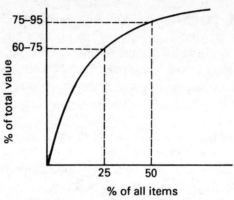

Figure 5.9 ABC analysis

THE MANAGEMENT OF CURRENT LIABILITIES

Current liabilities are all the debts owed by the company which are due for payment within a year. These payments must all be made in cash within the specified time, but while they exist current liabilities represent the short-term financing of the company.

The main components of current liabilities are:

◻ bank overdraft
◻ creditors
◻ tax holdings such as corporation tax, PAYE and VAT
◻ deferred current liabilities – these arise as a result of a firm's long-term commitments and often entail regular cash payments on specified dates, which may involve, for example:
  – interest payments
  – corporation tax payments
  – dividends
  which are scheduled for payment in the next accounting period.

There are two possible approaches to the modelling of current liabilities. First they may be ignored and instead the financing costs incorporated into the appropriate current asset. For example, the creditors can be incorporated into the inventory model (Haley and Higgins, 1973). Alternatively they may be incorporated into the short-term finance element, i.e. cash. This latter approach requires the treatment of short-term finance as multiple elements and thus programming techniques are appropriate (Cohen and Hammer, 1967).

Bank overdraft

Over recent years bank overdrafts have been a major source of short-term funds for UK companies. Overdrafts are negotiated lines of credit at call where the bank reserves the right to alter the rate of interest charges in accordance with changes in the bank's rate. Interest charged is usually one or two per cent above base rate. Since this is on the daily balances and subject therefore to fluctuating inflows and outflows it may work out cheaper than a comparable loan. The upper limit on the credit line is also subject to a downward revision in times of a credit squeeze. However, they can be negotiated quickly.

Most companies do not expect to pay off their overdraft within the year and it can, in some cases, be considered as part of the company's long-term funding. However, as this facility can be called at short notice and in full it is probably better to treat these funds as though they were short-term.

Bank overdrafts are also very flexible and simple to operate. In this respect they may be cheaper than other sources which have a lower interest rate in that the interest is only paid on the outstanding balance and the loan may be repaid as early as possible. So, overdrafts are particularly useful for financing exceptional workloads or seasonal fluctuations and for bridging the gaps in a company's financial requirements.

In general, banks like to lend to healthy companies with 'sound' liquidity ratios. They tend to prefer self-liquidating loans which are repaid automatically, such as financing a contract or finished goods stock.

Good relations with the bank are an important part of financial management and these are helped by negotiating loans well in advance and explaining why the loan is required, how much is required, and when and how it will be repaid. It can readily be appreciated that an accurate cash budget is vital in these conditions.

Small businesses and growth companies have particular needs for short-term finance (for stocks and debtors for example), but present in turn particular problems which will require periodic refinancing if the overdraft is not to grow out of control.

Managing creditors

Trade credit is a major source of short-term funds for UK companies, particularly for the smaller companies. This use of suppliers to finance a company's activities should be considered in the total financing policy as it provides a recognised and cheap form of borrowing (no interest is usually charged).

However, the level of trade credit, like all forms of financing, must not be taken beyond the capacity of the company's cash flow to service the payment requirements when they fall due. If one creditor takes legal proceedings to recover an amount due this may trigger off widespread claims by other creditors (and possibly the bank) that the company cannot meet in the short term. A company's image may also be important and a reputation as a slow payer may bring intangible costs which outweigh the value of the credit taken.

To control credit, a company should monitor the average age of accounts receivable as with debtors and match these payments in with their cash budget. Some suppliers offer cash discounts and unless a company is very short of funds it is usually a sound rule to accept discounts whenever possible. The cash saving can be compared with the cost of the most expensive source of short-term credit, often the bank overdraft.

The payment of the other elements of current liabilities are not usually at the discretion of the company's financial management. However, the longer a company can retain the funds the cheaper will be its overall cost of funds.

SUMMARY

A survey of the motor vehicle industry in 1984 revealed a cost advantage to Japanese manufacturing relative to the USA of over $2000 per vehicle. This advantage was distributed as follows:

	%
Just-in-time production	25
Quality control systems	15
Wages and benefits	25
Other productivity improvements	22
Miscellaneous	13

While this is historical, it was the competitive spur which in the recession of the late 1970s and 1980s led to large-scale revisions of behaviour in businesses.

Working capital management involves all aspects of the administration of current assets and current liabilities.

Firstly, there is the policy concerned with the level of current assets at any particular sales level and the risk acceptable to the company, i.e., a low level of current assets may entail stock or cash shortages though it should also entail high profitability as there is maximum utilisation of resources.

Secondly, there is the policy question of the level of current liabilities and short-term debt. Short-term debt is often less expensive than long-term debt and could be used to finance all current assets and possibly some fixed assets. However, this would increase the risk to the company as any difficulties in the future experienced by the company may result in an inability to make a payment when due and thus lead to insolvency.

In conclusion it is worth recalling that :

1. It is a false economy to attempt to finance a business at the expense of suppliers. Any initial savings resulting from taking extended periods of credit must inevitably affect the goodwill of an undertaking.
2. The co-operation of suppliers can often have a beneficial effect upon stock levels particularly where suppliers can be regularly phased according to production requirements. Such co-operation will not be forthcoming to the same extent if suppliers do not have their accounts paid promptly.
3. Prompt payment of accounts also increases the level of discounts which become receivable by a company.
4. Use of such things as sale or return, special terms including bills of exchange.
5. Remember bank overdrafts and loans can be recalled at short notice.

FURTHER READING

Chapters 15 and 16 of Franks and Broyles *Modern Managerial Finance* (Wiley, 1979), and Chapters 9 to 11 of Gitman's *Principles of Managerial Finance* (Harper & Row, 1982) are both very readable on the management of working capital.

Other useful supplements to this chapter would include Weston and Brigham's *Essentials of Managerial Finance* (Dryden Press, 1987), Firth M, *Management of Working Capital* (Macmillan, 1976) and Bass R M V *Credit Management – How to Manage Credit Effectively and Make a Real Contribution to Profits* (Business Books, 1979).

REFERENCES

Baumol, W J (1952) 'The transactions demand for cash: An inventory theoretical approach', *Quarterly Journal of Economics*, Nov, pp 545–556.

Cohen, K J and Hammer, F S (1967) 'Linear programming models for optimal bank asset management decisions', *Journal of Economics*, 22, pp 42–61.

Gitman, L J and Maxwell, C E (1985) 'Financial activities of major US firms: survey and analysis of Fortune's 1000', *Financial Management*, 14(4), pp 57–65.

Haley, C W and Higgins, R C (1973) 'Inventory policy and trade credit financing', *Management Science*, 20, pp 464–471.

Richards, V D and Laughlin, J (1980) 'A cash conversion cycle approach to liquidity analysis', *Financial Management*, Spring, pp 32–38.

Investment Appraisal

INTRODUCTION

Investment appraisal can be defined as the process of planning expenditure on assets whose returns are expected to extend over more than one year. It is a topic which is both well documented in the literature as well as being the subject of many formal procedures in organisations. It is perhaps surprising, therefore, that there is so much controversy over the topic, and in particular a significant difference between what the textbooks may recommend and the current practice within organisations.

The importance of such decisions to the firm can be judged by the degree of corporate risk which accrues should the project fail. At one extreme the project may incur losses which, at a minimum, will destabilise corporate earnings and threaten the overall liquidity and solvency of the firm.

Methods of capital budgeting are well documented but still much controversy exists between what is 'good practice' and what 'practice' is. We do not intend to cover this debate as it merits a book in its own right. Instead we will merely raise indicators of areas of concern as we introduce the methods particularly in operationalising the techniques.

The projects which are the subject of investment appraisal (which is sometimes known as capital budgeting) can be classified as follows:

- replacement decisions – maintenance of the business resources, cost reduction;
- expansion decisions – of existing products and markets, launching new products/markets;
- safety or environmental;
- other.

While both replacement and expansion decisions may easily be quantified in cost/benefits, problems arise with safety and environmental projects in which the costs may be all too obvious and the benefits difficult to quantify or intangible. Consequently while techniques of investment appraisal have been developed which, in conjunction with economic measurement concepts, provide comprehensive capabilities, there still remains a dependence on judgement and, often, the incorporation of other political and social perspectives. It is necessary therefore not to limit the scope to the techniques of investment appraisal alone, but also to consider the life-cycle of projects and their management.

PROJECT LIFE-CYCLE

The project life-cycle may be broken down into five distinct phases:

project identification;
estimation of cost/benefits;
choice;
implementation;
post-completion audit.

Project identification will have different origins according to the type of project. Replacement decisions may result from the management of the asset life-cycle or from the routine maintenance of the assets of the business. Alternatively it may stem from the sudden irrepairable failure of a vital piece of equipment in which case it is more than likely that procedures of appraisal and approval will be cut short or even followed after implementation. In the case of expansion projects the origin may be in research and development or marketing and clearly the nature of future cash flows may well have a different degree of confidence from those associated with replacement.

Having identified a project a procedure needs to be followed in order to ensure the application of rational choice. In many organisations strict timetables and documents have to be followed to gain approval from appropriate managers. Normal investment appraisal decisions are frequently seen as significant to organisations; consequently the approval of the board of directors is often needed. However, since capital expenditure may range from a few pounds in the case of the acquisition of a pocket calculator to millions of pounds for a new factory, it is normal to apply a threshold value to differentiate between those items which require formal approval from the Board or investment committee and those which may be approved by the respective budget heads within their annual expenditure budget.

These procedures form the elements of the project life-cycle and so the next stage is the estimation of the cash flows. The relevant costs and revenues for an investment decision are the incremental future cash flows attributable to the project (not the accounting income which incorporates depreciation which is not a cash flow). Sunk costs should be ignored as should commitments already made. In measuring the costs and benefits the opportunities taken up as well as given up should be incorporated as well as changes in working capital requirements resulting from the project. It is in the area of estimation of cash flows that the information about a project may be viewed as being most subjective. The subsequent manipulation of these estimates in the appraisal appears then to give the process a degree of accuracy and hence certainty which may not reflect the true nature of the estimation process. We will return to this aspect when we consider uncertainty and risk.

Once the cash flows have been estimated we may proceed to financially model the project and apply investment appraisal techniques. This will enable identification of those projects which fulfil our requirements and those which we should reject. This exercising of choice will also be dependent on the nature of capital rationing. Where capital rationing exists then selection of projects will be on the basis of ranking, where projects which are viewed as offering the greatest return are ranked higher than those offering a lower return. Clearly the number of projects approved will be dependent on the availability of capital and where projects are mutually exclusive then the project with the greater return will be selected. However, an organisation may be subject to self-imposed capital rationing where it seeks to limit capital expenditure to that which can be financed from within. In such circumstances it is conceivable and even probable that should a project be identified which offers exceptional opportunity and for which additional finance could be sought from outside then the decision will rest not upon a ranking but rather upon a hurdle criteria. In such a case the hurdle must be the cost of borrowing to finance the project.

A further aspect of choice which we shall return to later is the riskiness of the project and the decision maker's attitude to risk and uncertainty. Clearly any project is subject to a degree of risk, some of which we may make provision for in our choice criteria, but the attitudes of decision makers cannot easily be incorporated and may reflect qualitative aspects of the decision. The uncertainty in respect of the data may be incorporated through the use of probabilities or the use of high–low estimates.

Once the project has gained approval then it must be implemented in accordance with the approval. Clearly this requires the management of the implementation process to ensure that the project takes place on time and in accordance with the estimated cash flows. Deviation from the approved project should lead to a review process and additional approval. Only in this way is it possible to control the implementation of the project. Deviation in timing and cash flows is not uncommon and should be no surprise given that it is based on estimates made, probably significantly in advance of the event. However, the process of project management provides a comprehensive range of methods to manage and quantify the consequences of deviation:

- □ Gantt charts for project scheduling;
- □ critical path analysis to identify bottlenecks; and
- □ Project Evaluation Review Technique (PERT) – costing of alternative courses of action.

Once a project has been implemented a post-completion review will provide not only a critical appraisal of the specific project, but also an important learning vehicle for future projects. The use of post-completion audits is unpopular primarily because it exposes the project proposer, implementer and the approval body to review, in terms of their decisions, actions, and opinions. However, only by learning from previous mistakes will it be possible to improve the identification, estimation, choice, and implementation of projects.

Life-cycle costs

Increasingly the life of an asset is being viewed as a whole in which not only is the initial project subject to assessment through investment appraisal but also the subsequent life of the asset up to and including its replacement are viewed as one continuous project. This approach, referred to as *terotechnology*, incorporates the disciplines of finance, economics, and engineering. The emphasis is on the long-run average cost curve which is monitored through identifying not only the initial costs of the asset but also its subsequent repair, maintenance and improvement. The objective is to maintain the asset at the least cost position and provide early warning of increasing costs thus signalling replacement.

Figure 6.1 illustrates the average costs of a project which could be seen as one of many short-run average cost curves, collectively forming the long-run cost curve. Clearly in order to minimise the long-run cost curve the move from one short-run cost curve to another is critical and this is the replacement decision.

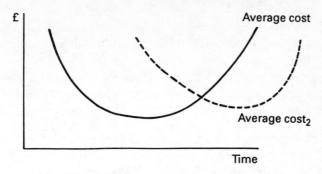

Figure 6.1 Project life-cycle costs

INVESTMENT APPRAISAL METHODS

Investment appraisal is the process by which investment projects are reviewed and selection is made as to which project to approve. The methods reflect decision rules which are being exercised for choice. Essentially there are two categories of decision rules:

☐ heuristics;
☐ formal methods.

Heuristics, or 'rules of thumb', are decisions rules based on experiential rules which have been found to work in the past. These rules may range from simplistic methods such as the precept: 'replacement is authorised if the capital cost and running costs of the new machine are less than those of the existing' (which is quite probable with high technology items), to systems of approximation and the use of hurdle criteria such as payback within six months.

The validity of such systems may only be judged in the context in which they are used and it is likely that if they were ineffective they would have been replaced.

Formal methods have been comprehensively covered in texts such as Bierman and Smidt (1971) but a summary will be presented here. It is important to recognise that each of the methods has support, and conflicting results may be found when applying the methods to the same projects. It is necessary to consider why conflicts may be generated and take these into consideration in making choices. The conflicts provide additional information for the decision maker rather than confusion, consequently it is common to find more than one method in use in an organisation. The main methods are:

☐ accounting rate of return;

- payback; and
- discounted cash flow methods: net present value, internal rate of return.

Accounting rate of return

The accounting rate of return as the name suggests is based on the ratio of average annual profits from the project to the average investment in the project. It owes its origin to the similarity to the calculation of return on investment used for evaluating ongoing activity.

The average annual profits are calculated on the incremental revenues and cost arising from the investment divided by the life of the project. The incremental costs include the net investment divided by the life of the project. The incremental costs include the net investment costs or the total depreciation charge. Similarly the average investment will be affected by the depreciation policy being pursued.

$$\text{Accounting rate of return} = \frac{\text{Average annual profits}}{\text{Average investment}}$$

n − depn
yrs

inv + scrap.
2

For example:

Project costs	25,000
Residual value	5,000

depreciated over 5 years (straight line method) is 4,000 per annum depreciation.

Net cash flows year 1	2,000
2	4,000
3	6,000
4	7,500
5	6,000
Total	25,500

Average profit	= (25,500/5) − 4,000	= 1,100
Average investment	= (25,000 + 5,000)/2	= 15,000
Accounting rate of return	= 1,100/15,000	= 7.33%

This method has the advantage of measuring profitability, and relating that to the return on the business as a whole. It is deficient in that it ignores the timing of the inflows and uses profit rather than cash.

Payback

This is the simplest method. The assumptions are that the cash outflows occur at the beginning of the cash stream and are followed by cash inflows. The payback period is the number of years it takes for the cash inflows to recover the initial outflows. The decision rule applied to accept or reject a project or to rank projects is based on an agreed number of years.

The payback period is calculated as follows:

Year	Profits project A	Cumulative profits A	Profits project B	Cumulative profits B
0	−10,000	−10,000	−10,000	−10,000
1	1,000	−9,000	3,000	−7,000
2	3,000	−6,000	3,000	−4,000
3	3,000	−3,000	3,000	−1,000
4	3,000	0	1,000	0
5	3,000	3,000		
6	4,000	7,000		
Payback period		4 years		4 years

This is indicated by the year in which the cumulative profits break even. Profits are calculated before depreciation and after tax.

There are two possible ways of using payback as a decision aid:

□ Accept any project which repays the initial outlay within a target period.
□ Rank projects according to the time taken to repay the initial outlay.

The advantages of payback may be summarised as follows:

□ It is easy to calculate.
□ As a measure of liquidity it may be useful because projects which provide a more immediate return of cash are preferred.
□ It may build in a safeguard against risk if risk increases as the payback period lengthens.
□ It could serve as a simple initial screen in project appraisal.

The problems with payback are as follows:

□ Defining the target payback period.
□ There is no way of coping with projects which have different pre-production periods.

- Variations in the timing of cash flows within the payback period are ignored.
- Cash flows outside the payback period are ignored.
- No allowance is made for interest on the initial capital invested.

Compounding – the terminal value of £1

Compounding interest is a familiar feature of most people's lives. Take for example a bank deposit account which yields an annual rate of interest of 9.5 per cent. If £1 is deposited in the bank at the start of the year and interest is added at the end of the year the amount at the end of the year will be:

$$1 + (1 \times 9.5/100) = 1 + 0.095 = £1.095$$

Note that the rate of interest, which will be called r, equals 0.095 which is 9.5/100 or 9.5 per cent. It is correct to talk of the rate of interest either as r (£0.095 in this case) or as $100r\%$ (9.5 per cent) but not as $r\%$. Thus the amount in the bank if £1 is invested for one year is $(1 + r)$.

If £1 is invested for two years and the interest is accumulated annually (and is not withdrawn) the amount left in the bank after two years will be £1 plus interest on one pound plus interest on one pound plus the first year's interest. This may be written as:

$$1 + 1 \times 0.095 + (1 + 1 \times 0.095) \times 0.095$$
$$= (1 + 0.095) (1 + 0.095)$$
$$= (1 + 0.095)^2$$
or $(1 + r) + (1 + r) r = (1 + r)^2$

Similarly at the end of three years the amount in the bank will be:

$$(1 + r)^2 + r(1 + r)^2 = (1 + r)^3$$

In general if £1 is invested for n years at an annual rate of interest r and interest is accumulated, after n years £1 will have grown to:

$$T = (1 + r)^n$$

Discounting – the present value of £1

It is often useful to calculate the amount which must be aside now, which with interest, will give £1 at the end of a specified number of years. This is known as the present value of £1. For example how much must be deposited in the bank to give, with interest, £1 at the end of one year? Call the sum required v then it is possible to write:

$$v\,(1 + r) = 1$$
$$v = 1/(1 + r)$$

The present value of £1 to be received one year hence is v, 'discounted' at the rate of interest r.

Similarly, what is the amount of v_2 which deposited for a period of two years gives with interest £1 after two years? Write:

$$v_2\,(1 + r)^2 = 1$$
$$v_2 = 1/(1 = r)^2$$

and so on. In general vn or $1/(1 + r)^n$ is the present value of, or the amount which with interest accumulates to, £1 after n years.

Table A (at the back of the book) shows the present values of £1 discounted for various numbers of years n and various rates of interest.

For example,

$$v^2 = 0.8264$$

for

$$r = 10\%.$$

The present value of £1 discounted annually at an annual rate of 10 per cent is 0.8264. This is the same as saying it is the sum which if invested for two years at 10 per cent compounded annually becomes £1. The following example shows what the bank deposit account would look like:

Present value invested	$v^2 = 0.8264$
First year's interest	$rv_2 = 0.0826$
Balance $v_2\,(1 + r)$	$= 0.9090$
Second year's interest	
$rv_2\,(1 + r)$	$= 0.0910$
Balance	$v_2\,(1 + r)^2 = 1.00000$

If the present value of any sum other than £1 is required then multiply the sum required by the appropriate discount factor. For example, the present value of £1,000 to be received after 10 years discounted at 7 per cent is:

$$1,000\,v_{10} = 1,000 \times 0.5083 = £508.3$$

Net present value method

The net present value (NPV) method of investment appraisal involves calculating the present value of the cash flows of a project in each year and summing the results (see Table 6.1). Suppose we wish to calculate the net present value of project A using a discount rate of 10 per cent. The cash flows of the project each year are set out below. The cash outlay is treated as being paid immediately and cash receipts are at the end of each year. The method of calculation is as follows:

- □ Supply the discount factors in column (3) for each year by looking at Table A in the 10 per cent column. These give the present values of 1 received at the end of the specified number of years.
- □ Calculate the present value of each cash sum by multiplying cash flow (column 2) by discount factor (column 3) for each year to give column 4.
- □ The sum of column 4 is the net present value of the project.

Table 6.1 The net present value method for project A

Year (1)	Cash flows (2)	v_n (3)	PV (4)
0	-10,000	1	-10,000
1	1,000	0.909	909
2	3,000	0.826	2,478
3	3,000	0.751	2,253
4	3,000	0.683	2,049
5	3,000	0.621	1,863
6	4,000	0.564	2,256
Net present value			£1,808

Any project with a positive NPV would be accepted providing there are no other competing projects when more complex rules must be adopted.

Net present value is the preferred method of most theorists in that it includes the time value of money and all the cash flows associated with the project.

Internal rate of return method

If the NPV of a project is calculated for several different rates of interest the results might be plotted on a graph of NPV against rate of interest. Figure 6.2 shows the shape of the curve which might result.

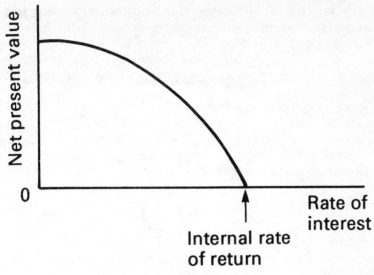

Figure 6.2 NPV/IRR graph

Most projects would show a smaller NPV the larger the rate of interest became. At one rate of interest a zero net present value would result. This rate is known as the internal rate of return (IRR) of the project (or the discounted cash flow (or DCF) yield.

The IRR is based on the same principles of time value of money as NPV. The IRR represents the rate of discount that will exactly discount the future cash flows to equate to the current cash outflow thus giving a zero net present value. The advantage of IRR is that it produces a rate of return which may be interpreted as the highest rate the company can afford to pay for finance for the project. A disadvantage is that the method assumes that surplus cash may be invested at the same rate of interest as the overall project and this may not be possible. The fixed interest method overcomes this shortcoming by investing cash at the normal discount rate.

There are two ways of calculating the internal rate of return:

☐ Trial and error: repeat the calculations shown above for the NPV but varying the rate of interest. Eventually you will find one which gives a zero or near zero IRR. Table 6.2 shows the NPV of project A using a discount rate of 15 per cent. If 16 per cent were tried a negative NPV would result and so the IRR is between 15 and 16 per cent (which is close enough).

☐ Advanced mathematical methods for solving equations. Computer programs are available which do the calculation using both methods (most spreadsheet and modelling systems offer NPV and IRR as financial functions).

Table 6.2 The NPV for project A using a 15 per cent discount rate

Year (1)	Cash flows (2)	$v_n(15\%)$ (3)	PV (4)
0	−10,000	1	−10,000
1	1,000	0.869	869
2	3,000	0.756	2,268
3	3,000	0.657	1,971
4	3,000	0.571	1,713
5	3,000	0.497	1,491
6	4,000	0.432	1,728
Net present value			£40
IRR = 15%			
NPV = 40			

A project which has a positive NPV at a given discount rate will normally have an IRR greater than the discount rate. Therefore, accept projects with IRR greater than the discount rate.

WHICH INVESTMENT APPRAISAL METHOD?

Many studies have been undertaken to establish 'what methods of appraisal are used in practice?' and 'what is good practice?' The evidence from studies such as Klammer (1972) and Hakka *et al* (1985) are that there is no correlation between the adoption of sophisticated investment appraisal techniques and corporate performance. The influencing factors are more likely to be the size of the business and the degree of uncertainty in the environment. Larger businesses are more inclined to use formal and sophisticated methods while smaller organisations will shift to simple methods or heuristics. Uncertainty encourages both the use of multiple methods of appraisal as well as encouraging simpler models. This summary of the surveys should be treated with caution as the evidence is that there is significant variety in behaviour including cultural differences.

The preferred method appears to be payback in the UK (Pike, 1982)

which was justified in its simplicity of calculation and comprehension. However, it is more than likely that multiple methods are used including IRR and NPV. The preference for IRR may be due to the psychological linking of the rate with the concept of return on capital employed.

There are good grounds to support the use of IRR which is not sensitive to size or timing differences when rankings are sought. But IRR has a particular weakness where the cash flows are mixed – both positive and negative. If the cash flows move from negative to positive and then oscillate it is probable that multiple rates of return may be computed and any single solution should be treated with caution.

Particular care should be taken with mutually exclusive projects as the assumption implicit in the appraisal of such projects is that they are of similar cost and lives. The NPV and IRR methods may produce conflicting rankings, particularly where there are scale differences, in which case the NPV result should be used. If projects are not mutually exclusive then care should be taken both with the method and the comparison of the projects. If projects are compared, then they must be compared on the basis of equal life, scale and timing. This may require the assumption of reinvestment which is normally taken to be at the cost of capital. However if projects are not mutually exclusive the complementary nature could be assessed using portfolio analysis.

Critics of the use of DCF methods can find support when high rates of discount prevail as they result in a very low weighting of medium- to long-term cash flows. Thomsen (1984) demonstrated that with a 15 per cent discount factor half the total time horizon is effectively included in the first four years. Thomsen shows, for example, that at a discount rate of 15 per cent, the whole of the twenty-first century counts the same as 7.7 months in 1984. Note that Pike's survey found that most respondents used a rate of 15 per cent (Pike, 1982, p 26).

There are a number of problems in evaluating potential projects, for example:

□ uncertainty of the life of the project;
□ determining the cost of capital;
□ cost volume profit relationships and flows;
□ future cash flows;
□ timing of planned expenditure and income;
□ residual value; and;
□ risk of obsolescence due to: technical innovation, wear and tear, value decline.

Particular areas of difficulty are found with projects involving research and development and high technology. One method of overcoming these problems is to use heuristics, but it is possible to adapt the basic investment appraisal methods by incorporating more sophisticated techniques which may be handled through separate models or incorporated into the overall capital budget model.

The assumption often taken is that the cost of capital is the cost of borrowing. However, this fails to reflect the sources of finance and so theoretical costs of capital reflecting the weighting of sources and their costs should be used (see Chapter 3). Further approximations which are used reflect inflation and some opportunity cost or risk. The cost of capital may also be affected by the size of the project, particularly if new sources of finance are required.

The cash flow methods all assume certainty in respect of the future cash flows which is most unlikely. To overcome this, simulation methods have been proposed in which the elements of the cash flows are broken down to the fundamental factors which are then estimated in the form of probability distributions. Probability distributions are applied to the estimated cash flows to arrive at an expected value. This may then be subject to the normal investment appraisal method. In the case of complex cash flows, decision trees may be used to analyse all the flows and the probabilities. Care should be taken with the use of probabilities and the associated expected values as the method is founded on the assumption of multiple recurrences and not on a single occurrence. Alternatively the distributions may be used in the simulation to construct the cash streams. This method known as risk analysis (Hertz and Thomas, 1983) allows either NPV or IRR to be applied to the resulting cash streams.

In place of obtaining probability distributions the adjustment of the discount rate has been used to reflect the management's attitude to risk. This method known as risk-adjusted discounting may exploit the CAPM to establish the appropriate rate of discount.

An alternative to risk analysis is the use of stochastic decision trees in which the stages of the investment form the branches (Hespos and Strassman, 1965). Markowitz (1959) proposes the use of portfolio analysis as used in investment decisions and this may be appropriate for decisions in which projects are not mutually exclusive and form part of the overall corporate strategy.

It is appropriate to mention at this point that information theory would guide us to seek more information, whether perfect or not, to improve our position in the face of uncertainty. Furthermore the costs and benefits of additional information may be weighed against each other and consideration of market research or even underwriting may be evaluated.

Financial models

The simplest financial model we could build would be the percentage of sales model in which the change in sales leads to a proportional change in working capital and fixed assets. This results in the need for additional finance and the level of finance is defined from the model. If one applies financial constraints of mix along with relative costs of finance it is possible to identify the least cost financing policy. Criticism of the model helps identify more comprehensive approaches but the linking of operations with finance is established.

There have been two distinct financial models developed which are particularly relevant to investment appraisal: linear programming and simultaneous equations. While all the models had as their objective the identification and estimation of finance requirements, in their development the linking of the financial requirements to the operations of the firm was the starting position. The output of the models was the pro forma balance sheet, profit and loss account and the vital sources and applications statement which linked the financial uses with the identification of source (see Chapter 2).

The first type of model is the linear programming approach developed by Carlton (1970) which sought to optimise the shareholders' interest through dividend and terminal share value. The model incorporated sales growth which then influenced the operating profit and the fixed assets required to support this level of sales. This in turn defined the additional investment requirement which optimised the mix of possible sources of finance. While the model contained simplifications it offered an optimising approach which linked uses of finance with sources.

Warren and Shelton (1971) pursued a different approach in which the interaction was through a series of semi-simultaneous equations. A similar approach was followed by Francis and Rowell (1978) but their model also incorporated risk and reflected demand and market share in establishing sales volume. Neither Warren and Shelton nor Francis and Rowell followed the optimising route; instead they favoured the simulation approach. Their models offer the same interaction of sources and uses of funds through the mechanism of simultaneity.

The important aspect of simultaneity is the linking of profit with interest and debt. In arriving at the retained profits and hence the level of self-financing, interest payments on debt must be deducted, but the interest payments will be dependent on the level of debt which is itself dependent on the level of self-financing. The alternative approach practised by many is the lagging of interest to debt thereby avoiding simultaneity.

An important development from these models is the simulation approach in which both alternative scenarios are modelled or the sensitivity of the variable is established. This approach is also achievable with the basic investment appraisal technique but all simulation is dependent on the availability of suitable low-cost computing power which is now readily available.

SUMMARY

This chapter has covered a wide area very briefly. We identified four main types of investment appraisal decision: replacement, expansion, safety or environmental, and other. We noted that obtaining all the necessary information for a rational decision may be problematical.

Following our discussion of the project life-cycle and our identification of how life-cycle costs may behave, we addressed the various methods of appraising investment opportunities. The methods outlined included:

□ accounting rate of return;
□ payback; and
□ discounting (NPV and IRR).

The advantages and disadvantages of each technique were briefly outlined. The chapter concluded by considering some financial modelling techniques which are now available.

This chapter has considered some very complex issues which go to the very heart of long-term corporate performance. In making investment decisions managers are asked to address themselves to longer timescales than normal day-to-day activity, and quite probably, to larger, more significant, operational, market and financial implications than they may be used to. What should be clear is that there is no easy answer. The manager is required to make a decision, a subject to which we return in Chapter 9.

FURTHER READING

Chapter 8 in Bowman and Asch's *Strategic Management*, Macmillan, London 1987, places the use of investment appraisal techniques in a broader organisational context.

REFERENCES

Bierman, H and Smidt, S (1971) *Capital Budgeting Decision – Economic Analysis and Financing of Investment Project*, Macmillan, New York.

Carlton, W T (1970) 'Analytical model for long range financial planning', *Journal of Finance*, 25, p 291–315.

Francis, J C and Rowell, D R (1978) 'A simultaneous equation model of the firm for financial analysis and plannng', *Financial Management*, Spring, pp 29–44.

Hakka, S F, Gordon, C A and Pinches, G E (1985) 'Sophisticated capital budgeting techniques and firm performance', *Accounting Review*.

Hertz, D B and Thomas, H (1983) *Risk Analysis and its Application*, John Wiley, New York.

Hespos, R F and Strassman, P A (1965) 'Stochastic decision trees for the analysis of investment decisions', *Management Science II*, pp 213–24.

Klammer, T (1972) 'Empirical evidence on the adoption of sophisticated budgeting techniques', *Journal of Business*, July.

Markowitz, H (1959) *Portfolio Selection; Efficient Diversification of Investments*, John Wiley.

Pike, R H (1981) *Capital Budgeting in the 1980s*, CIMA Occasional Paper, London.

Thomsen, C T (1984) 'Dangers in discounting', *Management Accounting*, January, pp 37–39.

Warren, J and Shelton, J (1971) 'A simultaneous equation approach to financial planning', *Journal of Finance 26*, pp 1123–42.

7

Budgeting and Control

INTRODUCTION

In this chapter we will focus our attention on budgeting and control. Before considering the complex issues involved in this area of managerial activity we need to place it in a broader organisational context.

> It is management's responsibility to ensure that an appropriate strategy is both formulated and implemented, for without the latter, precise formulation is of little use to the organisation. (Bowman and Asch, 1987, p 195)

So, budgeting and budgetary control can be seen as methods of ensuring that management's strategy happens. Indeed,

> Most of the time and effort of most managers is spent on strategy implementation, and the amount of this activity increases as the observer moves from top management to lower levels. (McCarthy *et al*, 1983, p 362)

Otley argues that in monitoring and evaluating performance budgeting is at the heart of organisational activity.

> Budgeting cannot sensibly be viewed solely as a technical accounting activity divorced from its organisational context. It is intimately bound up in much wider and more complex activities and must be studied from this perspective. (Otley, 1987, p 31)

Discussion of the use of budgeting as a planning and control technique would be incomplete without a consideration of communication and motivation. The chapter commences with a discussion of the use of planning and budgeting as a method of implementing strategic decisions followed by a look at issues involved in control in a strategic sense. Behavioural issues in control are then addressed followed by a consideration of some more recent developments in the use of budgeting.

There is one further point to make which relates to the use in this chapter of the word *planning*. Planning in this context is a method of *implementing* the formulated strategy. The planning and control system in an organisation represents the main approach through which the strategic objectives and policies (and plans) are translated into specific, measurable and attainable goals and plans.

ISSUES IN STRATEGIC CONTROL

Underpinning most of our discussion of planning, budgeting and control is the assumption that managers can bring performance back into line with what was planned. Managers need the power to act which derives from either their position in the organisation, or their ability to manipulate essential resources, or perhaps their ability to cope with uncertainty. As we will see later most control reports are driven by data within the organisation, that is, they include, for example, sales to date compared to planned sales, costs actually incurred compared to the budget. However, such information may not be sufficient to provide a complete picture of the organisation's strategic position and its progress in fulfilling its strategy.

The challenge of assessing strategic progress relates to the necessity to integrate long- and short-term objectives. Short-term objectives and plans are critical to the achievement of long-term strategic ends. The successful implementation of strategy, which is what budgeting and control is about, depends upon the integration of and consistency between long- and short-term plans. Due to the longer time scale associated with strategic control, evaluation should include an analysis of external conditions and the assumptions based upon them that might not normally be the case with short-term performance. In the short term environmental or exogenous variables are likely to be relatively fixed (Asch, 1989).

In assessing progress in achieving the organisation's strategy it should be recognised that the relationship between means and ends is less precise and the certainty of cause-effect relationships is likely to be lower. Strategic control:

☐ requires data from more sources, and more data from external sources, than does conventional budgeting and control where the operation itself generates the only data used.

- □ is less precise than operational control, making analysis more difficult. The former aggregates approximations form a complex environment, while the latter focuses on more precise representations from a much smaller world.
- □ data tends to be less accurate and their receipt more sporadic than those derived from operational monitoring.

As a strategic control process budgeting has its limitations. The fact that there will usually be a hierarchy of control systems with difficulties of linkage between them can lead to a decoupling of budgeting from control. Because it is a means of resource allocation and information dissemination, budgeting identifies changes in emphasis across the organisation. The whole process can become politically difficult due to the status attached to the size of budgets and the power struggles that can occur.

PLANNING AND BUDGETING

The process involved in formulating strategy, the marriage of objectives and the method by which these will be achieved, constitute the strategy or policy to be pursued by the organisation. Managers also need to know how well the chosen policy is performing, so 'the system' includes a monitoring phase for evaluation purposes. It has been argued that this type of planning and control system is in fact a single process (Anthony and Dearden, 1980, p 5). While we will treat each separately for the purpose of discussion it should be recognised that there are continuous interrelationships in what is in effect an overall system, and that the planning and control system is part of the strategic management of the organisation.

The planning part of the system is concerned with the more immediate future and does not normally involve new objectives since the plans are drawn up in order to achieve the organisation's strategic objectives. This phase involves the interpretation of the broader strategic policies derived during the formulation of strategy and their translation into more specific shorter-range plans. As such it is a process which involves managers at all levels in the organisation because the plans demand broad support and significant detail. Management at all levels translate the strategic thrust of the organisation into management objectives for specified timeframes.

This process requires active participation throughout the enterprise, and should be structured in such a way as to gain involvement from all involved. A planning and control process requiring the participation of all levels of management in the development of future plans builds in an important motivational force. The planning and control systems necessary for implementation do not necessarily indicate the existence of highly formalised and documented procedures and less formal procedures may be more than adequate.

The budget is the common method for implementation as it should encompass the communication of attainable goals while engaging the participation and support of all levels of management. It also provides information for evaluation. The function of budgeting, in converting strategy into an action plan, requires:

□ planning;
□ co-ordination;
□ control; and
□ review.

Budgeting is crucial to the planning and control process because it converts all elements of an enterprise's plans into financial numbers. At one level this is crucial for comparing results of disparate areas or functions, but its utility may be diminished if the process itself is inadequate in some way.

Figure 7.1 illustrates some of the more common budgets which may be prepared and indicates some interrelationships. There are several points which emerge from a consideration of Figure 7.1. First, each of the budgets may be divided into smaller segments. Thus the direct labour budget, for example, may well be broken down into a variety of departments or sections.

Furthermore, the final figure appearing is likely to be a function of (at least) the numbers employed, their grading, expected pay scales, overtime earnings, anticipated sickness levels, etc. Thus the preparation of the direct labour budget is likely to involve production management, personnel and the accounting function. Second, budgets are interrelated so that a change in one element has an effect elsewhere. So, in addition to a fairly obvious impact on cash and purchasing, a decision to reduce raw material stocks may also have an effect on production rates and labour. The third and final point is that the process is not static. The individual budgets leading up to the overall master budget is, normally, a series of continuous budgets which incorporates a feedback system permitting managerial evaluation.

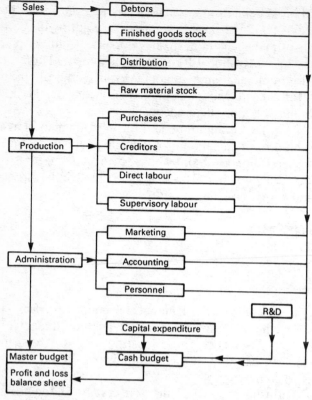

Figure 7.1 Budgets and their interrelationships

The *planning* phase of the budget should not be merely an estimate based on previous performance. The budget should be designed to articulate in greater detail the agreed strategic direction of the organisation; consequently the budget should be congruent with the strategy and may well use (indeed should use) the same future-orientated information in its preparation. For example, the more detailed analysis required will often entail segmenting elements into controllable or non-controllable costs. The variability of future revenues and costs will be subject to further analysis in an attempt to identify causal relationships. The last stage will entail the preparation of a projected income statement and balance sheet to ensure that the aggregate detailed action plan meets predetermined criteria, such as return on investment or profit levels.

The *co-ordination* of budgets requires the dovetailing of individual elements to ensure internal consistency. The classic case which often arises is to ensure a reasonable achievable match, for example, between sales, production, and stock-holding budgets. This represents a crucial communication link between differing functions and operations because it forces management to recognise the relationship of their particular function to others, and to the organisation as a whole. The co-ordination of the budgets in effect determines the iterative nature of the process. A properly prepared budget enables responsibility to be assigned and creates a situation where motivation and goal congruence is enhanced.

Before directing our attention to the control element of the process it is worthwhile identifying some areas where problems are inherent in budgeting:

□ Budgeting is dependent upon a range of assumptions and predictions about future performance, which are subject to error. The budget is not an exact tool but one which, if correctly utilised, can facilitate modification of plans and strategies in the light of the latest information.

□ Second, budgets are often misused particularly during the evaluation of results with the plan. Indeed it is all too common for attention to be focused on the Micawber-like qualities of the process, rather than on the more positive beneficial attributes.

□ Finally, as with any management information, the budgeting process involves the use of resources, office space, manpower, reprographics, and on occasion, the production of over-elaborate reports understood by no one. The process can only justify itself if it leads to actions which create more value than the cost of the process itself. Budgeting is, after all, an overhead cost.

BUDGETING AND CONTROL

As the previous section has discussed, the budget should represent the more specific way in which the chosen strategies are to be implemented. Providing, therefore, that the detailed budget is consistent with and conforms to the broader strategic elements, a comparison of the budget with the actual results will measure progress towards attainment of the strategic objectives.

For control to be effective a suitable *communication* system must exist. The communication system in most enterprises has both formal and informal features, which reflect the complexity of the organisation's operations and its environment. Formal measures would include, for example, written policy statements, procedural manuals, job descriptions, formal meetings and so on. Informal measures would include informal gatherings, say between supervisory staff and employees.

Fundamental to the exercise of control is reporting appropriate information at an appropriate level. Reports should be directed to those responsible for either controlling costs or generating revenue. Revenues and/or costs must be attributable to a particular manager's efforts and must be controllable by that person. The application of this responsibility concept is the basis of planning and control.

Most organisations are broken down into profit and cost centres which develop their own detailed budgets. To be useful such budgets need to be broken down into their key components with a system designed to feed results of operations to the appropriate manager. There are two preconditions for responsibility reporting to be of use. First, the budget should not be an imposed control. It should be accepted by managers who should have participated in its preparation. Second, where a manager is considered to be accountable for costs then those costs should be controllable by that person. Responsibility reporting is unlikely to be of use if managers are held responsible for costs over which they exercise no, or only partial, control. This sort of situation can occur in organisations whose costs are allocated and/or apportioned, and in enterprises where interdivisional transfer prices are arbitrarily set.

The reporting system provides the necessary feedback of results for comparison to the plan. Naturally there will be a time-lag between event and report. This delay should be acceptable in terms of a trade-off between the cost of reducing the delay and the benefits to subsequent management action.

As a general rule the reports received by managers at different points in the hierarchy will differ in terms of both the degree of detail and the time period to which they relate. Thus a managing director of a unit may receive a report detailing the output, material usage, labour efficiency and so on for the past week. The managing director's report is likely to allow a more direct comparison between results to date and the division's strategic objectives, so allowing implementation of the present strategy to proceed.

In looking at control Goldsmith and Clutterbuck found that controls were often very simple. Top managers tended to concentrate on their business. They quote that Lord Weinstock receives all his information on the giant GEC on three sheets of paper. The speed of reporting is another issue which they found to be common in successful UK companies. Numerous examples are quoted by the authors, but the focus is on tight financial controls, constant feedback of results, close attention to planning, and setting high standards and expecting people to stick to them (Goldsmith and Clutterbuck 1984, pp 47–58).

The results reported to management reflect historic performance.

This can only be of use if, in evaluating what happened against what was planned, it influenced future decisions. The reports need, therefore, to integrate the past with the future to provide a perspective on what may happen in the future.

Designing reports for management to enable them to control more effectively the direction of the organisation is made both easier and harder with the burgeoning growth of computerised management information systems. Computerisation has tended to lead both to speedier production of information and to the generation of masses of detailed data. Management requires information designed to assist decision making and control which effectively limits it in terms of its relevance. One way of determining relevance is to report only on deviations from expectations, in other words, *exception reporting*. This allows managers to concentrate on important variations from the plan; information relating to events conforming to the predetermined plan are screened out. Insignificant variations may not be reported. The degree of latitude in such matters will tend to vary according to the expectations of the managers in the organisation. What may be considered significant in one enterprise may not be considered as such in another.

> Planning and control are both concerned with expectations. Planning is concerned with future expectations and control in ensuring organisational response to changes that occur when what were future expectations become present expectations. (Machin and Wilson, 1979)

This sort of perception is important to the exercise of control because the budget or plan cannot control; people, managers control. Deviations from the budget (future expectations) are to be expected. The focus needs to be not on how accurate the forecasts were, but on unexpected results to see if the entity should alter its strategy in the light of this experience, and in what ways. Controllable variations from the plan warrant investigation to see how they occurred.

The comparison of actual results with the plan is of an historic nature – what is being reported has already happened. This review, focusing as we have indicated on significant deviations should be used to provide managers with important insights concerning the future implementation. The review may indicate that some of the earlier assumptions were incorrect or that unexpected events made the original plan unattainable. A strategic perspective is crucial in reviewing performance for two main reasons. First, the budget or plan should not be used as a constraining force which stultifies creativity or enthusiasm. Second, management should recognise that the plan is not 'cast in stone'. Subsequent events may well make it redundant as a tool for both strategy implementation and operational control. The relationship between short- and long-term plans is crucial here, because when the organisation decides to redraw the plan it will need to draw not only upon management's previous experience, but also what has been learnt so far about implementing the chosen strategy. So changes, say, in short-term budgets to make them a more effective vehicle for control, will need to feed through in a strategic sense to ensure that they are still consonant with the overall strategy. If the changes are brought about by unexpected environmental changes, then the alteration to the short-term budgets may effectively indicate other changes required to match the strategy to the 'new' environment.

BUDGETING AND MOTIVATION

In order to implement strategy the organisation needs to have a reasonable commitment to the achievement of the goals by those charged with ensuring that the enterprise succeeds. So motivation on the part of those managers is a most important part of the budgeting system.

Motivation may be accomplished by the reward-punishment system, part of which may be linked to the planning control system. A motivation system may use positive (bonuses, promotion, etc) or negative (demotion, etc) incentives. The establishment of a motivation system that blends the attainment of personal aspirations with goals of the organisation is a problematic task.

Cooper and Makin, having reviewed the literature and various theories on motivation, summarised them by saying that clear and moderately difficult goals should be set that are accepted by the person concerned. They also noted that valued rewards should be made upon achievement of goals, and rewards should be made through an explicit and fair system. They concluded:

> All of these terms will depend upon subjective judgements and hence the only source of objective information is the people concerned, and perhaps the only way of obtaining the correct information is by asking them. Never assume that people's perceptions of the same thing are the same . . . Participation is perhaps desirable, therefore, because more than anything else it is a source of information for all parties. (Cooper and Makin, 1984, p 114)

Once the budget is recognised to be an element that helps to motivate people in the organisation attention must be paid to individual and group needs and values. When these elements are incorporated in the overall planning and control process then the resulting budget is likely to fulfil its function as an aid to employees' motivation. If the process of developing plans and budgets, and their associated control systems, is properly conceived and utilised, involving real participation by all levels of management, then it becomes an indispensable motivational element.

THE PROCESS OF BUDGETING AND BUDGETARY CONTROL

Immediately an organisation introduces the use of budgets, this brings a forward looking approach into its information systems. The use of budgets encourages a more careful attempt at forecasting the future potential of the enterprise rather than the mere extrapolation of past results, or the addition of an arbitrary percentage to past figures. However, even more sophisticated approaches to management planning and control systems may tend to develop a rigid framework that become traditional.

Much of the discussion in this section will be equally applicable to the technique of standard costing. Both standard costing and budgetary control are based on some form of 'standard'. When the technique of standard costing is used, the standards are set for a number of reasons, although the main one is to enable the actual performance in terms of costs (with cost a surrogate for the measure of factor input efficiency) in the production of products and services to be compared with the standard originally set. An analogy is to compare the standard set by the athlete who is trying to break, say, a four minute 'standard' for the mile and runs 'against the clock'. The athlete measures the time actually achieved against the 'four minute standard' to see how far the performance was away from target – any difference being the 'variance'.

Thus the budget may cover income, expenditure (both current and capital), and budgeting is 'the process of drawing up a budget'.

Budgetary control can be defined as:

The establishment of departmental budgets relating the responsibilities of management to the requirements of an organisation's objectives and policies, and the continuous comparison of the actual with the budgeted results, either to secure by individual action the objectives of that policy or to provide a firm basis for the revision of that policy.

Thus an organisation plans in advance what the expected performance of its various functional departments is expected to be, and uses these budgets as a control device. In the development of an organisation's overall plan there will be a number of different budgets which all have to be co-ordinated in the budgeting process so that the firm's complete budgeting system will also act as a resource co-ordinating device.

Organisations using a system of budgetary control need to be clear how their budgets are formulated and what system of control will be used to follow up the plan when it is compared with later performance – and who will be responsible to take action when variances are found.

In large organisations where a number of departmental budgets are eventually drawn together in the overall master budget, the organisation needs to develop a system which links these together. Depending upon the size of the organisation and its organisational/administrative management structure, the budgetary process may be supervised by a budget officer or through the use of a budget committee. Generally when there is a budget officer he is likely to be equivalent to a permanent secretary to some group, or committee, of people who oversee the organisation's budgeting and budgetary control system.

As has been noted, the manager who is responsible for seeing that any budget set is met needs to be brought into the planning process. At the overall master budget level the people responsible for all the individual budgets of an organisation should be drawn into any reiterative process necessary to help in the formulation of the master budget. As the organisation's departmental budgets must ultimately be 'meshed' together it is important that a programme be drawn up showing timescale and any deadlines to be met in the preparation of departmental budgets. Such a programme needs to make allowances for any reiteration that may have to take place.

Generally budgets will be prepared on an annual basis. However, annual budgets are then usually segmented into shorter periods such as quarters, months, weeks, or even days. The number of periods into which an annual budget is broken down will be governed by a variety of factors including the industry concerned and its structural pattern. For example, a seasonal production or sales pattern (or both) will affect the way in which the time horizon and fragmentation of the budget is viewed, as will whether the industry uses labour or capital intensive production methods. The shorter periods that the budget is broken down into will be the ones that will be used for the day-to-day control of the organisation. The overall picture of the complete budget is more related to the organisation's long-term prospects whilst the immediate shorter periods into which it is divided are about the current situation.

Frequently large organisations have moved towards preparing budgets on a 'rolling' basis. In this the length of the budget period to which the firm looks ahead will vary from twelve to fifteen months, and the roll-over is achieved when one quarter of an original five-quarter budget passes adding another. In this process it is usual to divide the quarter nearest to the current time into months or thirteen weeks, with perhaps the nearest week being divided into days. With a rolling budget this means that organisations operating such a system will always face budgeted figures for at least one year ahead.

The advantages of this approach include:

- □ the ability to use fine tuning by segmenting the budget at the current quarter.
- □ the provision of a budgeting environment where the revision to budgets which go off-course is likely to be made reasonably quickly because the danger of waiting for an annual budget period to expire before making revisions is removed.
- □ the exercise of budgeting becomes an on-going process rather than an annual once-off process, which spreads the budgeting work throughout the year.

Limiting factors

There will always be some factors which eventually limit the extent of an organisation's activity. Eventually something must constrain the extent of a firm's operations. This may be the size of the market, availability of capital or factors of production, and will generally be found to show itself in one or other of a firm's subsidiary budgets. For example, there is not much sense in a firm producing goods or services for which there will be no demand and moving it towards an excess supply situation thus putting the firm into a position where it builds up large stocks with their associated holding costs. On the personnel side labour shortages, especially if there is long lead time before skilled labour can be trained to the required standard, may provide the limiting factor. At other times capacity may provide 'limits' to what an organisation can produce. Actual examples of this would have been: 1974 – oil shortages; 1975 – potato shortages; 1976 – water shortages; all of which would have affected particular industries where firms relied upon these as one of their factors of production.

The master budget

The master budget is the term used to refer to an organisation's overall budget which is built up from subsidiary budgets. Subsidiary budgets are often referred to as component, departmental, or functional budgets. Depending on the size of an organisation, it will be divided into a number of areas for budgetary purposes. These are likely to be departments or some other unit which is convenient for the budget process. The budgets for the various departments of an organisation are then built up into an all embracing comprehensive budget which covers all the firm's activities. Figure 7.1 (p 166) showed a number of possible subsidiary budget areas.

A problem frequently found in budgeting is that an organisation may put itself into a straitjacket once the annual budget has been drawn up. This is because management may be reluctant to change the budget even when there are changes in such things as production techniques, factor prices, markets and so on which would make it reasonable to make revisions to the budget even in the middle of a budget period. Thus management should not shy away from the need to revise budgets if this becomes necessary.

Budget preparation

We will now turn our attention to the preparation of some of the budgets identified in Figure 7.1. The ability of a firm to make sales is normally the major constraint to its growth. It is, therefore, our starting point, and indeed the focus of most of the remainder of this section as the remaining budgets will tend to flow from, or be significantly influenced by, the sales budget.

The accuracy of the sales budget hinges on the ability of an organisation to make good sales forecasts. The difficulty of making a sales forecast, and the extent to which it can be relied upon, depends upon a number of factors. For example, it is easier to make a good sales forecast for an established product which has little seasonal demand. In such a situation the simple technique of extrapolation may be used with some reliability being attached to the result obtained; for a new product, especially if it is likely to have seasonal demand patterns, market research and test marketing techniques may have to be used to help predict its likely sales.

When extrapolation is used an attempt must be made to adjust the base of past data so that any of the extrapolated results fit in as nearly as possible with any changes in the environment and other influences which are likely to affect the forecast. Even then the results from extrapolation need to be carefully examined in the light of information from other sources as a sales forecast model is built up. For example, information from people such as the customer/dealer/agent/retailer/user, and the firm's sales force and managers can be helpful. Then the use of statistical approaches and techniques such as the use of averages, samples, statistical models, leading indicators and correlations with such things as GNP, levels and growth of incomes, employment and population, etc can be considered. There is also market research, test marketing and other techniques which provide information that can be used to help in sales forecasting.

Because of the variety of sources from which data and information about potential and feasible sales can come is so vast and varied, and because the cost of collecting and processing such information can be high, there is a need for selectivity in the collection of this information. In making a decision about the extent of the information required to help make the sales forecast, the costs and benefits associated with various sources of information need to be taken into consideration. Once the information has been assembled, a forecasting team, probably drawn from the various departments providing input to the sales forecast, will both make new forecasts and monitor the old ones to see how successful these have been, and whether anything can be learnt from them.

Sales may be classified in a number of ways for forecasting purposes, for example, by:

- areas;
- products;
- customers; and
- salesmen.

It is useful to consider using more than one of these classifications when making the sales forecast. Thus a forecast for the firm's sales based on, say, areas and then products could be made. This will enable a comparison of the results obtained from different forecast bases to be made and enable those involved to see whether the forecasts are the same, and, if not, to ask why not. It should be noted that such classifications include a number of possible sub-budget centres that could be used for sales.

A question frequently asked concerning the sales budget is whether the sales recorded in it should be shown in terms of physical units or money terms. Obviously a statement of forecast sales in physical terms has advantages, and anyway physical units can easily be converted into money values. However, there may be a problem when there is price elasticity of demand because the price at which the goods are sold will have an effect on the number of units demanded. In such cases this factor would have to be taken into consideration in the conversion of the unit sales forecast into money terms in the sales budget. This point may also apply when the question about whether the production budget should be in .physical or money terms arises.

The preparation of a sales budget, especially when it provides the limiting budgeting factor within the master budget, has a number of uses to an organisation. These include the following conditions:

- It provides the major input into the formulation of the production budget.
- It enables the planning of optimum stock levels of finished goods. Information from the sales budget can help to reduce the possibility of under- or over-stocking thus eliminating any adverse effects that non-optimal stock-holdings have on working capital.
- It can be used to help in the provision of targets for sales people. This may help in the motivation of the sales force, especially when sales targets are geared to incentive schemes of bonuses. However, it should be remembered that if sales personnel are responsible for preparing their own sales budgets and know that any incentives will be geared to these then they may be inclined to set the budget at as low a level as looks reasonable to enable them to obtain a higher commission. To avoid such a possibility, it has been suggested that a salesperson's salary should be based on the budget that they set but that there is a deduction from their salary in the form of a negative commission when the budget is not reached. This approach may then provide salespeople with an incentive to fix their budgets as high as possible to enable them to obtain high salaries.

Figure 7.2 provides an example of a simple sales budget, drawn up from the following data:

Budgeted sales for 1995
10,000 units of EL at 15p per unit
5,000 units of QI at 18p per unit
15,000 units of TC at 12p per unit

Actual sales for 1995
9,000 units of EL at 16p per unit
4,000 units of QI at 20p per unit
17,500 units of TC at 12p per unit

Budgeted sales for 1996
9,000 units of EL at 18p per unit
5,000 units of QI at 20p per unit
18,000 units of TC at 12p per unit

Sales budget for the year to 31.12.1996

	1995 Budget			Actual			1996 Budget		
Prod.	price	qty	Total	price	qty	Total	price	qty	Total
EL	15p	10,000	£1,500	16p	9,000	£1,440	18p	9,000	£1,620
QI	18p	5,000	£900	20p	4,000	£800	20p	5,000	£1,000
TC	12p	15,000	£1,800	12p	17,500	£2,100	12p	18,000	£2,160
Total		30,000	£4,200		30,500	£4,340		32,000	£4,780

Figure 7.2   Sample layout for a sales budget

It is assumed that the budget for each year was based on a sales forecast made using a number of different forecasting techniques. However, the increase in sales for TC arose, and is predicted to continue, because of an increase in advertising directed towards this product.

In the layout of the sales budget to be found in Figure 7.2 it can be seen that for information purposes both the budget and the previous year's actual performance have been included. Once the budget for sales has been produced any marketing expenses and the sales department's costs can all be incorporated into a sales department budget.

The stock report

When sales is the limiting factor the sales budget can be used as the basis for a number of other budgets, including the production budget. However, before the production budget can be finally formalised adjustments have to be made for current and required stock-holdings. This is necessary because it is unlikely that an organisation will want to hold the same stock of products both at the commencement and the end of any budget period. Stock-holding requirements may be affected by a number of factors. For example stock-holdings are likely to be related to sales levels, and sales are likely to be changing from one period to the next so if sales are growing then stock-holdings are likely to be increased, and vice versa. The organisation's cash position will also have a bearing on its stock-holding possibilities.

Continuing the example but using product TC only, assume that the stock-holding at the commencement of the budget period is 4,000 units. To support a growing sales volume a stock-holding of 6,000 units will be required to be held in stock at the end of the period. This means that the production budget must be drawn up to take into consideration the 'growth' of 2,000 units of stock. There can be a separate stock budget or, as in the continuation of this example, allowances for change in stocks can be incorporated in the production budget.

The production budget

Once the sales budget and stock budgets have been established the production budget can be prepared. Remember the assumption made previously that sales are the limiting budgeting factor, whereas production imposed no constraints on the organisation's overall budget possibilities. The required production then simply becomes the forecast sales figure adjusted for any changes required in stock-holdings.

In practice it is likely that there will be separate production budgets drawn up for various products, product groupings, or departments depending upon the size of the organisation. Then these will be aggregated into the firm's overall production budget.

From the data already provided above, a production budget can be drawn up for TC in unit terms as has been done in Figure 7.3.

Production budget for year ending 30 December 1996

Product TC (in units)	*units*
Forecast sales	18,000
Closing stock required	6,000
	24,000
less Opening stock	4,000
	20,000
plus Allowance for substandard products (rejects etc)	1,000
Quantity to be produced	21,000

Figure 7.3   Production budget for TC in unit terms

Because experience has shown that in the production of TC there are likely to be a number of substandard units produced, an allowance, in this case for an additional 1,000 units, has been made for these to ensure that the total production of 'perfect' units will be at the level required. Normally such an allowance will be based upon past information and experience with statistical adjustments being made according to current circumstances and environmental changes.

From the production budget other related budgets such as: the materials budget from which in turn come the purchasing budget; the labour budget; the plant utilisation budgets; and so on, can all be drawn up.

A production budget can be converted into a production cost budget by multiplying the standard cost of the product by the number of units to be produced, which will show the cost of producing the quantity concerned.

The cash budget

This budget is very important especially as any profits that an organisation generates do not necessarily equate to the cash holdings of the concern (see Chapters 2 and 5). Enterprises, which on the face of it were profitable, have got into financial difficulties because their liquidity position has been unsound. This is because they did not have 'ready cash' available to enable them to meet debts as they fell due. When a cash budget is drawn up this shows the actual movements of cash into and out of the organisation.

Any credit transactions are not included in the cash budget until they are turned into cash, it is only the movements of cash from both revenue and capital expenditure that are shown in it. Therefore the cash budget is basically a planning and control device which reveals whether there are either shortfalls or surpluses of cash. It provides a warning signal to the organisation which enables it to make arrangements well in advance to cover any likely periods of cash shortfalls or make investments during periods when there is a surplus of cash.

The capital expenditure budget

The time horizon of the capital expenditure budget is generally much longer than that for the normal budget although any actual capital expenditure made during the year ahead will be incorporated in the organisation's annual budgeting process.

In the capital expenditure budget estimates will be made about the likely expenditure to be incurred in the acquisition of fixed assets necessary for the organisation's future survival. These estimates will be based upon such things as: expected sales and the production capacity required to support forecast profitable sales; possible changes in production technology; and so on. Frequently sophisticated investment appraisal techniques will be used before an investment decision is made. Any necessary replacement of machinery through either the possible obsolescence or wear and tear of plant, machinery and equipment will also be considered (see Chapter 6).

To support any changes envisaged in production or distribution patterns, items like expenditure on buildings, services for these, including administrative systems, transportation, etc, must all be brought into the analysis.

Budgetary control

Once the budget has been formulated after the process of drawing up the functional and other sub-budgets and the reiteration to obtain the co-ordination of these into the organisation's master budget, the use of the budget as the basis for budgetary control can be examined.

First, it is necessary to ascertain which managers are responsible for certain budgets and to ascertain over which aspects of their budgets they have some control. These managers must then have the details of their budget targets communicated to them, preferably by supplying them with a copy of their budget. Hopefully they had some say in it at the formulation stage.

On a regular basis, they should get reports showing their actual position in comparison to their budget, i.e. showing whether they are under- or over-budget. This information is usually provided to them in the form of a variance which is expressed in both absolute and percentage terms. Also the report will usually show the cumulative effect of any variances. In the traditional approach to budgetary control variance percentages are usually taken to be an indicator of the 'efficiency' of a department. However, this point is subject to much debate.

A budget control report is a convenient way of collecting information about a budget and the performance related to this. An example of a budget control report is given in Figure 7.4.

Even when the traditional approach is taken to budgetary control it is important that only controllable expenses are examined when the efficiency of a manger is being appraised. For it is only the controllable expenses over which a manager has some influence, and it is such items that can be examined using the management-by-exception principle.

When a manager receives the budget control report for his department he should examine any variances and produce a report to higher management which clearly states why they occurred. This will help them to decide whether any corrective action is required, and if so the form it may take. This report should cover both favourable as well as

Budget control report for the month of March
Department AB1
Budget Centre No AB1 015

Element of Cost		Month			Year to date		
Code	Item	Budgt	Act	Var	Budgt	Act	Var
Direct costs							
101	Material	2,000	2,025	(25)	7,200	7,403	(203)
201	Labour	1,120	1,114	6	3,400	3,210	190
302	Expenses	500	560	(60)	1,600	1,610	(10)
Indirect costs							
404	Material	250	188	62	750	591	159
502	Supervision	510	600	(90)	1,500	1,625	(125)
607	Misc. Exps	100	100	nil	1,400	1,284	116
910	Total	4,480	4,587	(107)	15,850	15,723	127

Performance	Month	102.4%	Cumulative 99.2%

Figure 7.4 An example of a budget control report

unfavourable variances. In the past all too frequently emphasis has been placed upon highlighting any unfavourable variances with there being less, if any, attention paid to favourable variances. However, information on ways of improving efficiency may be gained from an examination of favourable variances. It may even be that a favourable variance still does not indicate an efficient performance, especially if a slack budget had been drawn up in the first place. Also, although variances are frequently presented in percentage form, if details of the absolute amounts involved can be provided as well this may also give important information to controllers who can decide upon the materiality of the variance concerned. For example, a variance which shows up high in percentage terms may be immaterial in absolute terms (and vice versa). Any time and effort spent in examining such a variance may be wasted in comparison to true resources consumed in this examination and taking any control action necessary and the benefits to be gained from so doing.

In budgetary control it is extremely important that reports are presented quickly. This will enable any corrective action required based upon the budget control report to be taken quickly. For timeliness is the essence of budgetary control. The longer the delay in reporting on variances the more difficult it will be to provide any accurate information on the reasons for these variances. Where there is a long delay in reporting variances, by the time any control action is taken, the less effective this is likely to be because the situation will probably have changed further by the time the corrective action is instigated.

When control action is taken the reasons as to why it was taken, and information on the expected effect of that action, should be provided. Finally, it is important to follow up and see whether the control action had the desired effect.

DEVELOPMENTS IN BUDGETING

Having discussed some of the traditional views of budgeting let us turn to some more recent developments in budgetary control. We will emphasise the provision of additional information to the mangers of an organisation. In doing so particular attention will be paid to ways in which the traditional budgetary control system can be improved. In general, none of the developments require a major upheaval in an organisation's management information system, or in particular in its budgetary control system. The effect of any change is dependent upon: the depth to which any of the techniques are applied; the additional costs involved in their implementation; and any additional benefits that they would provide.

If an organisation has any form of budgeting at all it is usually quite a small step to prepare budgeted financial statements. These include a budgeted profit and loss account, a budgeted balance sheet and a budgeted sources and application of funds statement.

Budgeted financial statements enable management to ask whether they like the look of what is planned to be achieved. If not they still have the opportunity of reformulating their plans. Such statements also indicate whether the organisation's overall financial objective for the period will be attained if the budgeted figures are realised.

Probabilistic profit budgeting

One relatively recent development in budgeting, which has its roots in statistics, concerns the use of probability. What are termed probabilistic profit budgets (PBB) can be drawn up to help provide better budgeting information for decision-making purposes, especially under conditions of uncertainty. However, before discussing probabilistic profit budgeting it is useful to briefly remind oneself about flexible budgeting. This is because it is possible to confuse flexible and probabilistic profit budgets. Although flexible budgets will be drawn up on an *ex ante* basis their use tends to be *ex post* in that they help to analyse the actual performance against that section of the budget drawn up for the level of activity achieved; the probabilistic profit budget is both drawn up and used on an *ex ante* basis as an aid to decision making.

A flexible budgeting approach is frequently taken in situations where the activity actually achieved is likely to vary around some expected norm. In such situations if an organisation simply established its expected 'one-point' budget, when it came to analyse any variances between this and the organisation's actual performance it would be difficult to draw any sensible conclusions.

Therefore the organisation will produce a budget which is based on more than a one-point estimate. Flexible budgeting can be defined as follows:

A flexible budget is one which by recognising the distinction between an organisation's fixed, semi-fixed and variable costs is designed to change in relationship to different levels of attainable activity which may be achieved by the organisation.

When a flexible budget is prepared it shows what is expected to happen at the level of capacity that it expects to operate at. This is the 100 per cent part of the flexible budget. However, it is unlikely that the organisation will precisely achieve this 100 per cent level of activity. Assuming that past experience has shown that actual performance was likely to fall 5 per cent either side of the 100 per cent level, then additional 'budgets' could be established which would show what the organisation's financial results would be if either of these levels of activity were attained. These three 'budgets' can now be put together in tabular fashion and be incorporated in the analysis (Figure 7.5).

Management can now look at this flexible budget to see what the effect of different levels of activity will have on the profitability of their organisation. For example, an examination of the flexible budget provided in Figure 7.5 shows that because of the incidence of fixed costs a 5 per cent drop in activity from the 100 per cent level would reduce profits by 50 per cent, whereas a 5 per cent increase in activity from the 100 per cent level would increase profits by one-third. The influence of such a multiplier effect will depend on the proportion of the organisation's fixed to its variable costs. The information thus provided should, therefore, be useful for planning purposes.

Although flexible bugeting brings in a way of introducing some variability into the budgeting process, the percentage changes involved all have a direct linear relationship to the appropriate parts of the 100 per cent model. For planning purposes probability should be introduced into the budgeting process to get away from flexible budgeting's linear relationships. In establishing such a budget questions will have to be asked about the probability of the occurrence of individual budget items at their various possible levels.

	Percentage of expected activity		
	95%	100%	105%
	£	£	£
Sales	190	200	210
Costs			
Variable	95	100	105
Fixed	90	90	90
	185	190	195
Profit	£5	£10	£15

Figure 7.5 A flexible budget

The major assumption upon which the concept of PPB is based concerns the use of probability to provide an indication of the potential variability of each item within the budget. Flexible budgeting, although moving away from the traditional approach of the single point, most expected budget, does not consider the potential variability of individual items within the budget. It merely extrapolates the expected budget to various levels of possible activity on either side of the single point most-expected estimate. The probabilistic approach to budgeting also provides a range of budgets, but draws these up under quite different assumptions. The technique also associates subjective probabilities with the various levels of activity that could occur, to provide probable or expected values for each major budget classification or item. This provides management with an aid to decision making under conditions of uncertainty. Management is then provided with a range of probabilistic budget information to examine which enables them to carry out a deeper analysis of potential situations before they decide upon their profit plans.

At its simplest the probabilistic profit budget may be based upon three-level estimates. These will show the most likely, the optimistic, and the pessimistic figures that could be either associated with global budgets or various, probably major, items within a budget. This immediately introduces a high degree of sophistication in the budgeting process. Simulation can also be used in conjunction with this approach to further enhance the quality of the decision-making information provided. (Although the discussion in this section revolves around probabilistic profit budgets based upon three-level estimates, the range of estimates made in such a budget will depend upon the situation and circumstances involved.)

Probabilistic profit budget based on three-level estimates

	Attitude towards expected activity		
	Pessimistic	Most Likely	Optimistic
Sales (units)	70	80	100
	£	£	£
Revenue	[90p] 63	[£1] 80	[£1.2] 120
Variable costs	[60p] 42	[50p] 40	[45p] 45
Contribution	21	40	75
Fixed costs	35	30	25
Budgeted profit/ (loss)	(14)	10	5
Probability	0.2	0.7	0.1
Expected monetary value	(£2.8)	£7	£5
Expected monetary value (overall)	£9.2		

Figure 7.6 Sample probabilistic profit budget

Figure 7.6 provides an example of a probabilistic profit budget which is based on three-level estimates, and where probability has been introduced to enable expected values to be calculated. It can be seen that the most likely column, (which would be the 100 per cent budget under a flexible budgeting system), is based upon the expected outcome of future performance. This is the first column to be established. The next stage is for management to discuss their view of the possible outcome of the budget if they take a pessimistic approach. Sales and other items would be less favourable under this approach. In fact, both unit sales and the price that could be charged for the items would be lower if things turn out badly. The overall effect is to make the budgeted profit position very much worse than it would have been if a linear relationship had been considered for all the items involved.

A repeat of this exercise is then carried out, but this time taking an optimistic view of the future.

Although an examination of the columns of a probabilistic budget, just as they stand, will provide useful management information, an additional stage would be to assign subjective probabilities to each of the columns. Such probabilities are referred to as being subjective because they are established based on the 'subjective views' of those who assign them.

Armed with subjective probabilities the expected values associated with each column can then be computed. The columns can then be summed to provide an expected value of the overall outcome of the situation.

The ultimate extension of this would be the production of a probabilistic profit budget showing the likely outcome of operations in situations of uncertainty using a broader range of operations and a wider range of assumptions than those associated with three-level estimates. For example, a pessimistic view of sales in units could be taken together with an optimistic view of the prices that would be obtained for each unit sold. Or a pattern of pessimistic costs could be matched with one of optimistic revenues. In fact there are numerous possible combinations that could be used in the analysis of even three-level probabilistic profit budget information.

Using a computer enables an organisation to deal with the numerous possible relationships and interrelationships. The various elements of many more than three-point estimates could be combined to produce dozens of different relationship profiles by use of a suitable program. Simulation can also be used to show the effects of any changes, or the interrelationships of changes, in the budget's components.

Measures of Variability

A number of approaches can be taken to measure the variability of an item, or items, within a probabilistic profit budget. Measures that can be used for this purpose include those associated with the following parameters:

☐ *Probability intervals*. Probability intervals enable an analysis to be made of the percentage of items which are seen to fall within given ranges of distribution.

☐ *Confidence intervals*. Where the parameters concerning the probability are not known with any reliability these will have to be estimated. Confidence intervals are all about the level of confidence associated with the estimates of parameters.

☐ *Co-efficients of variation*. To enable the variability of discrete probability distributions to be described co-efficients of variation can be used. These concern the percentage relationship between the standard deviation and the mean of the distribution. They enable the prediction of the potential variability of the items within a budget. This variability will be large when the co-efficient of variation is high.

PPB can be used to provide a range of data and information to decision makers on the possible outcomes of budgets and the probability of the occurrence of these outcomes. They assist decision makers who examine them by enabling them to evaluate the information presented and which of the profiles presented they would prefer to work towards. This enables management to ensure that effort is focused in the right direction.

Zero based budgeting

Zero based budgeting (ZBB) is a fairly recent development to the formulation of budgets which was introduced in the United States. It originally concerned budgeting in the public sector. However, since its initial development in the public sector it has increasingly been applied in both commerce and industry.

Basically it is a 'start all over again' process. The budget is formulated as if its compilers were in an *ab initio* situation, that is they start from a zero base. Its concept is based on avoiding the dangers associated with using a previous period's budget (or performance) as a base for the next period's budget and making what are felt to be appropriate changes to this. Therefore in ZBB the executive or manager has to consider and state the complete budget requirements from a starting point of zero. Furthermore, this must be in full detail and the expense items from which the budget is comprised must be ranked in order of importance. ZBB firmly places the burden of proof for the budget on the manager, whereas in the traditional approach to the formulation of the budget it generally appears to be the norm to assume that past budgets will continue into perpetuity and it is only when people wish to change them that they may have to prove that any changes they request are necessary. The emphasis of proof has a dramatic change of direction when the concept of a zero base is introduced.

Obviously there are costs associated with the use of ZBB, and these will depend upon the detail of the analysis required by the system developed. Therefore before establishing a system for ZBB it is important to try to quantify the costs and benefits associated with its introduction and operation, to try to ascertain how justified its use will be.

The major areas of application of ZBB concern situations where the budget inputs cannot be directly measured against the outputs that they generate. In commercial and industrial organisations the use of the technique is particularly associated with things such as: expenditure on overheads; costs associated with central services, such as computers; marketing and distribution costs; and so on. However, it does not concern itself with direct expenditure. This is because direct expenditure is automatically justified on a variable basis in relation to the items with which it is associated.

One of the stages of ZBB is the ranking of budget items in order of their importance. This can cause difficulties associated with deciding upon the ordering of the budget items. Second, and more problematic, are the difficulties which arise if some of the budget items are interrelated, and dependent upon each other, or where they are not in discrete units and yet the uses of such composite budget items may have quite different rankings for different purposes.

The objective of ranking items is to enable them to be added to, or cut from, a particular budget. However, difficulties arise when trying to draw such lines as far as the various departmental budgets are concerned. The question arises as to whether items which, although having low priority in one department's budget, should really be ranked lower than those which are near the top of another's budget. In the answer to such questions consideration must be given to what is likely to benefit the organisation as a whole.

A number of alternatives have been developed, although they could be looked upon as watered-down versions of the full-blooded version of the ZBB concept. Nevertheless they do provide useful forms of the technique, especially where its full implementation would be either too difficult, or too costly, to operate.

Change justification budgeting

The use of change justification budgeting (CJB) is basically only useful in situations of expansion or where a particular budget is increasing, although theoretically it could also be applied to contraction situations. However, it does not overtly encourage budgets to be reduced from the levels that they reached during previous years. Therefore in practical situations CJB is applicable when management wishes to increase a budget, in real terms, from the level at which it stood during the previous year. In such a situation they have to justify the increase required in full detail. Therefore instead of assuming a zero base, the base of the previous year is considered to be the norm and any increases required to this would have to be justified.

Budget performance auditing

One way to overcome the problems associated with trying to encourage appropriate reductions to budgets is to audit a budget centre's performance. By definition an audit can only take place after the event and in itself it does not lead to the ranking of a budget's items in importance to the budget area concerned.

Therefore, whereas ZBB tries to identify areas of slack on an *ex ante* basis and to eliminate them before they occur, with budget performance auditing (BPA) the areas of slack are only identified on an *ex post* basis, and so must occur at least once. However, the use of BPA should hopefully stop the recurrence of excessive budgets. Thus, in situations where operations are contracting, the use of BPA does at least encourage reductions in the future budgets of such areas.

Review period budgeting

In the USA review period budgeting (RPB) is referred to as the sunset concept. This is the approach that the 'sun will eventually set', in this case, upon the budget. Built into the budgeting system is a mechanism which provides for the 'extinction' of the budget and for it only to be re-established after it has been rejustified from a zero base.

This is really saying that the ZBB exercise should not be carried out on an annual basis but, rather, after certain predetermined reasonable time intervals. The disadvantage is that changes that become necessary shortly after a review, would be delayed until the next review period came along.

Where zero based budgeting in its 'pure' form is inappropriate the use of the alternative of CJB, BPA and RPB, or the welding together of some of their approaches into a modified ZBB system may become a real operational alternative. A modified system would move an organisation in the direction of ZBB without all the costs and difficulties associated with it, and still provide many of the benefits that it gives in its pure form, as well as perhaps being more realistic operationally. This is an area where it would be appropriate to use a cost-benefit approach in the collection of the information required to help make a decision about how far towards ZBB an organisation should go.

Continuous business forecasting

Two basic assumptions underpin the concept of continuous business forecasting (CBF):

1. Management decisions can only relate to future events and therefore, by definition, all managers must be continually forecasting the future, either informally and/or formally in order to make these decisions.
2. The senior management of a business collectively requires an overview of where the total business is going, as well as where it has been, if it is to effectively direct a business in the medium term.

As a totally integrated detail prediction method on a fully continuous basis is impractical, a means is needed to pull together the significant individual views of the future into a coherent forecast for the whole business at appropriate time intervals. Until recently, this objective has been attempted by updating the annual budget exercise throughout the year with 'outlooks' or 'forecasts'. These quarterly exercises have basically been viewed as 'accountants' exercises which concentrated on reviewing the annual forecast and the period-by-period forecasts attracted little management emphasis. Therefore, these exercises have not really contributed to medium-term business decisions.

In deciding how forecast information can be used in the tactical direction of the business, the key question is how often the plan needs to be revised. The philosophy of budgetary control assumes that changes will be infrequent. The weakness of this is exposed in volatile economic or commercial climates when the plan becomes out of date. The original objectives may no longer be appropriate, certainly at the detail level, and there may be better methods of achieving the current objectives than by moving back on to the original plan. Where frequent changes are needed, continuous business forecasting provides an alternative for controlling and redirecting the business.

Continuous business forecasting (CBF) aims to draw together the significant individual formal forecasts from each discipline on a regular basis, at appropriate time intervals, to provide a total business picture for tactical direction and action in the six weeks to twelve months timescale. The output from CBF, expressed in a common language (+s), ensures that individual forecasts are compatible one with another and ascertains whether the overall direction of the business is acceptable or not. If not, the individual actions can be modified.

The approach of CBF is to 'model' the business rather than to indulge in monthly detail rebudgeting. Control comes from monitoring expected performance against current objectives; and by monitoring year-on-year changes to establish whether the forecast is compatible with what has already been achieved. Any 'redirection' needed is planned by concentrating on the assumptions made and actions required to take the business from where it is now to where it needs to be.

The objective of CBF is to provide the directors with a regular forward view of business progress and a proper quantification of the major assumptions, influences and uncertainties that are impacting the business. The forecasting procedures used can quantify those aspects of the decisions which are amenable to financial evaluation. Such financial information must be forward looking: it must focus on a time horizon of up to a year ahead; show individual period forecasts up to six months ahead; and it must say something both concise and relevant about the decisions that have to be taken.

By alerting management to the need to take action while there is still time for it to be effective, CBF can make a significant contribution to quantifying the direction which such action should take. The benefits of CBF lie not only in formalising the forecasts themselves but in the extra information available from the forecasting procedures, and the action which is taken as a result.

To produce credible forecasts CBF requires:

□ Proper involvement and input from all the functions of the business, to ensure that it is a business forecast rather than an accountant's forecast.

□ Identification and quantification of the major issues and alternatives so that management attention can focus on items of real significance.

□ Identification of areas of risk and evaluation of alternatives. It is here that business forecasting procedures are intended to support management by answering the 'what if?' questions.

□ A reliable statement of the actual position to date as a base.

In practical terms this requires a joint effort by all the management of the business, with the financial function providing a framework discipline and an administrative resource. During the preparation of the forecast the finance director/accountant acts as the prompter and inquisitor, challenging the major assumptions, evaluating the alternatives, and ensuring that the key issues are identified and kept in focus.

For regular forecasting to be feasible it must be based on efficient procedures and a minimum of detail. If continuous forecasts are to be of positive value to the business, they must be:

- reliable enough to act as a spur to action by management;
- seen as playing a necessary role in the medium-term direction of the business and have the full commitment of the directors;
- actually used to make decisions which would not have been made without them;
- revised on a monthly basis to include the latest management thinking on a reasonable timescale; and
- economical to prepare.

The goal of CBF is better management. The central purpose is to develop a more accurate overall forecast of the business to enable management to identify problem areas early, to make decisions more quickly, to take action and to achieve the required results. No forecasts can guarantee success, but financial forecasts coming from a sound continuous business forecast system can quantify the conditions for success. In the end, however, it is management input, commercial judgement and action taken which are critical.

SUMMARY

As we draw this chapter to a close it is appropriate to reflect on the need to shift from treating financial figures as the foundation for measuring performance, to treating them as one among a broader set of measures. Eccles (1991) argues that managers should be tracking quality, customer satisfaction, market share and human resources alongside, and with equal status to, financial measures for corporate performance to be properly evaluated. The impetus for this was the realisation that financial measures alone may undercut strategy. Indeed, Eccles argues that enhancing competitiveness requires managers to address the question 'Given our strategy, what are the most important measure of performance?' He reports that many managers believe that financial figures report only on the consequences of yesterday's decisions rather than indicating tomorrow's performance. The 1980s saw many companies' strong financial performance deteriorate because of unnoticed declines in quality or customer satisfaction, or because competitors were taking market share.

This chapter has covered a wide range of issues which affect managers in organisations. Budgeting was considered to be part of the planning and control process, and as such was the main way in which broad strategic aims were translated into measurable objectives. In looking at budgets as a control mechanism the importance of a suitable communication system for the feedback of results was stressed.

The influence of the budgeting and control system on the motivation to work was highlighted in terms of reinforcing the need to involve a wide range of mangers in the construction of usable budgets. The process of budgeting focused attention on the use of forecasts and on the issues involved in the preparation of budgets. Problems associated with the use of traditional 'techniques' were considered in the final section of the chapter. Techniques considered included probabilistic profit budgets (PPB), zero based budgets (ZBB), and continuous business forecasting (CBF).

FURTHER READING

Chapters 2, 3, 4, 5, 6 and 7 of Otley's book referred to above discusses, in more depth, the issues raised in this chapter.

REFERENCES

Anthony, R N and Dearden, J (1980) *Management Control Systems: Text and Cases*, 4th edn, Irwin, Homewood, Illinois.

Asch, D (1989) 'Strategic control: An overview of the issues', in Asch, D and Bowman, C (eds), *Readings in Strategic Management*, Macmillan, London, pp 397–408.

Bowman, C and Asch, D (1987) *Strategic Management*, Macmillan, London.

Cooper, C L and Makin, P (1984) 'Motivation at work', in Cooper C L and Makin P (eds), *Psychology for Managers*, Macmillan, London, pp 94–117.

Eccles, R G (1991) 'The performance measurement manifesto', *Harvard Business Review*, Jan–Feb, pp 131–137.

Goldsmith, W and Clutterbuck, D (1984) *The Winning Streak*, Weidenfeld & Nicolson, London.

McCarthy, D J, Minichiello, R J and Curran, J R (1983) *Business Policy and Strategy*, Irwin, Homewood, Illinois.

Machin, J L J and Wilson, L S (1979) 'Closing the gap between planning and control', *Long Range Planning*, Vol 12, April, pp 16–32.

Otley, D (1987) *Accounting Control and Organisation Behaviour*, Heinemann, London.

Strategy and Financial Planning

INTRODUCTION

A number of issues have been considered in the preceding parts of the book. Chapters 8 to 10 will seek to draw together some underlying strands which have emerged and which deserve consideration by managers involved in making decisions. First, we place financial planning in a corporate context by considering issues which are often taken for granted but which we believe warrant a degree of exploration to enable us to better understand some of the influences on managers.

The chapter commences with a brief discussion about organisational strategy, both content and process, before moving on to considering financial planning. We have illustrated the chapter with the example of the stock market flotation of Jaguar, and we would wish to acknowledge Professor K N Bhaskar for granting permission to draw on *Jaguar: An Investor's Guide*.

CORPORATE STRATEGY AND CORPORATE PLANNING

Strategy can be broadly defined as the match an organisation makes between its own resources and the threats or risks and opportunities created by the external environment in which it operates. So strategy can be seen as a key link between what the organisation wants to achieve – its objectives – and the policies adopted to guide its activities. We need to recognise that an organisation can have a single strategy or many strategies, and that strategies are likely to exist at a number of levels in an organisation.

We start by explaining the differences between the *content* of strategy and the *process* of strategy. By the content of strategy we mean 'what the strategy is about'. To explain this we explore the different levels of strategy: corporate, business and operational. The process of strategy refers to the ways in which the strategy came about, which includes its implementation. There is a good deal of evidence to suggest that the way a strategy is derived critically affects the chances of it being successfully implemented.

The content of strategy

We usually distinguish between different levels of strategy:

□ corporate strategy
□ business strategy
□ operational strategy

It is important to separate these levels, otherwise it can lead to confusion in strategic thinking. We shall first consider corporate strategy (see Figure 8.1).

Corporate strategy

A corporation would be, typically, a large organisation which is divided into a number of discrete and essentially autonomous units or divisions. Corporate strategy is the responsibility of those managers at corporate headquarters. The fundamental issue at corporate level is the *logic*, or rationale for the corporation. Put simply, 'what is the point of grouping these separate businesses under one corporate roof?'

Various arguments have been advanced to justify the corporation. These would include 'synergy' (by combining these units the whole performs better than the sum of the parts, often written as 2+2=5). The thinking here is that business units can benefit in some way from being under the corporate umbrella. These potential benefits may include the sharing of expertise, or exploiting scale economies (e.g. in bulk purchasing).

Some corporations are run almost as holding companies, where there is minimal interference in the management of a division or business unit from the corporate centre (e.g. BTR, Hanson). Others are justified on the basis of core competences which are nurtured, developed and leveraged into many diverse product markets (e.g. 3M,

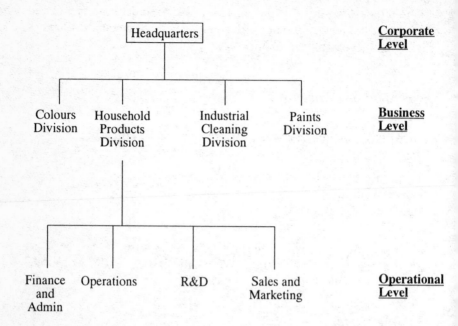

Figure 8.1 Levels of Strategy

Honda or Canon). In addressing the fundamental logic or rationale for the corporation, key questions that would need to be answered would be: what businesses should be in the portfolio and how should they be managed?

Business Strategy

The key strategic issue at business level is determining competitive strategy. This involves addressing the following questions:

- What markets should we be trying to compete in? What segments of those markets should we really focus on?
- How should we try to compete in those markets?
- What competences or capabilities do we need to compete successfully?

□ What do we look like now? What might be preventing us from changing?

□ How can we move forward?

Operational Strategy

Operational strategy underpins business level strategy. The key question at this level of strategy is: 'what is the role of this function/ department in delivering the business level strategy?' Operational strategies would include marketing strategies, production strategies, human resource strategies, information systems strategies and financial strategies. Ideally, once business level strategy has been set, the role of functional departments in delivering this strategy becomes clearer. Marketing should know what is expected of them, finance would know the likely demands for funds to implement the strategy, and so each function can plan accordingly.

However, the process is not usually as logical and rational as this would imply. Often the links between business and functional level strategy are tenuous. In determining business level strategy, functional heads may be more concerned with pursuing their own functional concerns. And if there is no clear direction at business level, functional strategies or plans are unlikely to be mutually supportive and consistent. This takes us into our exploration of the *process* of strategy.

In looking at the development of financial plans we need to recognise that they need to be built upon the firm's competitive strategy. Therefore, we will explore competitive strategy before looking at the process of strategy.

To explore competitive strategy we will use the 'Strategy Compass' (Figure 8.2). The vertical axis (perceived use value) refers to the value perceived and experienced by the buyer. The horizontal axis is perceived price. These two axes represent the components of value for money; the strategy compass separates them out to enable competitive strategy to be analysed.

There are two basic options facing a firm seeking competitive advantage: either compete on price or add perceived use value. If the firm chooses to compete on price it is imperative that the firm has lower costs than its competitors. Otherwise it is likely that, if a price war develops, price levels will reach the point where the firm is forced out of business.

In order to add perceived use value it is essential to be clear who the target customers are, and what their needs are. From this understanding the firm can develop approaches to adding perceived use values in ways that are difficult for competitors to imitate. The firm can choose to either try to sustain a *static gap* between itself and the competition (e.g. through developing and defending a strong brand), or it can sustain advantage by continually adding perceived use value (sustaining a *dynamic gap*).

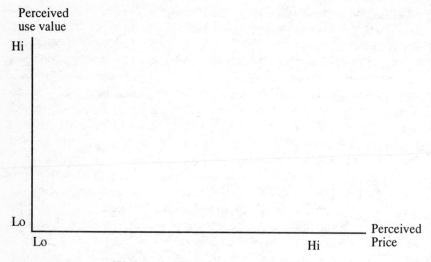

Figure 8.2 The strategy compass

Whether the firm is seeking to compete on price, or to compete by adding perceived use value, it should strive to be a low cost producer. The firm needs to be low cost compared to those firms the target customers perceive it to be in competition with. Achieving a low cost position through a strategy of adding perceived use value is attainable if market share advantages enable the firm to realise the cost advantages accruing from scale and experience effects. In addition, the firm may be able to achieve cost advantages through technological, locational (in a low wage economy) and/or system developments (e.g. just-in-time) that are difficult for rivals to imitate. But there will also be significant opportunities to eliminate costs from the product through a thorough understanding of what it is that customers value: if it isn't valued, cut it out.

A firm may choose to add perceived use value and to charge a premium price for these added values. If buyers are prepared to pay premium prices, and if competitors cannot imitate the added values, then the move will lead to sustainable advantage. However, great care must be taken to understand the nature of demand (the natural, need-based segments that exist), and the structure of competition in relation to these segments. A move northeast (adding perceived use value, and charging higher prices) may involve a shift from one segment to another. Care needs to be taken to ensure that the firm can achieve a competitive advantage over firms serving this different segment of demand.

Moving north by continually adding perceived use value, while at the same time striving to be the lowest cost producer is not an easy strategy to implement. In some respects the two aspects of the strategy (product/service innovation and achieving lowest costs), might appear to place contradictory demands on the organisation. To achieve these twin aims is difficult; but that is why it is a source of sustainable competitive advantage. If it was easy, everyone could do it. A more comprehensive discussion of competitive strategy is set out in Bowman and Asch (1996).

STRATEGY PROCESSES

By the process of strategy we mean 'how the strategy came about'. There are two critical process issues:

□ The quality of the strategy that emerges from the process, that is how appropriate is it for the situation the organisation is facing?
□ The commitment to implementing the strategy.

There is little point in having a high quality strategy that no-one is committed to implement, equally it would be dangerous to have high levels of commitment to an inappropriate strategy. Our main concern here is to address the quality of the strategy (for an in-depth discussion of strategy processes see Bowman and Asch, 1996). We will commence by considering a conventional planning process (Figure 8.3) and follow that by looking at some new ideas for considering the development of a strategy that addresses the challenges of the arena faced by the organisation.

We will now consider each of the components in the process. Although each of the major stages is dealt with individually, as Figure 8.3 reveals, they are interconnected. Also, while we will discuss the elements in a sequential manner, this is not to indicate that this represents the way in which the process might work in practice. Because of the interrelationship between the elements the corporate planning process is likely to be of an iterative nature,

200 / Financial Planning

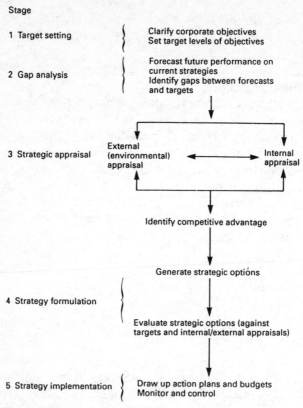

Figure 8.3 A corporate planning process in outline

containing negotiation and compromise, for example, between those involved.

The present situation (stages 1 and 2)

The formulation process in an existing organisation does not and cannot commence in a vacuum, constraints usually exist that impact on the process. The firm's current situation, strategy, plans, or commitments obviously present a starting point for analysis. Thus the firm may be in a situation where 'formulation' as such is unnecessary as the requirement is to develop and fine-tune existing strategies, or to modify short-term objectives to fit with the long-term aims.

The present situation of course should not preclude the firm from taking advantage of opportunities in unrelated areas. The key point is that the existing organisational structure and what the firm does well will have an effect on the formulation process.

Environmental and internal appraisal (stage 3)

A firm can be viewed as an open system with respect to the environment in which it operates. It is involved in a continuous process of exchange with external parties – suppliers, customers, employees, government bodies with the other organisations for these resources. As such the environmental appraisal is a central element in formulating strategy.

Additional analysis is required to identify strategic options, involving an appraisal of the organisation's own resources with the objective of identifying the firm's strengths and weaknesses. Such analysis will reveal the capability of the firm to counter external threats and to take advantage of the presenting opportunities. An important feature of this process concerns the identification of 'distinctive competencies', that is, those things at which the organisation is particularly good in relation to its competitors.

Strategic options and strategic selection (stage 4)

The generation of strategic options is not a random process but may be stimulated, for example, by a shortfall in current performance and the level of performance expected by key decision makers. It is also more complex than merely seeking to fit a range of variables affecting the firm and its environment.

The method of evaluating which strategic option(s) will be selected will vary from organisation to organisation. Chapter 6 looked at some of the most widely used methods. Although strategic decisions emanating from the formulation process may often be presented as utilitarian, in most cases the decisions are reached as a result of, or in spite of, a wide range of influences on those involved. Such influences will include, for example, individual needs, values and perceptions, coupled with wider societal values and expectations impacting on managers as individuals and the organisation as a whole.

Strategic implementation (stage 5)

We have already discussed most of the issues involved in implementing strategic decisions, for example in our consideration of budgeting and control in Chapter 7.

In summary, therefore, some of the benefits that can be derived from the process of corporate planning are as follows:

- 'Rational' techniques can assist choice even if (because of the pressure of complex qualitative variables) they cannot make the choice.

- Systematic planning can encourage an orderly approach to the study of strategic problems.
- An analytical approach can help in defining the strategic problem.
- The process of rational analysis can generate useful information which can shed light on 'softer', or value-laden issues.
- Rational analysis can force the decision makers to confront the value judgements that need to be made.

Bowman and Asch (1987, pp 335–8) have summarised the major criticisms:

- For many firms, the dynamic nature of the environment makes the corporate plan rapidly redundant unless it is couched in the most generalised terms.
- Information is never available in the quantity and quality required to undertake a comprehensive analysis of the internal and external environment, or to permit an exhaustive exploration of alternative strategies.
- Decision makers are not capable of comprehending much more than a very limited and simplified set of interrelated variables. In fact, decision makers deliberately employ devices to simplify complexity, for example, breaking the problem down into discrete, manageable chunks, which are dealt with in sequence.
- Systematic, formal planning activities can stifle the emergence of radical, 'maverick', but potentially successful ideas.
- Where the corporate plan is drawn up by specialist planners, line managers (who have to implement the plan) often display resistance to decisions in which they have not been involved. In addition, staff planners often lack access to vital information held by line managers.
- Peters and Waterman (1982) point out that fewer than one in ten US companies produce a corporate planning strategy that is achieving its goals.
- Many problems with corporate planning crop up at the implementation stage:
  - (a) implementation of changes proposed in the plan always seem to take longer than expected;
  - (b) unforeseen big problems surface; and
  - (c) competing activities and, especially, crises within the firm deflect attention from implementing the plan.
- Problems often arise in the introduction of the corporate planning process. Like many eagerly grasped management panaceas (for example, MBO, quality circles, management audits) insufficient

attention is paid to developing the organisation and the management in preparation for the successful introduction of the new planning system.

AN ALTERNATIVE TO CORPORATE PLANNING?

In recognising that corporate planning as a process may not necessarily benefit the organisation we should take account of some useful empirical research. Quinn (1980) observed:

□ the planning activity often tended to become a bureaucraticised, rigid and costly paper-shuffling exercise;
□ most major strategic decisions seemed to be made outside the formal planning structure, even in organisations with well-accepted planning cultures, but especially so in smaller and entrepreneurial companies;
□ management literature on planning seemed to be producing more and more sophisticated but unworkable models.

Whereas formal, logical planning models seemed not to be followed in practice, Quinn, does not hold that the major descriptive theoretical alternative 'muddling through' is an adequate explanation of actual strategic behaviour. Managers purposely blend different processes (labelled behavioural, power-dynamic and formal analytical) together to improve both the quality of the decisions and the effectiveness of their implementation.

As a result of his research Quinn came to the following conclusions:

□ The most effective strategies tend to emerge step by step from an iterative process in which the organisation probes the future; experiments and learns from a series of partial (incremental) commitments rather than through global formulations of total strategies.
□ Logical incrementalism is a synthesis of logical, global analysis (e.g. corporate planning) and political or power-behavioural decision making which operates through a process which:
   (a) improves the quality of available information;
   (b) establishes critical elements of available information;
   (c) creates needed participation and commitment, thus enhancing decision quality and the likelihood of successful implementation.
□ The quality of each subsystem's strategy is improved if executives move forward incrementally, modifying their conclusions from

broad conceptions towards specifics as more information, confidence and personal commitment are achieved.

□ As each subsystem 'pulses' forward it interacts with the strategies of other subsystems creating:
  (a) new opportunities;
  (b) new demands; and
  (c) new constraints for all subsystems.

□ Because of this continuing complexity and uncertainty executives should manage each subsystem incrementally in keeping with its own imperatives.

□ Therefore effective strategic managers try to shape the development of both subsystem and total enterprise strategies productively in a logically incremental fashion. Thus they:
  (a) accept ambiguity;
  (b) ensure that the subsystems do not work at cross purposes;
  (c) define overall strategy in such a way as to encourage movement in the 'right' directions; and
  (d) consciously avoid overspecifics which might impair flexibility or commitment.

Quinn sees the major obstacle to successful strategic planning as the trap of thinking of strategy formulation and implementation as separate sequential processes: '[Executives] have relied on the awesome rationality of their formally derived strategies and the inherent power of their positions to cause their organisations to respond', whereas, successful managers build the seeds of understanding, identity and commitment into the very processes that create their strategies. By the time the strategy begins to crystallise in focus, pieces of it are already being implemented.

Logical incrementalism is perhaps not an alternative to corporate planning, rather it is one empirical derivation at the overall complex strategy process. As such we believe that it does indeed shed some light on how managers in organisations shape and influence their firm's strategy.

A RESOURCE BASED VIEW OF STRATEGY

An effective strategy will make realistic use of the true resources available to the organisation. Prahalad and Hamel (1990) argue that 'the critical task for management is to create an organisation capable of infusing products with irresistible functionality or, better yet, creating products that customers need but have not yet imagined'.

They go on to note that while in the short term competitiveness derives from the price/performance attributes of current products, in the long term competitiveness derives from an ability to build core competencies that lead to unanticipated products. The key lies in management's ability to consolidate corporate-wide skills and resources into competencies that enable individual businesses to adapt quickly to changing environments. Prahalad and Hamel define core competencies as '. . . the collective learning in the organisation, especially how to coordinate diverse production skills and integrate multiple streams of technologies.' Grant (1991) develops this theme and argues that, where environmental features are rapidly changing, the firm's own resources and capabilities are a better basis on which to develop strategy. He states '. . . a definition of a business in terms of what it is capable of doing may offer a more durable basis for strategy than a definition based upon the needs which the business seeks to satisfy.'

The organisation's resources are inputs to the business process. As such, most individual resources have little value. Grant (1991) defines a capability as the capacity for a team of resources to perform a task or activity. Resources then are the source of an organisation's capabilities, and capabilities are the main source of competitive advantage. Prahalad and Hamel (1990) define these central strategic capabilities – they call them core competencies which we referred to earlier as 'the collective learning in the organisation, especially how to coordinate diverse production skills and integrate multiple streams of technologies.' They go on to note that core competencies also involve the organisation of work, delivery of value, communication, involvement, plus a deep commitment to working across organisational boundaries.

The key task is to assess the organisation's capabilities relative to its competitors. A successful strategy can then be developed which exploits these relative strengths. Because capabilities involve complex patterns of coordination between people and between people and other resources, Grant (1991) identified a number of issues which illuminate the relationships between resources, capabilities and competitive advantage:

- □ The relationship between resources and capabilities while not predetermined does have an impact on what the organisation can do. An important element in the relationship between resources and capabilities is the ability of the organisation to achieve cooperation and coordination between teams. The style, values, traditions and leadership are key dimensions here.

□ The trade-off between efficiency and flexibility concerns limits to the organisation's ability to articulate its capabilities, because many of its routines involve a large element of tacit knowledge. So, while a limited number of routines can be performed highly efficiently, this may limit the organisation's ability to respond in novel situations.

□ Economies of experience derive from the organisations's ability to perfect organisational routines over time and usage. However, while this may give established organisations an edge over newcomers in some industries, in industries where technological change is rapid this experience may hinder the established firm due to their commitment to old routines.

□ The complexity of capabilities refers to the idea that some capabilities derive from the contribution of a single resource, while others involve a complex series of interactions from many different resources. Complexity may lead to the development of sustainable competitive advantage.

Grant goes on to identify four characteristics of resources and capabilities which determine the sustainability of competitive advantage: durability, transparency, transferability and replicability.

1. Durability

The durability of resources, that is the rate at which they depreciate or become obsolete, varies considerably. The pace of technological change tends to shorten the lifespan of capital equipment and technological resources. Reputation, brand and corporate, appears to depreciate relatively slowly. Capabilities have the potential to be more durable than the resources on which they are based because the organisation can replace individual resources as they wear out or move on. The longevity of capabilities depends upon managers ensuring their maintenance and renewal.

2. Transparency

The sustainability of an organisation's competitive advantage depends upon how quickly competitors can replicate its strategy. A competitive advantage derived from a superior capability in relation to a single performance variable is easier to identify and comprehend than a competitive advantage stemming from multiple capabilities. In addition, a capability which requires a complex pattern of co-ordination between large numbers of diverse resources is more difficult to identify and comprehend.

3. *Transferability*

Having established the sources of superior performance an imitator must then acquire the resources and capabilities to develop a competitive challenge. If the resources can be acquired on similar terms then the competitive advantage will be short lived. However, most resources and capabilities are not freely transferable between organisations, so potential competitors will be unable to obtain them on equal terms. Imperfections in transferability may arise from several sources:

□ *Geographical immobility*. The costs of relocating large items of capital equipment and highly specialised employees puts firms which are acquiring these resources at a disadvantage to those which already possess them.
□ *Imperfect information*. Assessing the value of a resource may be difficult due to the heterogeneity of resources and by imperfect knowledge of potential productivity of individual resources. The established organisation's knowledge of resource productivity gives it an advantage over any prospective purchaser of the same resources.
□ *Firm specific resources*. The value of a resource (e.g. a brand reputation) may fall on transfer due to a decline in its productivity. Where a brand reputation is associated with the firm that created it a change in ownership of the brand name will tend to erode its value. Employees may also suffer a similar decline in productivity when transferred to another organisation.
□ *The immobility of capabilities*. Because capabilities require interactive teams of resources they are far more immobile than individual resources. Even if the resources that constitute the team are transferred, the nature of organisational routines, especially the role of tacit knowledge and unconscious co-ordination, make the recreation of capabilities uncertain.

4. *Replicability*

Given the difficulty of transferring resources and capabilities it may be possible to imitate them by internal investment. Some can be easily imitated by replication. Capabilities which are based on highly complex organisational routines are much less easily replicable.

The implications for developing the organisation's strategy are clear. The organisation's most important resources and capabilities are those which have durability, are difficult to identify and comprehend, are not easily replicated, and are clearly owned and controlled by the organisation. These need to be protected and maintained. Furthermore, designing a strategy around them limits the scope of the organisation's strategy to those areas where it possesses clear competitive advantage, the sustainability of which is determined by the durability, transferability and replicability of the resources and capabilities. This in turn will influence the time frame of the strategic planning process. In industries where competitive advantage tends to be short lived (e.g. retailing, fashion, toys) then the organisation should focus on creating the flexibility and responsiveness that will enable them to create new advantages at a faster rate than the erosion of existing advantages.

In using capabilities as a cornerstone for the development of a competitive strategy, Stalk et al (1992) identified four principles. Firstly, they stated that strategy should be based on business processes as opposed to products and markets. Secondly, they argued that success depends upon transforming key processes into strategic capabilities to provide superior value to the customer. Thirdly, these capabilities are created by investing in support infrastructure that links together and transcends traditional SBUs and functions. Finally, because capabilities are cross functional their development needs the support of the CEO.

A danger of focusing on capabilities is that the firm becomes too inward looking. Stalk et al, in addressing this issue, note that a capability is only strategic when it begins and ends with the customer. Using capabilities as the focus does allow the organisation to create processes that may be robust and flexible enough to serve a wide range of businesses. In reinforcing the need to examine the organisation's resources and capabilities managers must first identify the strategic capabilities which are crucial to sustain and develop. Prahalad and Hamel (1990) identify three tests in the identification of core competencies:

- [] It must provide access to a wide variety of markets.
- [] It should make a significant contribution to the perceived customer benefits of the end product.
- [] It should be difficult for competitors to imitate.

Prahalad and Hamel note that few companies are likely to build world leadership in more than five or six fundamental competencies. They also note that it seems strange that managers are willing to compete for cash in the capital budgeting process, but are unwilling to compete for the organisation's most prized asset – its people.

FINANCIAL PLANNING AND MODELLING

The previous sections of this chapter have set out to explore a wide range of dimensions which impact on the planning process. We believe that some understanding of the difficulties and complexity of the strategy-making process are necessary prior to addressing financial planning.

The organisation's financial plans are often the most tangible output of the overall planning process. A particular plan of action is chosen because managers believe that it will reduce the gap between objectives and forecasts.

But the factors which contributed towards the choice of strategy – strengths, weaknesses, opportunities and threats – are not static. They will change over time as a result of internal or external factors or both. If suitable responses are not forthcoming, or if planned actions are not taken, confidence will be lost.

> The confidence that managers feel in a given strategy is less dependent upon actual results than upon the company successfully taking those actions prescribed in the plan and on their confidence in the continuing validity of the assumptions, forecasts, opinions, etc that went into their original strategic decision. (Argenti, 1974)

Discrepancies between planned and actual performance can arise for a variety of reasons. Intelligent use of a computer model, however, should enable ready identification of some of the underlying causes of variances. Here, too, confidence is a factor. In 1974, Grinyer and Wooller conducted a survey of the use of computer based financial models and found six main reasons connected with the success of a financial modelling exercise:

1. Sponsorship and continued support were given by top management.
2. Top management understood and had confidence in the model, and were prepared to place at least some reliance on forecast results.
3. The model met specific management decision-making needs.
4. The data required as input was readily available and not voluminous.
5. The model was embedded in the planning process (i.e. was used as a matter of course during normal planning procedures).
6. The model was properly documented throughout its development.

Failure tended to result if any three of these conditions were not present. It is our opinion that their findings would not be quite so relevant today, partly because of the PC revolution. Grinyer and

Wooller were talking of an era when models took a great deal of manpower and mainframe resources. Today modelling is more an extension of the desk calculator. Nevertheless, it is worthwhile learning from earlier mistakes.

Scenario planning can be described as a means of modelling the future. By taking the current state of the business and building in certain assumptions about the environment, a projected position is formulated. Utilising a dynamic model will allow the impact of these assumptions on the organisation's future performance to be assessed. The need for proportion is summarised by Argenti (1974):

> The key to a good scenario is that it should describe a *feasible* sequence of events that are consistent with each other and with the relevant features of the real world.

In constructing a scenario a variety of internal and external options may be considered which will encompass both qualitative and quantitative factors. Examples of internal options include:

increasing or reducing the workforce;
adding to or deleting from the product range;
changing products;
expanding or contracting production facilities;
changing production technology;
changing advertising;
changing distribution and marketing methods;
moving into new markets.

Some or all of these may be combined to form a scenario. It might be decided, for instance, to combine new markets, new products, new production facilities and new marketing to produce a particular scenario. Another scenario might be to take no action. Both can then be processed using a dynamic model and the results of each compared against a number of criteria, in particular the corporate objectives to which we referred in the previous section.

Also to be considered are external options. A variable such as sales volume, for example, is not entirely independent of assumptions about pricing and advertising/marketing expenditure. However, given a situation in which prices are determined and in which there already exists a pricing/advertising budget, the sales volume may very well be a function of factors and variables which are normally outside the company's control. These include exchange rates, inflation rates, interest rates and wage rates. Exchange rate movement, for instance, an area in which some fairly drastic developments have occurred in the past few years, can completely eliminate the profits of one market and open up competitive new opportunities in another part of the world. Similarly, wage rates are not entirely independent of production and capacity utilisation rates to the extent that low wage rates can impact adversely on industrial relations. So the overlap and mutuality of external and internal factors must constantly be borne in mind.

Table 8.1 (see page 215) shows some sample output from a hypothetical model. Each strategy has a range of different assumptions concerning capital investment, plant capacity, the quality or reliability of the product (and hence the competitive price that might be changed), industrial relations variables (e.g. production losses through strikes and the labour shedability factor), productivity and cost variables. Strategy A is a labour intensive, low capacity method of operation, while D is the reverse. Overtime can be incurred to provide up to an extra 25 per cent of capacity.

In the example, three different demand levels are considered for each strategy. Strategy A loses 20 per cent of production through strikes but by working overtime can actually achieve its theoretical capacity at the higher demand levels. The additional overtime costs ensure that the firm is profitable only when overtime is not being worked. It is interesting that in this example strategy D, the most capital intensive, is not as profitable as strategy C for the demand levels shown on the output.

Complexity versus simplicity

An important consideration when building a model is the number of variables to be used. On the whole, the greater the number the more realistic the model is likely to be. Equally, a simpler model is an easier vehicle for experimentation as the number of variables and assumptions are smaller and more easily remembered, and their impact more readily understood.

If an attempt is made to build a model that closely reflects reality, it is likely to become too complex. The Ford Motor Company, for example, probably offers well over 4,000 derivatives of its products. For short-term production forecasts this data may be vital to ensure accuracy. Producing a long-term plan based on over 4,000 derivatives would introduce enormous complexity. Data input requirements would be too great and probably too inaccurate; the modeller could not keep track of the effect of 4,000 sales variables; and experimentation with the model would be very difficult. In a longer-term model, therefore, it may be desirable simply to concentrate on either volumes of car sales or on major model derivatives (e.g. Fiesta/Escort/Orion/Sierra/Granada).

Another example lies in timber wholesalers. There are thousands of types of timber and typically it is cut into varying lengths, widths, depths, quality, type etc. For one model, just three key types of product – softwood, hardwood, plywood – were important variables for a long-term plan.

Taking account of external and internal factors, any number of scenarios can be drawn up for any given company. Some limit is clearly needed and for planning purposes the norm is three (although in some situations only two are used in order to force a choice). Where three scenarios are used, they can be presented in terms of high-, medium- and low-achievement. In these circumstances, however, there is a tendency always to choose the middle way. The more accepted approach is to project the so-called 'surprise free', i.e. expected scenario for comparison with two alternatives respectively representing better than expected and worse than expected outcomes.

An illustration of scenario planning is contained in *Jaguar: An Investor's Guide* which was prepared by Professor Bhaskar and members of the Motor Industry Research Unit prior to the return of Jaguar to private ownership (1984). The overall approach to its use of scenarios is described below. Since we are using it only as an example, however, much of the modelling output has been omitted; for the sake of brevity and simplicity we have restricted the inclusion of tables of figures to those which illustrate the process. A range of predictions of Jaguar's future profitability were produced in the following way.

Organisational strengths and weaknesses were identified as:

production and productivity;
components;
innovative manufacturing systems
capacity utilisation;
capital investment;
engineering resources – research and development;
personnel;
marketing.

Threats were identified as:

industrial arrest;
European competitors;
Japanese competitors;
take-over by a large vehicle manufacturer;
risks attached to new product acceptability.

With this data in mind, three different product scenarios were drawn up and combined with four alternative sales scenarios.

The three product scenarios were:

☐ Maintenance of existing range. It was assumed that what was then called the XJ40 would replace the XJ saloon range in 1985. (As readers will be aware it has been launched as the new XJ6.)
☐ Existing range plus replacement of the XJS by the XJ41 in or soon after 1987.
☐ Full range comprising the two strategies outlined above and an additional new small saloon introduced around 1990.

The sales scenarios were:

☐ Low: a pessimistic view
☐ Mixed: initially in line with the medium but subsequently falling to low as competition increases.
☐ Medium: between high and low.
☐ High: an optimistic view.

Two central cases were highlighted from the outset. For both it was assumed that the second of the three product strategies above, i.e. existing plus sports range, would be employed. The two cases were:

☐ The *mixed central case* which assumes that each new model introduced sells well initially. However, due to a combination of the novelty wearing off and aggressive action by competitors, sales figures subside to a lower level.
☐ The *medium central case* which assumes that initial sales figures hold up, and that Jaguar's competitors take no aggressive action to counteract the company's success.

Certain assumptions were made about:

incremental sales;
pricing structure;
geographical spread of sales;
capital investment;
numbers of engineering personnel;
other revenue (spin off products and consultancy);
advertising costs;
labour;
raw materials;
dividends;
exchange rates.

The assumptions about each of these were expressed in terms of each of the three product strategies.

The four sales scenarios were assessed against the three product strategies and the results are shown in Table 8.1.

Reference was made to other assumptions which had been made ranging from raw material costs to short-term debt interest rates. In conclusion, however, it was noted that: 'It should be borne in mind that the art of building financial models is to strike the correct balance between complexity and simplicity so as to reflect the real world in a meaningful way.'

Having established four sales scenarios for each of the product strategies, forecasts of profit before interest and tax (PBIT) and net profit were made for each (Table 8.1). The figures for 1984 and 1985 show no difference between the mixed-, medium- and high-scenarios because similar performance in these early years was assumed for each of them. From 1986 the differences become much more marked.

Summary statistics for the twelve permutations were calculated to show:

sales quantity;
revenue;
PBIT;
net profit;
cash flow;
assets employed;
working capital;
return of sales;
total debt/equity;
return on capital employed.

Full income statements and balance sheets were produced for the two central case projections. To summarise, they showed that the mixed case would generate sales up to 54,000 in 1989, stabilising at around 45,000 in the 1990s. Revenue would peak at £689 million in 1992. Peak net profits of £130 million were projected for 1989 decreasing thereafter to a sustainable level of £72 million. The medium case showed a higher sustainable level of sales (55,500) and revenue (£843m) in 1992 after peaking in 1990/1. Net profits were sustainable at the 1992 level of £118 million.

Having demonstrated that all twelve scenarios would show profits, consideration was given to problems which might arise and which could have a detrimental effect. These included a 10 per cent fall in the $/£ exchange rate from that assumed in the model, a 10 per cent rise in raw material prices which was not passed on in higher prices, a 10 per cent reduction in the price of all cars and a prolonged strike (for these purposes a strike of three months was assumed). The

Table 8.1 An example of a strategic model

	Strategy A			Strategy B			Strategy C			Strategy D		
		Low	Medium	High	Low	Medium	High	Low	Medium	High	Low	Medium	High
Capital investment ($)		10,000,000			20,000,000			25,000,000			30,000,000	
Plant capacity (units)		50,000			75,000			100,000			115,000	
Price ($)		660			728			735			742	
Labour shedability factor (%)		50			40			25			10	
Strike factor (%)		80			85			88			93	
Average wage ($)		7,000			7,500			10,000			12,000	
Theoretical productivity		24			42			54			63	
Fixed overheads ($)		375,000			400,000			430,000			440,000	
Variable overheads per unit ($)		25			30			35			37	
Warranty costs per unit ($)		20			19			17			15	
Material costs per unit ($)		100			98			97			96	
Demand	Low	Medium	High	Low	Medium	High	Low	Medium	High	Low	Medium	High
Demand (units)	40,000	65,000	90,000	40,000	65,000	90,000	40,000	65,000	90,000	40,000	65,000	90,000
Actual sales (units)	32,000	50,000	50,000	34,000	55,250	76,500	32,500	57,200	79,200	37,200	60,450	83,700
Actual productivity (units)	17	24	24	23	33	43	22	34	44	22	35	47
Capacity (%)	80	100	100	53	87	100	40	65	90	35	57	78
Theoretical no of employees	2,083	2,083	2,083	1,786	1,786	1,786	1,852	1,852	1,852	1,825	1,825	1,825
Actual no of employees	1,875	2,083	2,083	1,452	1,690	1,786	1,574	1,690	1,806	1,706	1,746	1,786
Income Statement												
Revenue ($'000)	21,120	33,000	33,000	24,752	40,222	55,692	25,872	42,042	58,212	27,602	44,854	62,105
Material costs ($'000)	3,200	5,000	5,000	3,332	5,415	7,497	3,414	5,548	7,682	3,571	5,803	8,035
Labour costs ($'000)	13,125	24,299	24,299	10,893	12,679	21,423	15,741	16,898	18,056	20,476	20,952	21,429
Warranty costs ($'000)	640	1,000	1,000	646	1,050	1,454	598	972	1,346	558	907	1,256
Overhead costs ($'000)	1,175	1,625	1,625	1,420	2,058	2,695	1,662	2,432	3,202	1,816	2,677	3,537
Depreciation ($'000)	1,000	1,000	1,000	2,000	2,000	2,000	2,500	2,500	2,500	3,000	3,000	3,000
Profit before interest ($'000)	1,980	76	76	6,461	17,022	20,623	1,956	13,691	25,426	-1,819	11,515	24,849
Interest ($'000)	90	90	90	215	215	215	295	295	295	295	295	295
Net profit ($'000)	1,890	-14	-14	6,246	16,807	20,408	1,661	13,396	25,131	-2,114	11,220	24,554

financial model was re-run to take account of these figures and to show the effect of each.

The final step in the process was to assess each of the product strategies in terms of low-, medium-, mixed- and high-sales scenarios, again with special reference to the two central cases, and to suggest a probable optimum product strategy.

Decision support systems

In closing this section on financial planning and modelling it is worth looking briefly at decision support systems. We return to decision support systems in the next chapter. The term decision support systems (DSS), which describes computer-based analytical aids to decision making, was coined way back in 1970 by Peter Keen. A key difference between DSS and data processing (DP) was the interaction with the end user, typically a manager using the computer system without assistance or formal training. The system would therefore be 'user friendly'.

We would encourage managers to employ a variety of systems appropriate to the situation together with their own skills. Long dormant expertise in mathematics, statistics, operational research and econometrics subjects which underpin much of this area, may be re-awakened, particularly in relation to the new user friendly mathematics processors and statistics packages which guide the user through the intricacies and overcome mundane number crunching. An added bonus is that many of these packages produce results as graphic output, providing less experienced users with easily comprehended information. Recommending the use of the right system does, of course, assume a knowledge of what systems are on the market and what those systems offer. In talking to managers at all levels, we are constantly surprised at how little is known about the availability of even quite elementary tools.

One underlying unease remains. Even in our own text we have been guilty of simplifying reality into known accounting structures which are themselves models. Although better, more refined tools will continue to be developed, their value can only be optimised if we, the modellers, improve our understanding of reality and build more sophisticated and verifiable models.

Bhaskar and Housden (1983) summarised the difference between existing and potential financial models:

> Clear cut accounting models deal with accounting relationships that involve mainly addition and subtraction . . . Representational models deal with the underlying economic relationships.

Only through careful and thorough analysis can we adequately generate a richly drawn picture of the firm's environment and the influences on it. Using a variety of methods to establish a model structure of the environment will enhance our ability to produce effective and efficient decision support systems.

SUMMARY

Corporate strategy and strategy processes were then discussed in order to place the use of financial planning and modelling into a broader corporate setting. We recognised that the seemingly rational corporate planning approach was subject to much criticism and rated that it may lead to restrictive choices for the organisation. Nevertheless, many techniques associated with corporate planning are widely used in organisations so we concluded that providing the *process* was not allowed to dictate, then its use could assist in understanding the complexity facing organisations. Having explored a wide range of issues we concluded by considering financial planning and modelling by focusing on the use of computer-based models. The return of Jaguar Cars to private ownership as an example of financial modelling was used to illustrate the process.

FURTHER READING

Bowman and Asch (1987) discuss the issues surrounding the development of corporate strategy. Kaye G R and Bhaskar, K N have written a series for Economist Publications Ltd, *Financial Planning with Personal Computers* which explores the latter part of this chapter in greater depth:
  Volume 1, Cash Flow Forecasting (1985);
  Volume 2, Management Accounting Reports (1985);
  Volume 3, Budgeting (1986);
  Volume 4, Scenario Planning (1987).

REFERENCES

Argenti, J (1984) *Systematic Corporate Planning*, Nelson, London.
Bowman, C and Asch, D (1987) *Strategic Management*, Macmillan, Houndmills, Basingstoke.
Bowman, C and Asch, D (1996) *Managing Strategy*, Macmillan, Houndmills, Basingstoke.

Bhaskar, K N and Housden, R J W (1983) *Accounting Information Systems and Data Processing*, Heinemann, London.

Bhaskar, K N and members of the Motor Industry Research Unit (1984) *Jaguar: An Investors Guide*, University of East Anglia, MIRU.

Grant, R M (1991) 'The resource-based theory of competitive advantage: implications for strategy formulation', *California Management Review*, Spring, pp 114–135.

Grinyer, P H and Wooller, J (1978) *Corporate Models Today*, ICAEW, London.

Peters, T J and Waterman, R H (1982) *In Search of Excellence*, Harper & Row, New York.

Porter, M E (1983) *Competitive Advantage*, Free Press, New York.

Prahalad, C K and Hamel, G (1990) 'The core competence of the corporation', Harvard Business Review, May–June, pp 79–91.

Quinn, J B (1980) *Strategies for Change*, Irwin, Homewood, Illinois.

9

Decision making

INTRODUCTION

In Chapter 8 we looked at the role of financial planning in a wider organisational context. The modelling approach adopted in this book tends to presuppose a rational decision process. Such an approach may be viewed with suspicion so we will in this chapter try to redress the balance with a discussion of firstly the role and styles of management followed by individual and group influences on decision making.

We will also provide a description of the decision making process and how it may be supported through *decision support systems* that may include financial planning models.

THE MANAGEMENT ROLE

> *'I won't keep a dog and bark myself.'*
> Jonathan Swift (1667–1745)

Lessem (1989) suggests there are four domains of management theory represented around the globe. The rational or scientific approach has been championed by Peter Drucker (1979), but dates back to the movement founded by F W Taylor and is embedded in the mass-production era of industry, with machine paced workers. In contrast, Tom Peters (1982) encourages us to return to basics and 'thrive on chaos'. The third emerging domain is the 'corporate culture' in which the myths and beliefs of the organisation, as practised in its rituals, are the focus of attention (Owen, 1987).

The fourth approach is developmental and is firmly based outside the USA, and while it is associated frequently with Japanese management styles owes its origins to Central Europe at the turn of the century (Lievgoed, 1973). The industrialising countries in the nineteenth century were characterised by the enterprising personality and the spirit of national independence. These metamorphosed into those of organisational man and the dependence on the institution. Today this is interpreted to mean individual and local autonomy, combined with institutional and global interdependence. To quote the current slogan, 'think global, act local'.

The 1970s saw the start of a new economic force from Japan. As Europe and the USA saw their post-war economic miracles fade and the growth of the Pacific basin industries, management researchers turned to Japan for answers. The initial differences were obvious: aggressive market-based products, rational organisations, etc. However, the fundamental difference lay in another quarter:

> The trouble with the Japanese is that they have never really caught up with Adam Smith. They don't believe in the invisible hand. They believe that you cannot get a decent moral society, not even an efficient society, simply out of the mechanisms of the market, powered by the motivational fuel of self-interest. The morality has got to come from the hearts, the wills, and the motives of the individuals within it. (Dore, 1987).

Pascale and Athos (1982) compared and contrasted the eastern and western manager and concluded that:

> Eastern management lore sensitises its managers to be wary of illusions of mastery and to suspect the notion that at any one time anything is truly decided. Whereas western management beliefs tend to portray a decision as fixed and final, Eastern philosophical tradition emphasises individual accommodation to continuously unfolding set of events.

Western managers' ideals are based on Protestant ideologies of Smith and Weber, while Japanese managers draw on Buddhism and Confucianism. The latter emphasises reciprocity and is more in tune with 'serving the customer'.

Lessem (1991) suggests that the four main functions of an organisation are:

- Process Management
- Resource Management
- Relations Management
- Information and Communication Management.

The fifth leadership function is interdisciplinary, and this is the role of management. Lievgoed (1973) suggests a model that typifies the functions and their interaction within the organisation is the four leaf clover shown below:

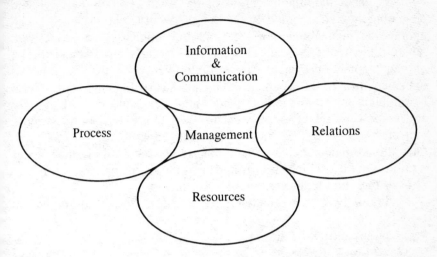

The four functions are shown as the leaves while the management is represented by the line encompassing and co-ordinating each of the functions but also linking with the external world. This particular metaphor removes the concept of a hierarchy and replaces it with a web or network that links the functions.

An important message from many current writers on management following Lievgoed, is the role of management in developing the organisation. This popular role reflects a shift from the stewardship model of early agricultural management. Management is now focused on change, both reactively and proactively. The proactive elements suggest some developmental role. Anthony (1965) suggested that planning and control systems within organisations could be classified into a hierarchy of:

He suggested that senior management is concerned with the long-term direction of the organisation. Middle management was concerned with the tactical implementation of the strategy. This required the development and acquisition of the capability and resources. The operational management of the front line managers was to ensure the fulfilment of the goal. This mechanistic and hierarchical model of management has been a powerful influence on the literature of management and reflects the military models of line and staff. These hierarchical models have been under attack recently with delayering and empowerment of employees. In many respects it is the middle management level that has found itself most severely squeezed. Operational managers have found themselves increasingly interfacing with the tactical which in turn has been closer to the strategy in the light of the volatile and turbulent environments.

Traditionally, management activity has been thought to involve:

- planning
- control
- decision making
- motivation, and
- co-ordination.

However many writers have described managers as having less structured activities with an inclination to 'muddle through' (Mintzberg, 1973).

DECISION MAKING PROCESSES

The processes of planning and control are arguably inseparable. Decision making is perceived as both the primary task and a wider role for management, whether for routine or ad hoc events. Motivation and co-ordination reflect the importance of the behavioural dimension in ensuring that management's intentions are carried out through other people. This later perspective cannot easily be modelled and hence is often omitted from models undermining their predictive capabilities.

Gilligan, Neale and Murray (1983) suggest that a decision cycle exists which links the elements together:

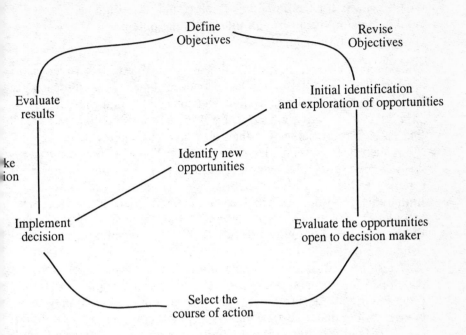

Define Objectives

Revise Objectives

Evaluate results

Initial identification and exploration of opportunities

Identify new opportunities

ke
ion

Implement decision

Evaluate the opportunities open to decision maker

Select the course of action

From the plan embodied in the objective to the decision and the subsequent control. To this end, management science has developed techniques to support decision making which form the tools of modelling:

- probability
- decision theory
- linear programming
- economic order quantity
- Pareto analysis
- discounted flow
- network analysis
- simulation.

See Bridges (1989) for the application of econometric modelling and operational techniques to decision making. Many of these techniques exploit computers to solve the mathematics and a range of application packages has been developed to support this work (Plane, 1986). These application packages are the founding fathers of modelling systems embodying the development of sub-routines for model building.

These rational approaches seek to optimise the decision assuming that:

- ☐ adequate information is available or estimable
- ☐ the criteria for the outcome are clear and unambiguous
- ☐ the decision maker has an interest in the outcome
- ☐ the problem is solvable.

The common criteria for the decision are cost benefits. However, these are not the only criteria, available or used. Quality has increasingly been a criteria of performance and decision making and while it may be expressed quantitatively, frequently it incorporates qualitative aspects that may be more subjective than objective measurement.

Frequently in making decisions we may have several criteria we wish to maximise. Mathematical techniques can accommodate multi criteria in the objective function and incorporate adjustments in limitations in order to achieve the defined goal. However, these techniques are very sophisticated and while available in user-friendly software, often require the aide of a facilitator (mathematician) to help define the model.

Decisions that are structurable into mathematical models may be developed into programs to support routine decision making. Linear programming models frequently incorporated into production systems were blending materials to achieve acceptable compounds at minimum cost (e.g. feed and flour compounding). Non routine decisions may still exploit some of these techniques through the increasingly available applications packages, some of which utilise spreadsheets as a form of data input template (e.g. Crystal Ball, Goal!).

Where rules are applied to the decision, these may be formally declared or implicit in heuristics. In the case of the formal declaration these may be programmed even when complex into application packages such as expert systems (Crystal). The expert system may be compared with the human expert to tease out the subtle nuances. Where rules are not easily discernible then actual behaviour may be monitored and the computer used to identify patterns of behaviour on which rules may be built (Neural Networks).

/Decision making may include an aspect of problem solving. The process of problem solving normally comprises four stages:

1. Recognition of the problem.
2. Search for courses of action which address the problem.
3. Evaluation of these alternatives.
4. Choice of one or more alternatives.

To these can be added control, whereby actual against planned results can be monitored, compared and contrasted.

Managers frequently solve problems, not by optimising, but by satisfising. The 'rules of thumb' or heuristics may have rational explanations or they may represent an approach to coping with uncertainty and risk. However, the mathematician will encourage the manager to quantify the uncertainty by drawing on past experience or expectations of feasible ranges of outcome. The use of probability and statistics of past events will allow increased confidence in the information available to the decision maker.

An important filtration process needs to be applied to the available data in order to only include relevant costs in our decision. A relevant cost is a cost that is expected to occur and which differs from the other costs in the other possible alternative courses of action being considered. The sunk cost (i.e. past costs) of what we paid for a car is not relevant to a decision on a cost of repair. The future value of the car after the repair *is* relevant. Any loss in value implied on the vehicle has already been lost. However, in making our decision to spend money on repairing the car we must include the opportunity cost of using the money for the car rather than leaving the money earning interest in the bank or spending it on a holiday. In examining the alternative of a holiday or repair to the car, both decisions have the same opportunity cost of lost interest on the money in the bank that is therefore irrelevant to deciding between either the holiday or car repair. It is the difference between the alternatives that we must focus on in making our choice.

Most decisions are based on examining the monetary values of the alternatives. Here care must be taken to compare like with like as the monetary unit may be based on different criteria. For example, materials may be valued at historic or replacement cost, while future income may be expressed in real or nominal values. Adjustment may be required to ensure the correct values are used in the calculations.

Care should be taken with the benefits as both tangible and intangible benefits may arise. A severe problem has occurred with a number of new technology investment decisions that have failed to identify all the costs and benefits. This is because both costs and benefits included in the decision will depend on the boundaries drawn for the decision. The investment in the desktop personal computer is unlikely to include the associated costs of medical care of the user which may arise from incorrect posture or overuse causing eye strain. While these may be treated as hidden costs and benefits, there may also be intangible benefits such as fewer letters despatched with spelling mistakes, such benefits may be unquantifiable.

We must not forget that the decision maker is exercising judgement and in doing so demonstrating preference. We should not rely on the computer program to make our decision but inform our decision

226 / Financial Planning

making. The computer program can include in its calculation that which we have coded in. In this way, subjectivity will be excluded and elements that cannot be coded in the prescribed manner may also be excluded. The mathematical model may only be a partial model of the decision, hence the decision maker may need to reflect on the information available and exercise judgement.

INDIVIDUAL AND GROUP INFLUENCES ON DECISION MAKING

Implicit in our discussion so far is the assumption that a rational approach to problem solving will produce a 'good decision'. In this section we will seek to develop further some of the issues flagged in Chapter 1 concerning the influence that individual managers and groups of managers may have. So, our first question is to determine what a good decision is. Janis and Mann (1979) suggest that high quality decisions are more likely to emerge if the decision-maker:

1. thoroughly canvasses a wide range of alternative courses of action;
2. surveys the full range of objectives to be fulfilled and the values implicated by the choice;
3. carefully weighs whatever he knows about the costs and risks of negative consequences, as well as the positive consequences, that could flow from each alternative;
4. intensively searches for new information relevant to further evaluation of the alternatives;
5. correctly assimilates and takes account of any new information or expert judgement to which he is exposed, even when the information or judgement does not support the course of action he initially prefers;
6. re-examines the positive and negative consequences of all known alternatives, including those originally regarded as unacceptable, before making a final choice.

This rational and comprehensive approach would appear to exclude an intuitive decision that nevertheless may result, for instance, in the introduction of a very successful product.

One of the dangers in an over-reliance on systematic approaches to decision making (of which the modelling method described earlier is one variant) is that it can stifle flair, intuition, inspiration and creativity, in favour of rather dull but highly justifiable, 'logical' decisions. The ideal solution might be to devise a process that incorporates the best features of both, that is, the comprehensiveness of the systematic approach combined with a capacity for generating and incorporating novelty and ingenuity into the process.

Individual factors

Whether decisions are made by individuals or by groups, there are factors affecting individuals that may help us understand why particular decisions are made.

Bounded rationality describes the limited perception of decision-makers, bounded by their experience, information, etc. The concept has been used to distinguish views of how decisions are actually made (for example, 'satisficing' decisions) from the omnisciently rational entrepreneur assumed in the more abstract economic models. An individual may, however, make 'rational' decisions, but these decisions are only *relatively* rational; rational in the context of the decision-maker's knowledge, perception and objectives. For example, an executive seeking a solution to a problem retains his perception of the presenting problem's major features while discarding complexities viewed as irrelevant. As a result:

1. satisficing replaces optimising – satisfactory levels of the criterion variable, rather than optimum levels, are required;
2. alternative courses of action are discovered sequentially through search processes;
3. repertories of action programmes are developed by organisations and individuals and these serve as the alternatives of choice in recurrent situations;
4. each specific programme deals with a limited range of situations and consequences;
5. each programme is capable of being executed in semi-independence of the others – they are only loosely coupled together.

Furthermore the range of possible alternatives considered is constrained by the organisation itself. 'The organisation represents the walls of the maze and, by and large, organisational decisions have to do with solving maze problems, not reconstructing the maze wall' (Katz and Kahn, 1966, p.459).

The concept of bounded rationality can be extended into the notion of 'psychological rationality' (in contrast, say, to 'objective' or 'economic' rationality). Here an individual manager may make a decision that is irrational in terms of the profit goal, but is rational in terms of his psychological disposition.

Perceptual biases and distortions stem largely from the need to simplify complexity, to make information and experiences manageable. A brief description of these biases and distortions is attempted below (the interested reader is referred to Katz and Kahn's *The Social Psychology of Organisations*):

Cognitive nearsightedness refers to the tendency to pay more attention to physical, quantitative, visible and immediate factors at the expense of intangibles and dimensions of the problem that are remote in time and place. This can seriously distort decision making, and the use of quantitative techniques, in forecasting for example, often exacerbates this tendency.

Global thinking refers to a way of simplifying the world to create a few categories (the fewer the better) and lumping people and things into them. Prejudice is one aspect of this tendency, literally pre-judging on the basis of some inappropriate categorisation, and the more psychologically remote a group is, the more susceptible it is to these distorted perceptions.

Dichotomised thinking (or 'black and white' thinking) means something is either all good or all bad, there are no in-between, curate's-egg positions. In reality, almost any problem concerning people introduces a fuzzy, unsatisfactory collection of contradictory factors that, if they are ignored in favour of a quick and easy assessment using extremes, will result in valuable information being lost in the decision process.

Oversimplification of cause and effect, that is, a problem of logical, 'straight-line' thinking refers to the tendency to search for one-way connections between variables: x causes y – whereas, not only may z affect y, but y may affect x. Again, in an effort to cut through complexity, we can oversimplify our analysis of the situation.

Positions and experiences may lead us to view the world from our positions in 'social space' (that is, class, income, culture, education, job) and from our place within the organisation. If we change our role in the organisation (for instance on promotion) not only is our overt behaviour likely to change, but the way we think may change as well. We can also tend to assume that everyone thinks as we do. For example, a manager might assume that a subordinate would be motivated by a prospect of promotion just because *he* is.

Because each of us can only enjoy a severely limited range of experiences, our perceptions must be limited accordingly. Unless a conscious effort is made to reverse this tendency, career and life-styles may lead to a narrowing of experiences.

Proactive v *reactive* refer to the fact that many management writers advocate that managerial work should consist of planning, organising, motivating, communicating and controlling (or some other permutation of these and similar laudable activities). In reality, too many managers could best describe their jobs as fire-fighting of one form or another. The management role is often seen as having to deal with problems, disturbances and interruptions to routine with which staff feel unable to deal (or the manager thinks they are not capable of doing so). 'Management by exception' elevates this situation to the status of a prescriptive theory of management. So a 'good day' is when the telephone never rings and no one knocks on the door!

It is not surprising, therefore, that the essentially reactive nature of much managerial work does not encourage the development of positive attitudes towards planning.

Commitment refers to the extent to which a person will be bound to the decision that he or she takes (either legally or psychologically). The degree of commitment will affect decision making behaviour.

Information preference relates to what sort of information managers seem to prefer. Mintzberg (1973) identified the manager's preference for 'live' information:

☐ Managers place greater reliance on up-to-date information even if it may not be thoroughly verified.
☐ Managers tend to favour verbal information, telephone conversations, formal and informal meetings.

As a consequence, much of the information upon which decisions are made is undocumented and qualitative. This tends to set up a resistance to decision-making techniques that rely on amassing large amounts of dated, quantitative information because vital qualitative information is locked in the manager's head, this information can only be incorporated in the decision if the particular manager is actively engaged in the decision-making process. No matter how sophisticated the techniques used, if a vital piece of qualitative information is not available to the analyst, the conclusions are likely to be rejected.

Group factors

There are numerous ways of making decisions, some ad hoc, some systematic, and some group processes. The cohesion that may result from the use of a group may be a positive outcome, but there are factors that impair the effective working of groups.

Janis has labelled the suspension of critical judgement that results from the individuals' effort to maintain group cohesion as 'group think'. In an effort not to rock the boat and be seen as a poor group member, doubts and criticisms which the individual may have about the decisions the group is taking are held in check.

Symptoms of the 'group think' phenomena are:

1. An illusion of invulnerability, shared by most or all of the members, which creates excessive optimism and encourages the taking of extreme risks.
2. Collective efforts to rationalise in order to discount warnings which might lead the members to reconsider their assumptions before they recommit themselves to their past policy decisions.
3. An unquestioned belief in the group's inherent morality, inclining the members to ignore the ethical or moral consequences of their decisions.
4. Stereotyped views of rivals and enemies as too evil to warrant genuine attempts to negotiate, or as too weak or stupid to counter whatever risky attempts are made to defeat their purposes.
5. Direct pressure on any member who expresses strong arguments against any of the group's stereotypes, illusions or commitments, making clear that such dissent is contrary to what is expected of all loyal members.
6. Self-censorship of deviations from the apparent group consensus, reflecting each member's inclination to minimise to himself the importance of his doubts and counter-arguments.
7. A shared illusion of unanimity, partly resulting from this self-censorship and augmented by the false assumption that silence implies consent.
8. The emergence of self appointed 'mind guards' – members who protect the group from adverse information that might shatter their shared complacency about the effectiveness and morality of their decisions. (Janis and Mann, 1979, p 130).

Janis suggested some ways of overcoming group think:

1. The leader of the group assigns the role of critical evaluator to each member, including himself. Doubts and criticisms are positively encouraged within the group. However, this suggestion may be rather hard to implement as nobody relishes criticism.
2. The leader should not bias the group towards a particular decision, wittingly or unwittingly, by the way that guidance as to what is to

be accomplished, is initially given. A group can easily become sensitive to the wishes of the leader, thus producing the 'right' decision.

3. Members of the group should seek advice from trusted colleagues who are outside the group. Fresh perspectives can thus be introduced.

4. A devil's advocate role should be assigned to a group member (or members). The role should have high status in the group and it should preferably be rotated.

5. A 'second chance' meeting should be held to permit members to express any residual doubts they have about the consensus the group has reached.

Other group-related problems include:

□ *Risky shift*, a term which describes a tendency for groups to make riskier decisions than individuals, because of factors such as: dispersed responsibility; influential members having more extreme views; the tendency for individuals to become more extreme in their views when placed on the defensive; 'moderate' members remaining silent.

□ *Interaction problems*, here we are referring to the behaviour of group members which acts to impair the working of the group: sniping at others; adopting hidden agendas (for example, criticising someone's ideas as a way of putting them down); over-talking; ignoring 'low status' contributors; protecting personal interests and reputations; distorting or withholding information.

□ *Procedural problems* refer to the fact that the way meetings are arranged and conducted can either oil the decision-making wheels or make them grind to a halt.

DECISION SUPPORT SYSTEMS

The previous chapter introduced the term *decision support systems* (DSS). A key difference between DSS and data processing (DP) was the interaction with the end user, typically a manager using the computer system without assistance or formal training. The system would therefore be 'user friendly'.

The recognition of the importance of the task context and organisational positioning and behaviour was not ignored by these developers but the available tools at that time severely restricted their capacity to deliver generalisable systems. Consequently the DSS in the 1970s/1980s were restricted to specific tasks and organisational situations.

With the proliferation of personal computers, user friendliness has become the norm, but DSSs have remained essentially associated with operational research techniques including linear programming and modelling. Recently, there has been a move back to DSSs as a result of the linking of corporate databases with personal computers, using Local Area Networks and Wide Area Networks communication systems. This has permitted the available data to be processed through a variety of user friendly, micro-based packages from linear programming, statistical analysis, etc, to established modelling systems. Some of these packages have their origin in cumbersome mainframe systems that, when revised to fit a micro, have been given completely new user interfaces. Others are entirely new systems.

Alter (1977) suggested a taxonomy of decision support systems spanning from:

□ The filing cabinet
□ Data analysis systems
□ Databases and small models
□ Accounting models
□ Representational models
□ Optimising models
□ Suggestion models.

While the lowest may be described as the systematic storage of data by main structures to enable ease of retrieval, the development of databases reflects advances in data processing to enable hierarchical, as well as relative, retrieval of data. The development of accounting models reflects the convergence of information processing systems from data processing with theoretical frameworks of knowledge and understanding. The subsequent development of higher level models exploits the management sciences to support rational decision making. However, the final category reflects the incorporation of intelligence and experience and may be seen in expert systems and the application of neural networks to problem solving with complex data. These latter systems incorporate not only data but knowledge represented by rules and evidence.

SUMMARY

To go forward we must learn from each philosophy and adapt it to our circumstances. Rejecting one for another fails to recognise the strength of each to its circumstance. This developmental approach recognises the cultural diversity, the influence of the environment and the historic location of the development. Steiner (1945) developed a

philosophy for economic and social renewal in the aftermath of World
War II, and while his work is more associated with caring communities,
important lessons on social organisations may be drawn. A key concept
underlying Steiner's work was the development of communities that
were *sustainable* and capable of growth and renewal.

In our discussion of individual and group influences, we identified
a number of issues, (but by no means an exhaustive selection) which
impact on the quality of decisions. It seems axiomatic to us, therefore,
that any of the processes outlined throughout this book must take
account of *all* aspects if we are to enhance and improve organisational
decision making. A truly sophisticated model would need to capture not
just the 'facts' (whatever they are), but also to some extent the meaning
of that information to the manager struggling with the problem.

FURTHER READING

For a fuller discussion of individual and group factors, Katz and Kahn
(1966) and Janis and Mann (1979) are well worth dipping into.

REFERENCES

Cretein, P D, Ball, S E and Brigham, E F (1987) *Financial Management Using Lotus 1–2–3*, Dryden Press.

Jackson, M (1985) *Creative Modelling with Lotus 1–2–3*, Wiley, Chichester.

Jackson, M (1988) *Advanced Spreadsheet Modelling with Lotus 1–2–3*, Wiley, Chichester.

Janis, I L and Mann, L (1979) *Decision Making*, Free Press, New York.

Katz, D and Kahn, R L (1966) *The Social Psychology of Organisations*, Wiley, Chichester.

Kaye, G R and Bhaskar, K N (1985) 'Cash Flow Forecasting', Vol 1 in *Financial Planning with Personal Computers*, Economist Publications Ltd.

Kaye, G R and Bhaskar, K N (1986) 'Management Accounting Reports', Vol 2 in *Financial Planning with Personal Computers*, Economist Publications Ltd.

Kaye, G R and Bhaskar, K N (1986) 'Budgeting', Vol 3 in *Financial Planning with Personal Computers*, Economist Publications Ltd.

Kaye, G R and Bhaskar, K N (1986) 'Corporate Planning', Vol 4 in *Financial Planning with Personal Computers*, Economist Publications Ltd.

Lewis, C (1989) *Business Forecasting in a Lotus 1–2–3 Environment*, Wiley, Chichester.

Mintzberg, H (1973) *The Nature of Managerial Work*, Harper and Row, London.

Osborne, C W Kyd (1986) *Financial Modelling Using Lotus 1–2–3*, McGraw-Hill, New York.

Person, R (1991) *Using Excel for Windows*, QUE.

Remenyi, D and Nugus, S (1988) *Business Applications in Lotus 1–2–3: A guide to forecasting, risk analysis, backward iterations and simulation*, McGraw-Hill, New York.

Sherwood, D (1983) *Financial Modelling Practical Guide*, G & Co.

Weizenbaum, J (1984) *Computer Power and Human Reason*, Pelican.

10

Planning and Modelling Tools and Methods

INTRODUCTION

Previous chapters have explored a wide range of financial and modelling issues. We considered what might be meant by the use of the word 'model' in Chapter 1 before going on to discuss financial statements (which are of course a model of the organisation) and financial structures in Chapters 2 and 3. Many areas of concern to managers were then considered, including costs and decision making (Chapter 4), managing working capital (Chapter 5), investment appraisal (Chapter 6) and budgeting and control (Chapter 7).

Clearly much of our previous discussion has involved us in building models of some description. Some of these models were fairly straightforward such as those depicting cost-volume-profit relationships, others were much more complex like the Jaguar model. In this our concluding chapter we will discuss an approach to modelling which can be applied to both simple and complex cases. We will also look at alternatives available for the development of models from spreadsheets to programming languages.

MODELLING TOOLS

There are a number of available technologies for model building. However, the most important requirements for the modeller are:

A brain.
Pencil and paper.

Without the ability to think and develop conceptual models that can be expressed in diagrams, words and mathematical relationships, we are unable to model. All models should first be developed on paper before encoding on the computer. Subsequent development may be done at the keyboard but even then there is a need not only to think but also to document thoughts on what is being developed.

Most planning and development today takes place in the micro-computer environment and much of the quest for increased speed and memory stems from developers' desires to continue to run large models on micros rather than transfer to mini or mainframe environments. This is justified on the relative costs of both hardware and software but security and integrity of micros is fragile and should not be overlooked.

Essentially a modeller has four alternative approaches for developing a computer model. Generally all four are available on the full range of machines from mainframe to micro. However, certain machines are restricted in the choices offered but generally any system in use for business applications should be able to offer:

☐ General Purpose Programming Language.
☐ Fourth Generation Languages.
☐ Modelling Systems.
☐ Spreadsheets.

The advantage of a modelling system is that it enables a model to be developed in less time (by a factor between 3 and 5) with the loss of some flexibility. On the other hand, it usually uses more computer time in processing (in micro seconds) for a given model than the general purpose language. Originally, modelling used to be carried out using cheap and readily available general–purpose programming languages such as BASIC, FORTRAN or PASCAL. A model developed using such a programming language could take a long time and hence could be costly, but was portable across systems. It usually involved not only programmers and computer operators but often operational research personnel and systems analysts who formally defined the problem, the logic and the output requirements to the programmers who wrote and debugged the code.

Fourth Generation languages (e.g. FOCUS) have increased program-ming productivity and allowed end-users to write their own programs, including faster models.

The choice of a modelling system is more difficult since there are increasing numbers on offer, with a more even distribution of usage. The first modelling packages, e.g. ICL's PROSPER consisted of named sub-routines within the programming language that formed a library available to the user as opposed to the programmer. However, the user needed to be skilled and often became a specialist modeller. The choice of a modelling system is restricted with some being offered on both mainframe and micro, e.g. EPS-FCS. There still remains a need for mainframe modelling, particularly with networked systems, large scale models, integrated office systems, etc.

Modelling systems in turn have a number of advantages including easier input and output operations. Modelling systems normally allow immediate output in a somewhat messy format, while with more effort a neat report can usually be generated. The main section of a modelling system deals with the logic of a model; modelling systems are not always as flexible as a general purpose programming language in this instance. There are six areas in which they do have an advantage:

1. *Multiple products.* Some (but not all) modelling systems allow the incorporation of multiple products in an easy way and/or facilitate the totalling of rows or columns.
2. *Functions or sub-routines.* A few modelling systems provide a comprehensive array of functions for calculating tax, depreciation, and so forth, which makes it very easy to program the model using these functions as part of the modelling system.
3. *Vector approach.* Modelling systems automatically adopt a matrix or vector approach to programming. The looping over time is also performed automatically by the modelling system.
4. *Consolidation.* Some modelling systems provide a facility that makes the consolidation of divisional or company models a less complicated task.
5. *Sensitivity analysis* and *'what if' questions*. Modelling systems are usually geared to the modeller performing this task.
6. *Totalling over periods.* Modelling systems are generally capable of totalling quarterly, half-yearly or cumulative results with a simple instruction.

With the explosion of the micro-computer market in the late 1970s and 1980s, a new type of software package was heralded in, i.e. 'the spreadsheet'. Dan Bricklin, in conjunction with Dan Fylstra and Bob Frankston, launched the first spreadsheet product Visicalc in 1976. This simple grid, conceived as a type of word processor for calculations, allowed statistical, financial calculations and cross referencing within a structure of rows and columns. What they failed to recognise was that accountants had been using such a tool for many years. It was known as 20 column analysis paper. Unfortunately at that stage computing power was supplied by the accountant who undertook recalculation of the spreadsheet when any variable was changed.

One of the classic applications for this manual spreadsheet was the budget. The 20 columns permitted the division of the financial year into

12 periods with provision for: description, variable values, fixed factors and totals, all within the single piece of paper. To achieve greater detail additional sheets could be used as subsidiaries (3 dimensional spreadsheets) or by attaching several sheets, large spreadsheets could be achieved. However, increased size led to increased processing time hence budgets were primarily a once a year activity with, in exceptional circumstances, half or quarter year reviews.

Spreadsheets are based on a large matrix structure in which the cells of the matrix may be thought of as the computer equivalent of a large, multi-column analysis sheet. The accountant has a natural affinity with analysis paper being the normal working document, so many found it easy to adjust to an electronic version. Traditionally, the accountant was restricted to about 20 columns by 30 rows on paper, in which data and relationships were expressed and subsequently subject to calculation in order to arrive at the answer on the bottom line or rightmost column. The electronic version, however, displays on the VDU (screen) only a limited portion of an enormous analysis sheet (e.g. 16,000 cells plus) which can quickly recalculate as data is modified. The display (the window) may be moved around the spreadsheet for constructing, editing and reading results. It may be used for a variety of purposes, not only by the accountant, but also by other managers and functions.

Each cell may have text, numbers or formulae entered in it. In this way, text may be used to define terms, months, sales, revenue, etc. Numbers may form data associated with the text and formulae may take more than one cell and process them against other cells or process the contents of a particular cell against some defined mathematical base. Additional functions allow graphing and desktop publishing of output reports. Most systems increasingly permit interfacing with other systems, such that data may be transferred into the model for automatic processing. At the same time the output may interface with communications systems for onward transmission, graphics packages for visual presentation of reports and word processing for the editing and presentation of reports.

In using a spreadsheet, the technique is to lay out the matrix, showing workings and reports, entering headings, relationships and formulae, subsequently followed by data that may be worked upon to produce results. A major danger with spreadsheets is that the first outcome is assumed to be correct when it may contain errors in logic. Subsequent editing and development of the reporting format are essential, as is a process of verification of logic (in a study carried out in California, 30 per cent of spreadsheet models examined contained fundamental errors of logic).

The crucial distinction between modelling systems and spreadsheets is that data, logic and reports can be separated and saved as separate files. Models are based on formally stated mathematical relationships expressed in the logic file that may be used in a variety of ways and in a variety of situations. Spreadsheets represent report output systems that will restrict the degree of flexibility of input. Spreadsheets use a cell referencing system to express the logical relationships of variables. Modelling systems such as Micro-FCS therefore allow the user to run different sets of data through the same logic, and produce a variety of reports from the same logic. This ability greatly facilitates consolidations: for example, where budgets for different departments are added together; a facility only available on the more advanced spreadsheets.

The alternative to both of these is the development of specialist programs. An example of this is the use of FORTRAN or other higher level language systems. This route has primarily been replaced by packaged software, but it still has some validity as the building of specialist models may exploit a freedom unavailable in the spreadsheet or modelling package that is constrained by the original design specification. For example, spreadsheets are primarily simulation systems and may only achieve an optimising model through iterations in a trial and error manner until optimum is achieved. Modelling packages have varying degrees of goal seeking abilities but again this tends to be in an iterative manner. For specific optimising techniques such as linear programming, a specifically written program using a language such as FORTRAN (mathematically based) or BASIC (general purpose) or their equivalents may be best or specialist programs.

The alternative approach is the building of simulation models in which 'what if' experiments may be undertaken, along with iterations, to achieve an optimal point. It provides not only a tool closer to the manager's own behaviour but also a learning process in which relationships are understood which may permit the development of complex relevant models of the problems being faced. Eventually this may require a shift to more sophisticated optimising, purpose-built models.

This rather conflicts with the traditional assumptions that decision makers always seek optimal solutions, e.g. profits maximisation, sale revenue maximisation, cost minimisation, etc. While optimising models may be built, they require a clear understanding of relationships and in a complex world this is not always available. The result is that optimising models tend to be over-simplifications of reality that, while elegant, produce results of little use to decision makers.

Finally, we will summarise what we believe are the important features of the tools.

1. The separation of input, process and output. The assumptions are incorporated in the inputs, which are separated from the logic of relationships. The product of the logic is presented in the proforma report output.
2. English like and/or mathematical expression of relationships.
   Sales = f(price × advertising × R&D × . . .) + e
3. Structured order of processing leading to accuracy and predictability of outcome.
   $Y=p(1+r)n/12$
4. Provision of subroutines of accepted convention.
   NPV
   IRR
   Average
5. Provision of database of names or chart of accounts to ensure consistency of usage. The principle of Data Dictionary as used in databases should be incorporated.
   CoG : cost of goods sold
   sales: sales volume
   SRev: sales revenue
6. Logic checking and auditability of process and model.
   Circular arguments ($a1..a1)
7. Ability to use alternative input data sets, output reports and maintain consistent logic structures.
8. Provision for housekeeping and security facilities. The automated backing-up of models is limited in many systems with file naming often user dependent.
9. An easy operating environment with icons, pull-down menus, windows and a mouse (a pointing device).
10. Operating facilities that allow a number of tasks to be performed concurrently and providing a stable interface.
11. The ability to transfer data between various stand-alone applications packages.

In the Appendix to this chapter we have included some simple instructions for starting to build models with spreadsheets.

MODELLING METHODS

In Chapter 1 we introduced the process of modelling. We shall now unpack this process and consider the individual elements involved thereby developing a method of modelling. The problem solving approach presented below can be applied to any financial modelling situation. There are seven stages:

1. Problem identification and definition – a process of analysis.
2. Analysis of constraints and variables, thereby identifying the relevant variables, including simplification of reality.
3. The formal definition of relationships between variables.
4. Specifying the model – including the algorithms.
5. Encoding the model – to suit the software.
6. Testing the model.
7. Applying the model.

All stages are viewed as iterative. Iteration is absolutely fundamental to stages 1 to 4 as conceptual models are developed and tested against reality in order to arrive at appropriate models, which may be subject to formal building and testing in stages 5 to 6. In addition, the whole cycle may be viewed as iterative as we move from simple models to more complex models.

1. Problem identification and definition

The information sought from the model by the decision-maker must first be specified. Those aspects of a system's behaviour of interest to the decision-maker should be stated and the types of questions for which answers are required should be summarised.

Assuming you have identified a problem the next stage is analysis. For example, consider the case of the owner of a small business who needs to either build new premises or move to new premises to allow the business to expand. Before a decision can be made on these two alternatives, the constraints must be identified together with the relationship between variables. An obvious constraint is the financial resources available. As part of the problem analysis process the owner must identify and predict future financial resources. This means forecasting future income and expenditure as well as knowing existing resources. Information on existing resources can be obtained from the control system, particularly the accounting information system. Forecasts of future income and expenditure must be calculated by predicting the behaviour of the elements of the business (the variables). This can be done by constructing mathematical functions of the relationships between variables and seeing if these reflect actual behaviour. This testing may be undertaken by looking at past records. Once a representative relationship has been found it may be applied

242 / **Financial Planning**

to predicting likely future events, such as income and expenditure. In this way one element of the decision portfolio becomes known, i.e. the company's financial status.

If we now analyse what has taken place above we will see the process of problem analysis was as follows:

1. *Problem identification.* In this case, we specified the problem as being one of the need for bigger premises that could be solved by moving or building an extension to the existing premises. While this problem could be broken down further we assumed the manager had this understanding of the problem. Problem identification essentially involves setting limits or boundaries to the problem that will enable us to define internal content and external influence.

2. *Analysis of the problem.* The analysis process identifies the content and influences in two forms: constraints and variables. Constraints are limits that may define feasibility and acceptability. When considering whether to move to bigger premises or build extensions, the availability of financial resources to cover the costs represents a constraint on the decision.

   Variables, on the other hand, reflect the interaction of elements of the problem. They may be sub-elements of constraints or variables. In the case above we looked at variables that were sub-elements of a constraint. The constraint was financial resource availability, and the variables were current financial resources, future income and expenditure.

3. *Disaggregation and aggregation.* In any modelling exercise, one of the first decisions is the degree of aggregation or disaggregation to be applied to the relative elements. An example of this can be given by considering the time element within cash flow forecasting: levels of disaggregation exist yearly, quarterly, monthly, weekly and daily. The degree of disaggregation will define:

   □ The degree of sensitivity of the model.
   □ The planning control horizon.
   □ The degree of variable disaggregation.
   □ The appropriateness to the task.
   □ The simplicity, as opposed to the realism, of the model.

2. *Analysis of constraints and variables*

The above process continues until two characteristics are established. Firstly, we must establish the relationship between variables in a structural form (normally mathematical):

For example: $\text{Current financial resources} = \text{Past financial resources} + \text{Change in financial resources}$

These relationships need to be tested and verified to ensure they are correct otherwise the model will fail. Secondly, the variables must be broken down until a known basis is established which will allow the inputting of data into the relationships to permit calculations. These known bases may be (as above) the existing financial resources or be forecasts of future elements, e.g. sales volume.

Before we rush to build any model we must rigorously test our conceptual model to ensure its validity. Otherwise our model, when built, may produce unexpected and unusual results – GIGO (Garbage In, Garbage Out).

The process is one of repeated analysis into elements until either a known factor is found or a relationship that has been tested and proved is identified.

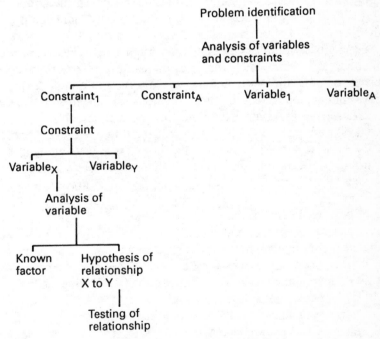

Figure 10.1 Problem analysis

The process of analysis is one of decomposition into primary elements. This process is somewhat eased in financial modelling that is built on the basis of financial accounting, itself a model of the business system. The mathematical relationships are implicit in the accounting model but in order for us to process them mechanically, we must make them explicit, for example

- □ IMPLICIT – Sales revenue is dependent on the sales volume and the price
- □ EXPLICIT – Sales revenue = sales volume × selling price

This process of making the mathematical relationship explicit is fundamental to the computer's operation. This is because the computer will receive instructions of what to do explicitly from the program and cannot assume the knowledge that the accountant has. This process may be eased by decomposition of the model into its constituent parts.

The questions asked of a model will usually relate to the values of endogenous variables, that is, those variables that are determined within the system. The endogenous variables will include those aspects of the system that are of interest, as specified in the first step, and also any other variables generated within the system in the course of deriving a final solution. All significant endogenous variables must be specified.

The exogenous variables complete the variables set. These comprise all other variables for which the relevant values are determined by influences outside the system and will be taken to include those variables under the direct control of the decision maker (sometimes referred to as controllable or decision variables) as well as non-controllable variables. The latter will include not only variables reflecting appropriate aspects of the firm's external environment, but also variables reflecting those aspects of the internal environment that comprise a set of constraints resulting from decisions made elsewhere in the organisation.

It will be seen later that the choice of the set of relevant variables will have a critical bearing on the quality of the model that is eventually formulated. In particular, it is important that no significant variables are omitted, since a mis-specified model that yields misleading results could be of less value to the decision maker than having no formal model at all. Yet while a degree of realism is important, the cost of building a model means that there is likely to be an optimal level of model complexity beyond which the cost of improving the degree of realism becomes prohibitive, where, in other words, the expected additional benefits do not outweigh the costs of elaboration. The model-builder can usually ensure at an early stage that unnecessary detail is avoided by differentiating between those variables that are likely to have a significant impact on the behaviour of the model, and those which represent less important items of detail. If the potential impact of a particular variable is uncertain however, it should be included because the sensitivity of a model can be tested at a later date and insignificant variables can then be excluded.

3. *The formal definition of relationships between variables*

The process of decomposing the model is one in which we specify each of the variables and their relationship. This is best explained through an example. Here we will draw on the cash flow model:

1. Firstly the closing cash balance may be defined as = opening cash balance + change in cash position for the month.
2. The opening cash balance for any period may be defined as = closing cash balance in the previous period. We may express this as being: opening cash balance period T = closing cash balance in period T–1.
3. Next, the change in cash position for the month = the income for the month – the expenditure for the month.

At this stage we have decomposed the original formula into two further sub-formulas, hence the closing cash balance may be defined as being dependent on the closing cash balance brought forward from a period plus the income for the period less the expenditure for the period.

Through decomposing we identify the relevant variables and their relationship. This is a process we shall have to follow repeatedly to identify all the elements within the model. In the course of this process we will draw out all the relationships which on occasion will only be achieved by further decomposition or even the introduction of previously omitted variables. In this way generations of models will start to emerge going further into the relationships and reflecting reality through testing and validating. This process is referred to by econometricians as estimating and validating, in that the conceptual models are given substance through estimating the parameters of the variables and testing the resulting model for validity.

It can be seen that the degree of decomposition reflects the degree of accuracy and representativeness sought in the model. The greater the degree of decomposition, the greater the complexity. An attempt to develop a comprehensive model immediately runs the danger of including a greater number of errors, as the number of variables and their interactions increase. It is recommended that a simple model is built, tested and proven before further decomposition and complexity are added.

4. Specifying the model – including the algorithms

Once the relevant set of variables has been defined, the relationships between them must be formally specified in mathematical terms. A relationship may be:

1. *Defined*, e.g. revenue = volume × unit price.
2. *Empirical*, i.e. obtained by some estimation technique, such as observing the past behaviour of variables (for example, a retailer may observe that the gross margin on sales has, on average, been X per cent of sales value).
3. *Derived*, by algebra from some other combination of relationships (for example, if the pricing mechanism in an industry is such that a manufacturer's price to a wholesaler is based on cost plus a fixed mark-up, and similarly the wholesaler sells to the retailer on a cost plus basis, it is clearly quite simple to express the retailer's cost of purchases in terms of manufacturing cost and to ignore the wholesaler).

The requirement to express the relationship in mathematical terms is necessary because simulation is a numerical technique producing output numbers from input numbers in a step-by-step fashion. Whether the computations necessary at each step are to be effected manually or with the aid of a computer, they must be expressed in a form that will allow one number to be derived from some combination of two or more other numbers according to a fixed rule. The rule is, in fact, the mathematical expression of the relationship.

5. Encoding the model – to suit the software

Assuming that the model is sufficiently large or complex to justify the use of a computer, the relationships developed and specified must be translated into a computer readable code and organised in the exact sequence in which the calculations need to be made. Clearly the characteristics of the software to be utilised must be considered, and if they should form unacceptable limitations then alternative software should be sought or alternative methods of implementation, such as general purpose languages, considered.

6. Testing the model

At this stage, prior to applying the model it is necessary to test that it is behaving correctly. The usual method used is to compare the output produced for some given set of input data against the expected output, probably in the form of actual observations from a previous period. Alternatively, it may be possible to derive estimates of some of the output variables, using other modelling techniques, for example statistical regression.

If it is found that the output values indicated by the simulation model are not significantly different from their expected values, the decision maker should be able to proceed to use the model with a fair degree of confidence. If, however, there appear to be systematic differences between the actual output and the expected output, then the model is probably mis-specified and steps will have to be taken to improve its design. This may involve changing the set of variables assumed to be significant and/or altering the form of one or more of the relationships between variables.

In many modelling situations, the testing process and any subsequent model revisions will be an important, continuous exercise. Whenever the system being modelled contains elements whose nature changes over time, it is important that changes in relationships are reflected in the model immediately. Otherwise, serious mistakes could be made as a result of taking decisions on the basis of information from a mis-speci-fied model. Hence the testing process should be regarded by the modeller as a regular exercise in all except the most stable systems.

In an earlier section we discussed the problem of capturing reality and apparently there will exist a development process of models. This process is no different to the development of any other product and is reflected in the short-run and long-run product life cycles.

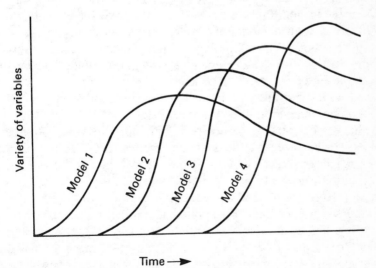

10.2 Life-cycle of models

As each model is developed, understanding of the problem is captured and built into the model. The failure of a model to achieve full representation of reality results in the development of a revised and improved model in which further elements now understood have been incorporated. This learning process permits the gradual improvement of validated models, for example:

Model 1 PROFIT = Sales Revenue – Total Costs
Model 2 PROFIT = Sales Revenue – (Fixed Costs + Variable costs)
Model 3 PROFIT = Sales Volume × Contribution – Fixed Costs

In the above example, the failure to capture the sensitivity of the model to changes in volume leads to the development of Model 2. Model 3 is the result of understanding the complex relationship of contribution, costs, revenues and profits to volume.

The target, then, of any modeller is not the development of the perfect model first time round but rather the gradual development of a more comprehensive and robust model that reflects the current understanding and knowledge, and will permit further improvement as additional experience generates understanding and knowledge.

It seems appropriate to emphasise that, since the modelling process is a long-term activity through which learning about a business and its behaviour is undertaken, the modelling task should not be seen as a separate specialist activity but rather the natural activity of management. The separation of the modelling task from management runs counter to the learning process. The learning process permits management to achieve a higher level of control and functional performance. In addition we believe that the investment in learning how to model with a modelling system pays dividends in the long term, not the short. We cannot expect immediate payback nor should we keep shifting from one modelling system to another. From our experiences, however, the rate of learning a new software system is increased with exposure to a variety of systems, but it must first be built on a competence in one system.

We have presented a structured, rational, analytical approach owing its origins clearly to systems analysis and design. While this approach ensures a robust, valid model it can be costly in development time and may fundamentally fail to adhere to the user's objectives. An alternative approach, now followed in systems analysis, which may be applied in modelling is prototyping. Prototyping is the approach in which a model is built and tested to gain experience to permit the building of a more robust and relevant second generation model that more closely approximates to users' needs. A series of generations of the model thus evolves.

This approach is feasible with many modelling systems. However, it may not be used efficiently in systems that demand the definition of all variables at the initial stage and do not permit subsequent editing. The systems that have this characteristic require a more structured approach.

7. *Applying the Model*

Once the model has been validated it can be used to produce answers to the questions originally identified by the decision maker in the first step. The behaviour of the endogenous variables which interest the decision maker may be observed for given sets of input data, as can the effects on the system of marginal changes in the exogenous variables, thus providing some idea of the sensitivity of the model.

Besides answering 'what if' type questions, it is possible to set up routines based on the simulation model that test the values of various items of output data automatically as the input data are changed in some way, for example to represent various decision choices available to the manager. By remembering the 'best' value of an objective function based on values of the output data, it is possible to identify an optimal action from a set of specified alternatives by simply re-running the model for each set of input data. This type of search procedure is sometimes described as 'iterative'.

SUMMARY

In this chapter we have reviewed the available technology for financial planning and modelling. As we stressed at the beginning, the technology cannot replace the intellect of the brain. The modeller may use technology to ease the modelling process but the time and effort in building and testing a model should not be underestimated. The documentation of the model, from the concept through to the coded and implemented system, must be retained as an audit and validation trail. The use of pencil and paper and independently worked test data is the only guarantee of reliability of the logic within the model. Reliance on the technology to debug and prove the model should not be used, particularly with new or recently upgraded software. The opportunity for 'computer assisted error' is very large with untried modelling systems and spreadsheets. The limitations of existing known software should be recorded and form a control criterion on the model. For example, one well-known spreadsheet is unreliable with data running to the seventh decimal place. While it seems unlikely that our model would be sensitive to this detail, it represents a serious limitation on the application of the package to certain model structures.

The most frequently used systems for modelling are spreadsheets, which have their own particular features that make them attractive to users. However, spreadsheets have significant weaknesses and these should not be ignored. In the appendix that follows this chapter we provide a series of key points to apply to developing models in spreadsheet systems that should improve the quality of models developed.

We then outlined a seven stage process for developing a model of a situation. This involves identification, definition and analysis, and depending on the degree of complexity, a considerable amount of sophistication.

This arguably ultra-rational approach, may be compared with earlier Chapter 9 where we discussed individual and group influences on decision processes. We identified a number of issues (but by no means an exhaustive selection) which impact on the quality of decisions. It seems axiomatic to us, therefore, that any of the processes outlined throughout this book must take account of *all* aspects if we are to enhance and improve organisational decision making. A truly sophisticated model would need to capture not just the 'facts' (whatever they are), but also to some extent the meaning of that information to the manager struggling with the problem.

It is, therefore, our belief that the development of financial planning must encompass both the technology and those using it. We would hope that if readers have got this far, then they will be better placed – by understanding both modelling and people issues – to understand and implement appropriate processes in their own organisations.

REFERENCES

Cretein, P D, Ball, S E and Brigham, E F (1987) *Financial Management Using Lotus 1–2–3*, Dryden Press.

Jackson, M (1985) *Creative Modelling with Lotus 1–2–3*, Wiley, Chichester.

Jackson, M (1988) *Advanced Spreadsheet Modelling with Lotus 1–2–3*, Wiley, Chichester.

Kaye, G R and Bhaskar, K N (1985) 'Cash Flow Forecasting', Vol 1 in *Financial Planning with Personal Computers*, Economist Publications Ltd.

Kaye, G R and Bhaskar, K N (1986) 'Management Accounting Reports', Vol 2 in *Financial Planning with Personal Computers*, Economist Publications Ltd.

Kaye, G R and Bhaskar, K N (1986) 'Budgeting', Vol 3 in *Financial Planning with Personal Computers*, Economist Publications Ltd.

Kaye, G R and Bhaskar, K N (1986) 'Corporate Planning', Vol 4 in *Financial Planning with Personal Computers*, Economist Publications Ltd.

Lewis, C (1989) *Business Forecasting in a Lotus 1–2–3 Environment*, Wiley, Chichester.

Osborne, C W Kyd (1986) *Financial Modelling Using Lotus 1–2–3*, McGraw-Hill, New York.

Person, R (1991) *Using Excel for Windows*, QUE.

Remenyi, D and Nugus, S (1988) *Business Applications in Lotus 1–2–3: A guide to forecasting, risk analysis, backward iterations and simulation*, McGraw-Hill, New York.

Sherwood, D (1983) *Financial Modelling Practical Guide*, G & Co.

Weizenbaum, J (1984) *Computer Power and Human Reason*, Pelican.

APPENDIX: SIMPLE INSTRUCTIONS FOR BUILDING MODEL WITH SPREADSHEET

(NB Commands shown in CAPITALS are specific to the software and here we have used LOTUS 1–2–3 as examples).

Two approaches are recommended for the design of models with spreadsheets. Firstly, it is recommended that the layout separates data input (assumptions and variables) from the logic of the model and the reporting. This approach assists operation, editing and debugging. The use of a diagonal or cascades structure is recommended by some authors to assist copying, and deleting, but can cause some problems of tracing not encountered with columnar approaches. The reporting area may contain multiple reports, e.g. for screen, graph, printout, to avoid formatting problems. Macros, sub-routines, commands, look-up tables and tables of range names may be allocated an area to the right of data input section.

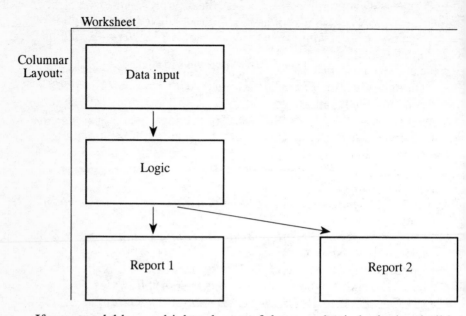

If your model has multiple columns of the same basic logic then build description and logic of column one first. Test and debug this before using /COPY to copy logic into adjoining cells. Editing of logic is possible after copying but use appropriate absolute and relative referencing to control copying process.

Description	Logic Column 1	Logic Column 2

If you place your description with the first column of logic right you can use /RANGE NAME LABEL RIGHT to label cells in the first column of logic. This will assist document debugging. Cells are like fish scales and while nothing is present in the cell to the right, over-flow of display will apply. This should not confuse the builder.

Description	Columns	Using range names
Sales	B2	Sales
Costs	B3	Costs
Gross profit	B2–B3	Sales − cost

Testing and Debugging: You should always apply test data to your model. This should come from a reliable source (manually worked up only if proof). Also useful are the following:

1. Use 1's in all data fields while building.

$$
\left.
\begin{array}{l}
1 + 1 = 2 \\
1/1\ \ = 1 \\
1 \times 1 = 1
\end{array}
\right\}
\quad \text{Simple easily spotted results}
$$

2/0 Use cross tabulations

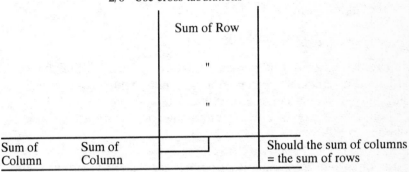

Formats: Use appropriate formats:
- fixed decimal place
- currency
- text mode

Remember the fixed decimal place does not stop calculation to higher decimal places (hence rounding errors). The value in the cell will be displayed as ** if it exceeds the character space available. Use the text mode to display logic formula (nb global and range order) for printing out logic in correct location (alternative is cell by cell listing facility within print options).

Modular Approach: Regularly used report formats may be saved as separate templates and *combine* allows the importing into new spreadsheets for re-use (but remember cell referencing will be invalid). Likewise EXTRACT may be used to save part of a spreadsheet for reuse.

Where similar spreadsheets are required, copying the files and using edits facility will be the quickest way to produce sub units.

Insert and Delete: You may insert a column/row or delete – but remember, the effect will be on the whole spreadsheet, not just the area you are looking at on the current view. Use *moves* as an alternative.

Zero: Do not suppress zero while building and testing – you can see where values, labels and formula are.

Recalculation: Recalculation speed will be affected by:

☐ the processor speed
☐ the Presences of a maths co. processor
☐ the logic layout
or
☐ size of spreadsheet.

   The default setting is automatic natural order of recalculation. To aid input to manual recalculation you may achieve speed increases through layout and column or row calculation order.
   Iterations apply to solving simultaneous equations (default is 1 maximum 50).

Tabular layout: Remember that reports are easier to read if they have subtotals and lines to break up the columns and rows. Only use the lines in report area as they will occupy cells and limit the ability to graph ranges without editing.

Justify: Improve your layout using justify to left, right and centre rather than using another column for titles.

APPENDIX – DISCOUNT TABLES

n \ i	2.5	3.0	4.0	5.0	6.0	7.0	8.0	9.0	10.0	11.0	12.0	14.0	15.0	16.0	18.0	20.0	25.0	30.0	35.0	40.0
1	.9756	.9709	.9615	.9524	.9434	.9346	.9259	.9174	.9091	.9009	.8929	.8772	.8696	.8621	.8475	.8333	.8000	.7692	.7407	.7143
2	.9518	.9426	.9246	.9070	.8900	.8734	.8573	.8417	.8264	.8116	.7972	.7695	.7561	.7432	.7182	.6944	.6400	.5917	.5487	.5102
3	.9286	.9151	.8890	.8638	.8396	.8163	.7938	.7722	.7513	.7312	.7118	.6750	.6575	.6407	.6086	.5787	.5120	.4552	.4064	.3644
4	.9060	.8885	.8548	.8227	.7921	.7629	.7350	.7084	.6830	.6587	.6355	.5921	.5718	.5523	.5158	.4823	.4096	.3501	.3011	.2603
5	.8839	.8626	.8219	.7835	.7473	.7130	.6806	.6499	.6209	.5935	.5674	.5194	.4972	.4761	.4371	.4019	.3277	.2693	.2230	.1859
6	.8623	.8375	.7903	.7462	.7050	.6663	.6302	.5963	.5645	.5346	.5066	.4556	.4323	.4104	.3704	.3349	.2621	.2072	.1652	.1328
7	.8413	.8131	.7599	.7107	.6651	.6227	.5835	.5470	.5132	.4817	.4523	.3996	.3759	.3538	.3139	.2791	.2097	.1594	.1224	.0949
8	.8207	.7894	.7307	.6768	.6274	.5820	.5403	.5019	.4665	.4339	.4039	.3506	.3269	.3050	.2660	.2326	.1678	.1226	.0906	.0678
9	.8007	.7664	.7026	.6446	.5919	.5439	.5002	.4604	.4241	.3909	.3606	.3075	.2843	.2630	.2255	.1938	.1342	.0943	.0671	.0484
10	.7812	.7440	.6756	.6139	.5584	.5083	.4632	.4224	.3855	.3522	.3220	.2697	.2472	.2267	.1911	.1615	.1074	.0725	.0497	.0346
11	.7621	.7224	.6496	.5847	.5268	.4751	.4289	.3875	.3505	.3173	.2875	.2366	.2149	.1954	.1619	.1346	.0859	.0558	.0368	.0247
12	.7436	.7014	.6246	.5568	.4970	.4440	.3971	.3555	.3186	.2858	.2567	.2076	.1869	.1685	.1372	.1122	.0687	.0429	.0273	.0176
13	.7254	.6810	.6006	.5303	.4688	.4150	.3677	.3262	.2897	.2575	.2292	.1821	.1625	.1452	.1163	.0935	.0550	.0330	.0202	.0126
14	.7077	.6611	.5775	.5051	.4423	.3878	.3405	.2992	.2633	.2320	.2046	.1597	.1413	.1252	.0985	.0779	.0440	.0254	.0150	.0090
15	.6905	.6419	.5553	.4810	.4173	.3624	.3152	.2745	.2394	.2090	.1827	.1401	.1229	.1079	.0835	.0649	.0352	.0195	.0111	.0064
16	.6736	.6232	.5339	.4581	.3936	.3387	.2919	.2519	.2176	.1883	.1631	.1229	.1069	.0930	.0708	.0541	.0281	.0150	.0082	.0046
17	.6572	.6050	.5134	.4363	.3714	.3166	.2703	.2311	.1978	.1696	.1456	.1078	.0929	.0802	.0600	.0451	.0225	.0116	.0061	.0033
18	.6412	.5874	.4936	.4155	.3503	.2959	.2502	.2120	.1799	.1528	.1300	.0946	.0808	.0691	.0508	.0376	.0180	.0089	.0045	.0023
19	.6255	.5703	.4746	.3957	.3305	.2765	.2317	.1945	.1635	.1377	.1161	.0829	.0703	.0596	.0431	.0313	.0144	.0068	.0033	.0017
20	.6103	.5537	.4564	.3769	.3118	.2584	.2145	.1784	.1486	.1240	.1037	.0728	.0611	.0514	.0365	.0261	.0115	.0053	.0025	.0012
21	.5954	.5375	.4388	.3589	.2942	.2415	.1987	.1637	.1351	.1117	.0926	.0638	.0531	.0443	.0309	.0217	.0092	.0040	.0018	.0009
22	.5809	.5219	.4220	.3418	.2775	.2257	.1839	.1501	.1228	.1007	.0826	.0560	.0462	.0382	.0262	.0181	.0074	.0031	.0014	.0006
23	.5667	.5067	.4057	.3256	.2618	.2109	.1703	.1378	.1117	.0907	.0738	.0491	.0402	.0329	.0222	.0150	.0059	.0024	.0010	.0004
24	.5529	.4919	.3901	.3101	.2470	.1971	.1577	.1264	.1015	.0817	.0659	.0431	.0349	.0284	.0188	.0126	.0047	.0018	.0007	.0003
25	.5394	.4776	.3751	.2953	.2330	.1842	.1460	.1160	.0923	.0736	.0588	.0378	.0304	.0245	.0160	.0105	.0038	.0014	.0006	.0002

^n_i Present value of £1 received after n years discounted at $100i$

Index